THE BLOCKADE BREAKERS

THE BERLIN AIRLIFT

HELENA P. SCHRADER

THE HISTORY PRESS

First published in the United Kingdom in 2008 by
The History Press · Cirencester Road · Chalford · Stroud · Gloucestershire · GL6 8PE

British Library Cataloguing in Publication Data
A catalogue record for this book is available from the British Library.

Hardback ISBN 978-0-7509-4388-8

Typeset in Photina.
Typesetting and origination by
The History Press.
Printed and bound in the United Kingdom.

To all the men and women who
contributed – in whatever way – to the success
of this remarkable and unique operation

CONTENTS

List of Illustrations and Maps

ILLUSTRATIONS

MAPS

ACKNOWLEDGEMENTS

This book could not have been written without the contributions of the many men and women who took the time to write, email or call me with their personal stories. Almost all who contacted me felt their own contribution had been small; most were hesitant about whether their stories were important enough for a book, yet it is precisely the contributions of everyone from cook to flight captain that I would like to honour here. I do not wish to distinguish between them now and I thank them all equally.

I also wish to thank Jonathan Falconer of Sutton Publishing who guided me gently but firmly in the right direction. Without his faith in this book, it would never have been written.

PREFACE

It was cold, wet and windy, as so often in Berlin. The dark clouds hung low over the city. Smoke oozing from the chimneys of the power plants and factories was trapped under the overcast sky, wrapping the city in ill-smelling smog.

Nothing in the city had seen paint or fresh plaster for nearly a decade, and so the grime of the smoke-laden air had blackened the faces of the buildings. What buildings there were, that is. Whole sections of the city resembled the ruins of Pompeii and Herculaneum: the pattern of the streets was visible, yet between the streets only heaps of rubble lay helpless and inert in the gloom.

But in Berlin in the winter of 1948 many of these ruins were inhabited. People lived in the cellars and in the decapitated lower stories of half-destroyed apartment blocks. They housed under the rubble in windowless caverns created by partially intact rooms. They had built shacks out of broken wood and masonry in the hulking wrecks of what had once been gracious courtyards. Plywood, newspaper and tarpaper 'glazed' the windows of these dwellings, and chalk messages scribbled on the dirty façades told visitors where the former residents of ruins might now be found.

The once gracious boulevards of the mutilated city led away from the dead heart towards the suburbs. The trees flanking the wide avenues struggled to survive; those trees, that is, that had not been incinerated by the fire-bombs or splintered by artillery and tanks. On the strip between the avenues, remnants of summer vegetable gardens lay fallow awaiting the return of spring. Open trams clanked along ringing their bells to warn the horse-drawn carts and bicycles to move out of the way. Workers in dungarees and young men in made-over uniforms with shabby briefcases clung to the outsides of the trams.

Gradually the buildings rose from the rubble in greater number and height. Their façades were pock-mocked from artillery and small-arms fire; large sheets of naked brick were exposed where the once elegant façades had shattered and fallen off. Here and there signs indicated a shop selling coal or food, and before these, crowds of women wearing head-scarves and shapeless winter coats stood awaiting their turn. And over all droned the continuous, relentless hum of aircraft engines.

A four-engine aircraft broke free of the cloud right over the rooftops of the five-storey buildings crowding the large airfield just south of the city centre. It was already on final approach. Undercarriage and flaps were down as it sank below the rooftops, level with the apartments on the top floor. The approach lights it was following ran through a graveyard and guided the aircraft on to a broad, flat airfield. The Skymaster throttled back, sank the last few feet and settled down hard with a short squeak of rubber on concrete and a puff of rubber smoke.

Ahead, an RAF York was just turning off the runway, and on the parallel runway a Dakota was taking off. Aircraft lined the taxiway like dutiful ducks waiting for the chance to trundle onto the runway and take off. On the hard standings beside the semi-circular terminal buildings which embraced the airfield from the north-west, dozens of Skymasters, Dakotas, Yorks and Hastings stood like docile workhorses, while crates of tinned goods, sacks of flour and bags of coal were offloaded into waiting lorries. Crews of stevedores worked like brigades of frenzied ants to strip the aircraft of their cargoes in the shortest possible time. Their faces, hands and dungarees were black with coal. Soldiers in jeeps dashed between the lorries delivering weather reports and orders to the aircrews.

From the cockpit of an aircraft that had just shut down its engines, the crew emerged, leather flying jackets concealing the rank insignia of the officers. Already the cargo of coal was being moved from the aircraft to the waiting lorry at a hectic pace. The pilot's trousers were crumpled from the flight, his hands dirty from the grime that had infiltrated every compartment of the aircraft, the coal dust from today, the flour from yesterday. . . .

From under the concrete overhang of the terminal two small civilians emerged. They moved forward hesitantly, intimidated by the bustle, dust and noise of the offloading, the purposeful movements of the heavy lorries and the hectic frenzy of military vehicles. Both civilians were dressed in their best. The taller wore hat and gloves and high-heeled shoes. The shorter wore a puffy skirt, white ankle socks and a ribbon in her hair. The woman had a bouquet of flowers, while the young girl clutched a brown teddy bear with the fuzz worn off its bottom.

The pilot noticed the approach of the two civilians and paused. This was not the first time he had been confronted with such a delegation. Grateful Berliners had increasingly brought tokens of gratitude to the men supplying the besieged city by air. They had brought hand-made gifts and family heirlooms, little plaques and inscribed books – anything they had salvaged from the ruin of their city and could afford to give away. Yet the flowers seemed like a tiny miracle. Where had this woman found fresh flowers in the dead of winter in a besieged city where every square inch of fertile soil was devoted to producing fresh things to eat? But here they were, a tiny burst of colour in the gloom of a wintry dusk, a remembrance of better times and a promise of a better future.

The pilot expressed his thanks to the donor and took the flowers. The ceremony, neither the first nor last of its kind, appeared to be over. But then the little girl offered a gift too. She offered the pilot her teddy bear. The gesture was not easy for her. She was fighting back tears as she handed him her beloved. 'Please take my teddy bear,' she pleaded in broken English. 'Good care take of him for me.' The pilot was unable to ignore the girl's tears. He did not need to *take* the teddy bear to understand the depth of gratitude expressed by the gesture. He assured the child that she could keep her treasured teddy. But the girl insisted. It would, she told him, bring him and his comrades good luck on their flights to Berlin. She knew because this teddy bear had comforted and protected her through the dreadful nights of cowering in the cellar beneath her home. Then, too, the drone of aircraft was unrelenting and merciless. Then, too, the four-engine aircraft filled the air, laden with heavy cargoes intended for Berlin. The fleet of aircraft behind the pilot bore the same markings as those that had filled the air then: the white star of the USAF or the roundels of the RAF. But now the pilot, who for all she knew had been flying then too, had become a friend.[1]

Chapter 1

CRISIS IN BERLIN

24 JUNE 1948

Just before midnight on the evening of 23 June 1948, the electricity network in the Western Sectors of Berlin collapsed without warning. Shortly afterwards, in the early hours of 24 June, the sole railroad artery into the city from the Western Zone, roughly 100 miles to the west, was closed to rail traffic. Likewise, the only autobahn by which the Western Powers moved personnel, goods and equipment to their garrisons in Berlin, was shut down. At roughly the same time, all barge traffic into the Western Sectors of the city was brought to a complete halt.

As the city awoke to a new day, the Soviet-controlled radio dryly announced to Berliners that: 'due to technical difficulties' the Transport Authority of the Soviet Military Administration in Germany (SMAD) had been forced to suspend both passenger and goods traffic on the railroad between Berlin and Helmstedt, the latter being the closest point in the British Zone of Occupation. But Berliners rapidly realised that much more was at stake. The triumphant Soviet Union, which had defeated the once invincible German Wehrmacht, captured Berlin and annexed large parts of Germany, was determined to eliminate an irritation. It wanted to get rid of a patch of territory, deep within its own Occupation Zone, that was not completely under its control: the Western Sectors of Berlin. For whatever reasons, the Soviets had chosen not to use their vastly superior military strength, but to employ an economic weapon instead. Just how powerful the chosen weapon was, however, was recognised at once by those with insight into the situation. The director of the utilities monopoly in the Western Sectors of Berlin, BEWAG, reported the same day that without electricity supplies from the power plants controlled by the Soviets, demand for electricity in the Western Sector could not be met. Furthermore, not only had the Soviets cut off the electricity produced in their own zones of occupation, they had halted the deliveries of coal needed to keep the few small and obsolete power plants located within the Western Sectors of Berlin operating. Therefore, even if electricity consumption was drastically reduced, the Western power plants would only be able to operate for roughly 10 days before their reserves of coal ran out. After that there would be no electricity in the Western Sectors of Berlin at all. No electricity would mean that the city's water pumps and sewage systems would cease to function. It would mean that the most important components of the public transport system, the trams and the underground railway, would come to a halt, the factories would have to close down and massive unemployment would ensue. In short, the entire economic activity of the city would cease.

This was not all. The Soviets also announced that all deliveries of goods, including food, medicine, coal and liquid fuels to the Western Sectors of Berlin from the Soviet Zone of Germany and Soviet Sector of Berlin were forbidden. Goods from the Soviet Zone, which completely surrounded Berlin, would henceforth only be delivered to and distributed in the Eastern (Soviet) Sector of the city. Control-points were established on the roads leading into the Western Sectors of Berlin from the surrounding Soviet Zone and all along the inner-city border between the Soviet Sector and the Western Sectors of Berlin. These measures, it must be noted, were not aimed solely at 'capitalist industry' but rather at every man, woman and child living in the Western Sectors of Berlin. To take just one simple example, the children of West Berlin were dependent upon the surrounding rural areas of the Soviet Zone for deliveries of 50,000l of milk daily. From one day to the next, that vital source of nutrition was cut off.

Throughout the city, stores, factories and private households had reserves of one sort or the other. Shop shelves and warehouses, household cupboards and pantries were not all empty, but the inhabitants recognised how precarious their situation was. Berlin had not been self-sufficient in food, much less energy, for decades. Traditionally, both came from the surrounding regions, near and far. With these abrupt measures, the Soviets had cut off the Western Sectors of Berlin, in which between 2.1 and 2.2 million civilians lived, from all sources of food and energy. Like a medieval city surrounded by a hostile army, the Western Sectors of Berlin were under siege.

The economic situation in the city was already dangerously fragile. At the end of the Second World War, industrial production in Berlin had been reduced by bombing and the final battle for Berlin, to just half of the 1936 levels. During the period of exclusive Soviet occupation, industrial capacity had been reduced even further by the systematic deconstruction of anything that appeared still functional, and the wholesale removal of their components from Germany to Russia in the name of 'reparations'. Although by 1948 factories were struggling to re-establish themselves, clearly the economy was still frail and vulnerable. Furthermore, that industry was completely dependent upon raw materials and component parts being imported into the city.

In consequence of the war, vast portions of the city's housing were uninhabitable, and the public transport system was severely lamed by the destruction of the city and the expropriation of rolling stock and rails by the Soviet Union. Telecommunications had been cut to less than 1 per cent of pre-war levels in the immediate postwar era and was far from recovered. Unemployment was high, over 15 per cent, but wages were almost worthless because of the confused currency situation. As of 24 June 1948 there were two currencies in circulation in Berlin; one of them was illegal in half of the city, while the other was virtually worthless. It was therefore hardly surprising that the black market was flourishing, while honest workers fainted from inadequate nourishment. The daily ration was still only three-quarters of the daily minimum recommended by the Red Cross.

Coupled with this dire economic state was an explosive political situation. Although the vast majority of the elected members of the City Council were members of non-communist parties*, the Communist Party of Germany exercised an effective veto over all political decisions via the Soviet Union, which possessed a veto in the occupation administration of Berlin, the Kommandatura. The Soviets had, among other things, prevented the democratically elected mayor from taking office. To make matters worse, the council members found it increasingly difficult to meet and make decisions, because whenever they tried to attend council meetings they were subjected to harassment and physical abuse from crowds of pro-Soviet agitators. Indeed, the delegates representing the vast majority of the Berlin population found that they were repeatedly prevented from going to their offices and performing their duties because their offices lay in the Soviet Sector and violent protesters blocked their way. They were not accorded police protection from the Soviet-controlled police force.

It was not only the politicians who were subject to terror. Ordinary citizens – journalists, professors, and scientists – 'disappeared' with increasing frequency. They were dragged from their beds in the dark of night by men often wearing the uniform of the city police. They were arrested without warrant and sent without counsel or trial to Siberia or the concentration camps in the Soviet Zone that were still operating. Meanwhile, orders had also gone out to the Berlin Fire Department that engines located in the Eastern Sector of the city were *not* to respond to alarms from the other side of the Sector border.

In short, by the end of June 1948, most city-wide services had ceased to function, from the municipal authorities and police, right down to the fire department and utilities. The city was officially divided into four sectors, but in reality torn in two: East and West; and to make the situation more absurd, one half of the city, the West, was under siege while the other half, the East, was not.

Yet Berlin in June 1948 was still one city. There was no wall surrounding it or dividing it in two. No less than 170,000 workers, who resided in the unaffected Eastern Sector of the city, worked in businesses located in the besieged sectors, while an estimated 45,000 residents of the besieged sectors worked in the East. In addition, countless residents had family and friends who lived on the opposite side of the political divide. Although they would discover that they were subject to ever more rigorous searches to prevent the movement of food-stuffs and other goods across the zonal border, the movement of people – and so the movement of information, ideas, and opinions – within Berlin was not yet prohibited. The city was thus at one and at the same time both divided and whole.

A second anomaly was almost as curious. Although the Western Sectors were clearly surrounded by an enemy army, they were 'defended' by the enemy as well. The army which encircled and besieged them, the 'Red' Army of the Soviet Union, was still officially allied to the United States, Great Britain and France, whose armed forces occupied the besieged sectors of the city. The Western Allied Forces of Occupation in Berlin numbered roughly 8,500 men: 5,000 Americans, 2,000 British and 1,500 French. They faced 18,000 Red Army troops inside the Soviet Sector of Berlin and roughly 300,000 Soviet troops in the surrounding Soviet Zone.

It was these foreigners, the wartime allies of the Soviet Union, which were the actual target of the Soviet measures. The method chosen to dislodge them from the Soviet Zone was, however, indirect. The immediate victims of the Soviet siege were the civilians living inside the Western Zones, yet the transparent objective was to make life within the Western Zones so intolerable that the population would force the Western Allies to retreat, leaving the Soviet Union in control of the entire city.

It was up to the Western Allies to find a solution to their predicament. As Clausewitz had written more than a century earlier, it was up to the *defenders* of the status quo to decide whether they preferred to preserve peace by surrendering to the aggression of the enemy or risk war by resisting. The Western Allies were given a choice between withdrawing from Berlin and thereby sparing the civilian population the hardships imposed by the siege, or of remaining and demanding that the civilian population – their former enemies and defeated subjects – endure hardship and discomfort for the rights of their erstwhile enemies and present occupiers to stay in Berlin.

Chapter 2

THE LONG, DIFFICULT ROAD TO A DANGEROUS DEAD END

RELUCTANT ALLIES

Before examining the Western response to this crisis, it is worth considering how the Western Allies got themselves into such an absurd situation in the first place. The position of the Western Allies in Berlin had its roots in the Second World War, which had been fought jointly by Britain, France, the Soviet Union and the United States in order to crush National Socialist (Nazi) Germany.

The four victorious powers were from the start strange bedfellows, who had been dragged into a war they did not want by the aggression of Nazi Germany. Britain had been the first of the Four Powers to attempt to call a halt to Nazi aggression by declaring war on Germany after its invasion of Poland on 1 September 1939. France reluctantly followed the British lead, but the Soviet Union was at that time an ally of Nazi Germany and very happy to participate in the invasion and partition of Poland. In the following months, while the Soviet Union engaged in aggression of its own against Finland, it tolerated indulgently Hitler's invasion of Norway, Denmark, Holland, Belgium, France, and eventually Greece. Not until the German Wehrmacht rolled across the Soviet border on 22 June 1941 did the Soviet Union recognise and treat Nazi Germany as an enemy.

The United States was the last of the powers to join the conflict. Strict neutrality at the start of the war had turned into open support for the British after President Franklin Roosevelt's re-election in the autumn of 1940. Thereafter the United States adopted a policy of increasing support for the UK and, after 22 June 1941, the Soviet Union. This support was primarily financial and economic in the form of loans and supplies, but included military components such as weapons, munitions, and naval escorts for convoys to the mid-Atlantic. Nevertheless, the support stopped short of war. America had declared itself the 'arsenal of democracy' but hoped to avoid taking a direct part in the conflict. It was not until the Japanese attack on Pearl Harbor on 7 December 1941 that the US was dragged into the Second World War. Even so, it is doubtful whether the United States would have gone to war against Germany if Hitler had not taken the initiative to declare war on it on 11 December.

By the time the United States entered the war against Germany, France had been out of the conflict for roughly eighteen months. The French Army had surrendered on 22 June 1940 after just six weeks of fighting. A rump puppet-state existed in the South of France, while the northern districts were occupied by the Germans. Remnants of the French Army had escaped to England, and in the French colonies some elements continued to favour the struggle against Germany while others favoured accommodation with the 'New World Order' created by Nazi victories. Thus in the critical years, when the tide finally turned against Germany and the bloody victories were being won, France was not a significant partner; the three nations that defeated Germany were the British, the Russians and the Americans.

It is important to remember that while the British and Americans shared a common heritage, language, and system of government that made them friends as well as allies, the Russians shared none of these. Since its inception in the Bolshevik Revolution of 1917, the Soviet Union viewed both Britain and the United States as arch enemies. They were representatives and advocates of the hated capitalist system of oppression – something that, according to communist theology, was doomed. The Soviet Union had engaged in ideological warfare against both Britain and the United States throughout its entire existence. The necessity of accepting British and American aid during the near-fatal struggle against Nazi Germany had not in the least changed the ideological position of the leadership in the Kremlin.

The ideological and political differences between the Anglo-American Allies and the Soviet Union were reflected in their war aims. Even before the US entry into the war, the British and Americans had agreed on their postwar vision: namely, no territorial aggrandisement by the victors and the right of liberated peoples to self-determination.

The Soviet Union never subscribed to these aims. On the contrary, Stalin made his goals explicit in a statement to the Yugoslav communist leader Tito in 1944 when he stated: 'whoever occupies a country also imposes his own system. Everyone imposes his own system as far as his army has power to do.'[1] Thus while the Western Allies prepared to march into Germany, thinking that their job was to eliminate an aggressor and free the way for a restoration of the *status quo ante*, the Soviet Union saw the Second World War as a continuation of their fundamental struggle against the capitalist system. While the Soviet Union might have been forced into tactical retreat or alliances – whether with Hitler's Germany or the capitalist powers of Great Britain and the United States – at no time did the Soviet Union give up its long-term goal of world communism.

In the short term, however, the Soviet Union was dependent on American food, supplies and equipment to sustain its fighting capabilities, and was unable to drive the Germans off its territory without incurring unsustainable casualties. It needed Western help to defeat the Nazi threat. Under these circumstances it was forced to compromise with the West, and it was in this period of pre-victory cooperation with the West that a series of decisions were taken concerning the future administration of a soon-to-be-defeated Germany. These decisions were taken incrementally during a succession of wartime meetings between the respective heads of government and in committee at the working level. The result was a consensus based on the fact that Germany would be occupied jointly by the three victorious parties (Britain, the Soviet Union and the United States), and that that joint occupation would take the form of Zones of Occupation, each roughly equal in territory, population and economic potential. Due to the symbolic and psychological importance of Berlin as the capital of Germany, it was also decided that Berlin too had to be occupied jointly. This was interpreted to mean that each occupying power would control a sector of Berlin.

Geography determined that the Soviet Union, whose Red Army was advancing from the East, would be given its Zone of Occupation in the eastern part of Germany, while the Western Allies would occupy the western portions of Germany. Initial plans saw Berlin on the border between East and West. Later, however, the border of the Soviet Zone moved roughly 100 miles further west, leaving Berlin deep inside the Soviet Zone of Occupation. This meant that the Western Sectors of the city were no longer a contiguous and integral part of their own Zones of Occupation, but became small islands of Western authority within the Soviet Zone.

At the time this system of occupation was agreed upon, none of Germany was occupied and everyone involved in the discussions was more concerned about winning the war than about the details of a still somewhat visionary postwar world. The issue of access routes to the Western Sectors of Berlin through the Soviet Zone was not considered important enough for it to be documented in any protocol. At all events, once the Allies' armies found themselves in occupation of Germany and had taken up their position within the agreed-upon Zones, the Soviets de facto controlled the access routes.

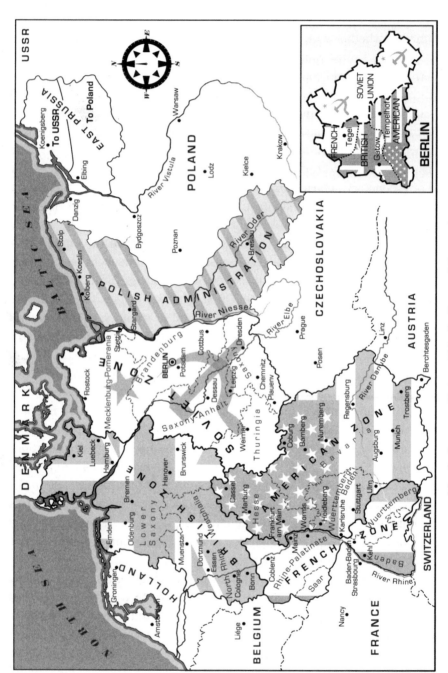

Map 1: Germany: States within the Zones of Occupation.

At no time did the Western Allies enjoy free movement of goods and persons across the Soviet Zone. It was only with much irritation and many difficulties that the Western Allies were even allowed to take control of their Sectors in Berlin as agreed upon. After the Red Army had won the race to seize Berlin, it remained in sole occupation of the entire city for roughly two months, while the Western Allies had to negotiate the terms and dates on which they would take control of their Sectors. These negotiations proved difficult and tedious and there were those in the West who felt that they should not withdraw their troops back to the agreed-upon zonal borders until Western troops were allowed into Berlin. These voices were overruled, however, by those – notably General Eisenhower himself – who were anxious to cooperate with the Soviet Union in the long run. They felt it was a matter of goodwill to withdraw within the agreed Zones of Occupation and trust the Soviets to let Western troops into Berlin in due course.

Two things need to be noted about this stage. Firstly, Western demands for 'free and uninhibited' access to Berlin were 'noted' but not accepted by the Soviets and, secondly, the manner in which the Western Allies were allowed to establish their garrisons in Berlin was a foretaste of things to come. When the first American and British troops set off on their separate ways to garrison their respective Sectors in Berlin, they encountered immediate and arbitrary interference at the zonal border. The Soviets not only prevented the Western Allies from making a triumphal entry into Berlin, but they demonstrated their ability to completely close down access to Berlin any time they wished to do so.

Colonel Howley, the newly appointed deputy commandant of the American Sector in Berlin, had his advance party arbitrarily reduced in size from 500 officers and men in 120 vehicles, to just 37 officers, 175 men and 50 vehicles before being allowed to enter the Soviet Zone. Then, just outside Berlin, this much-reduced force was again stopped by Soviet troops and blocked from entering the city itself. His column was diverted to Babelsberg, just outside Berlin, and prevented from proceeding for roughly one week. Finally, with an exaggerated display of Soviet hospitality, the Americans were allowed to enter Berlin. They were received at their future barracks by Soviet troops who withdrew with waving flags and fixed bayonets in a splendid parade march. They then discovered that their quarters had been stripped not only of furniture but of every oven, stove, light fixture, electrical outlet, window-pane, sink and toilet. The once well-appointed accommodations of the German Wehrmacht had been rendered entirely uninhabitable by the Soviet units that had housed there for two brief months before turning them over to their American 'Allies'. The American troops had to spend their first days in Berlin camping out in the forest of Grünewald.

The Soviets employed similar tactics against the British. First the advance unit of the Royal Army was told that 'all' the bridges across the Elbe in Magdeburg were 'closed for repair' and that they would have to wait indefinitely for repairs to be effected. Unfortunately for the Soviets, the British officers commanding this unit were experienced veterans and they very rapidly found a bridge which the Soviets had forgotten to guard. They redeployed and crossed the Elbe after only a few hours' delay. On reaching Berlin they again encountered bridge problems. In this case, a bridge over the Havel – clearly marked on their maps as intact – had been destroyed by the Soviets 'by accident'. Again the leading elements fanned out to look for alternatives, which they successfully did. To the sound of fife and drum the British advance unit entered Berlin in parade fashion, but they too had to openly camp on the former Olympic playing fields. Meanwhile, the advance party of the Royal Air Force, that had arrived to assume command of Gatow airfield in the British Sector of Berlin, was herded into a hangar and detained for 24 hours without any explanation, much less an apology from the Soviets.

BERLIN: ZERO HOUR

Berlin, which the Western Allies had now occupied after a long and costly war and after considerable diplomatic squabbling with the Soviets, was anything but the proud capital of a great, albeit defeated, nation. One of the German communists who returned to Berlin with the Soviet Army in May 1945 described it as 'a picture of Hell'. He found flaking ruins and starving people shambling about in tattered clothing, dazed German soldiers, drunk Red Army troops, long queues with buckets at pumps for water, and felt that everyone he met looked 'terribly tired, hungry, tense and demoralised'.[2]

This was not surprising. Fifty thousand Berliners were estimated dead. Many of the bodies had not had a burial and were rotting among the ruins, in streets, cellars, abandoned factories and military installations etc. Shortly before surrendering, fanatical Nazis had ordered the city's underground system flooded, and thousands who had taken refuge there, before the advancing Soviet tanks, troops and artillery fire, had been drowned. Their bodies only gradually worked their way into the canals and lakes.

Berlin's water mains had been ruptured in 3,000 places during the fight for the city and only 23 of the city's 84 sewage pumping stations were functioning.[3] The canals were filled not only with corpses and debris but with sewage as well, contributing further to growing health hazards in a city where only 9,300 hospital beds were available compared to a wartime capacity of 38,000. The water was unsafe to drink without boiling it first, but there was no electricity or gas with which to heat stoves and so boil the water. Coal and wood were also in short supply and typhoid and dysentery were spreading, the latter killing an estimated 65 out of every 100 babies born.[4] Furthermore, 1.5 million Berliners were homeless out of an estimated population of 3.3 million. In some boroughs of the city, those which had sustained the greatest bomb damage or those areas most fiercely contested in the final land battle for Berlin, the situation was even more acute. In central Schoenberg, for example, 45 per cent of all housing was completely destroyed, 15 per cent was heavily damaged, 35 per cent partially damaged and only 5 per cent still intact.[5]

Transportation was virtually at a standstill. Of the 150 bridges that had linked the various parts of the city across the rivers Spree and Havel and across the canals, 128 had been destroyed, and there were fewer than 40 buses and 100 street cars still in operable condition. There was absolutely no petrol for either public or private vehicles.[6] Three out of four of the city's fire stations had been destroyed and of the 125,000 street lights that had once lit up the city, only 4,000 were still standing.

This situation at German surrender was the result of war damage both through Anglo-American bombing and Soviet house-to-house fighting, but in the two months that followed, when the Soviets occupied the city alone, these desperate conditions were aggravated by a Soviet policy of private and public theft. While the individual Soviet soldier was given a blank cheque to take whatever he could lay his hands on and carry, the Soviet state set about systematically stealing anything that was not already destroyed. This policy was officially described as 'reparations', but the reality was that vast amounts of equipment and industrial plants were dismantled and transported out of Germany, although very little of it was ever reassembled in the Soviet Union. The Soviet policy of dismantling whatever remained of the German transportation and industrial capacity impoverished Germany without enriching the Soviet state or people. Berlin's telephone system, which before the war had serviced over 600,000 customers, was systematically taken apart until, by the time the Americans arrived, only 4,000 telephone connections remained.[7] In consequence of Soviet 'reparations', 90 per cent of Berlin's steel industry, 85 per cent of the optical and electrical industry, and 75 per cent of the printing industry was removed by the USSR.[8]

One particularly significant casualty of the Soviet demolition policy was the only major power plant located in the Western Sectors of Berlin. By the time the Western Allies arrived in Berlin this vital power plant (but not those plants in the Eastern Sectors of the city) had been dismantled by the Soviets and its component parts had disappeared into the 'East', leaving the Western powers dependent upon electricity supplied by the still-functioning power plants located in the Eastern Sectors of the city. Clearly, 'reparations' for war damage could have been collected more easily from a power plant located in the East. The dismantling of the only power plant in the Western Sectors of Berlin was a targeted move designed to weaken the position of the Western Powers in Berlin before they even arrived.

Such calculations were not noted at first. The first Western troops to arrive in Hitler's capital were too stunned by the scale of the destruction to fully grasp the Soviet game. What they saw instead was a shattered city, home not only to the decimated population of the city itself, but also to hoards of refugees displaced by the war. Although the figures for Berlin alone are not recorded, General Lucius Clay, the US Military Governor in Germany, claimed that 4.5 million German 'expellees' from the Sudetenland, Hungary, Czechoslovakia and Poland, as well as 2.1 million refugees from other parts of Europe, had swollen the population of the US-occupied territories.[9] A portion of these refugees, including former Nazi slave labourers and German refugees who had fled before the advancing Red Army, were stranded in dysfunctional Berlin simply because it had been a magnet and transportation hub until the last days of the war. When the city was surrounded by the Red Army, and the entire transportation network collapsed towards the end of the war, these refugees were trapped in the dying capital. Vast numbers of both 'expellees' and 'refugees' were now far too weak to continue their trek on foot.

Weakness was widespread because no one was getting enough to eat any more. The German system of provisioning the city had collapsed entirely in the last days of the war and so the Occupation Powers were responsible for supplying a city which had not been self-sustaining for generations. For the West this had been another surprise gift from the Soviets on their arrival in Berlin: the Red Army abruptly announced to the new Western commandants that now they were in Berlin, 'of course' they were entirely responsible for feeding the people in their respective Sectors, *not* from the Soviet Zone surrounding the city but from their own Zones, more than 100 miles away at best. In short, the Soviets dumped the provisioning of over 2 million people in the Western Sectors of Berlin on the Western commandants – without making the slightest concession with regard to the means of transporting those supplies into the city from the West. Initially, however, access was not the issue. The issue was simply finding enough food to prevent a catastrophe.

Even in peacetime, Germany as a whole had imported up to 30 per cent of its food. During most of the war, Germany had drawn upon the agricultural resources of the countries it had conquered from Norway to Italy and from the Aquitaine to the Ukraine. Hunger was a new phenomenon for the Germans, and it was spreading rapidly. The newly liberated populations of Western and Eastern Europe had known hunger under the Nazis and now they claimed their own harvests, while extensive war damage and the slaughter of farm animals had reduced the productive capacity of what was left of Germany. Adding to the problem was the fact that roughly one-third of Germany's pre-1936 territory (and a larger portion of its agricultural capacity) had just been annexed by the Soviet Union/Poland. Given the fact that the remaining rump state had to support a population swollen with refugees, it was clear that a crisis was in the making. The Occupation Powers were forced to fix rations at between 950 and 1,150 calories per day, or 'only half the caloric content deemed essential by nutritional experts to support a working population and about one-third of that available to the American people'.[10]

This was the situation in Germany in the summer of 1945, a point in time which the Germans came to call 'Zero Hour'. The complete and utter defeat of Nazi Germany, not just the unconditional surrender of Hitler's armed forces, had been achieved. This was the moment when the victors came together to work out a blueprint for the postwar world.

BLUEPRINT FOR A POSTWAR WORLD

Both Great Britain and the United States came to the first postwar summit conference, held at Potsdam between 17 July and 2 August 1946, with a very strong commitment to continuing the 'good working relationship' they had developed with the Soviet Union during the war. By contrast, the Soviet leadership came to the conference fully conscious that the Soviet Union was more powerful than it had been at any point in its history and that its armies were in occupation of vast areas of rich industrial and agricultural territories that were now theirs to exploit. From the Soviet point of view, the time for compromise with the ideological enemy was over. It was time instead to end the distasteful, tactical alliance with the class enemy and resume the strategic struggle against the capitalist powers.

This clear difference in attitude made it easy for the Soviet dictator, Joseph Stalin, to outmanoeuvre his counterparts. Stalin was also advantaged by the fact that both the United States and Great Britain were represented by new heads of state. Harry Truman had assumed the presidency unexpectedly at the death of President Roosevelt in April 1945, and as a result of a surprise victory in the General Election, Clement Attlee replaced Sir Winston Churchill in the very midst of the Potsdam Conference in July 1945. This left Stalin as the only veteran of what would later be called 'summit diplomacy' at the conference table in Potsdam.

Stalin won the first round before the conference was even convened. He did so by simply presenting the Western leaders with important *fait accompli* on vital topics that were supposed to be discussed and agreed at the Conference. Stalin had redrawn the map of Europe, turning over vast portions of Germany to the Poles, and annexing other parts directly into the Soviet Union along with large areas of what had been Poland. As one historian put it: 'All in all, Stalin had redistributed a quarter of Germany without a word or by-your-leave' to the West.[11] In addition, the Soviet Union had installed a puppet government in Warsaw, ignoring the Polish government in exile, which was still recognised in the West as the legitimate government of Poland. The only concession that the West gained was the belated acceptance of France as a 'victorious power', but only on the condition that France's Zone of Occupation be carved out of the British and American Zones; the Soviets gave up not one inch of territory to accommodate an 'ally' that from the Soviet point of view had never participated in the war.

At the conference itself, Stalin masterfully agreed to all the high-sounding principles that his Western Allies favoured, from 'democracy' to 'freedom of the speech, press and religion', but he carefully inserted the caveat that these rights would be exercised 'subject to security requirements' thereby creating an excuse for inhibiting them all. Both the Soviet Union and the West agreed on the need to 'de-Nazify, demilitarise and de-industrialise Germany', but the tactics for pursuing these aims were left intentionally vague. While all three Powers agreed on the need to prohibit Germany from the production of war materials, to limit the production of industrial products which could contribute to war production, and to reconstruct 'peaceful' and agricultural production, they were not in agreement on the size, nature or source of reparations. In fact, on the issue of reparations, Stalin singularly failed to get his way. By now the Western Allies had seen at first hand just how profound the destruction of German industrial capacity had been *and* they had had their first taste of reparations 'Russian-style'. It was rapidly becoming clear to experts and observers that the Soviets had been plundering without accounting ever since they crossed the German border, and that they plundered most thoroughly in those areas which they later turned over to the West.

A more important factor dictating Western firmness on the issue was the fundamental difference in the very concept of reparations. The Western Powers, being good capitalists, wanted Germany to pay reparations out of production and/or earned income. The Soviets wanted to expropriate the means of production. The West correctly foresaw that reparations in the Soviet manner would render Germany incapable of economic recovery, much less sustained growth. It was this, not any miserliness with respect to what the total sum might ultimately be, which made any agreement on reparations impossible.

Potsdam failed to produce any clear guidelines for the reconstruction of Germany or indeed any concrete agreements on key aspects of its recovery. There was no agreement on the reconstruction of transportation and communication networks, the re-establishment of a sound currency and banking system or the introduction of common policies on prices, wages, exports etc. Instead of establishing the framework for pursuing postwar recovery, the ad hoc wartime structure of joint, indeed unanimous, decision-making for anything affecting Germany in its entirety coupled with 'absolute power' for the individual Military Governors within their own Zones was retained.

The situation in Berlin was a microcosm of the situation in Germany as a whole. All decisions affecting Berlin 'as a whole' had to be made unanimously in the Kommandatura, yet the individual Sector commandants retained the right to rule their Sectors like absolute despots. The first meeting of the Kommandatura was a miniature version of the Potsdam Conference. Here, too, the Soviets presented the West with a series of important *fait accompli*. The Soviets blandly announced that 'naturally' all the orders they had issued while in sole occupation of the city had to be left intact and unquestioned 'until the Kommandatura saw fit to change them'. While this sounded reasonable enough, the Soviet veto in the Kommandatura meant that every single act of the Soviet Occupation Powers, from the day they took control of the city in May 1945 until the Western Powers arrived in July, was now immutable. As one observer put it:

> The Western Allies woke up to find that they had accepted a civil city administration in which the majority of the key posts were held by Communists; a banking system that was Communist controlled; a police force commanded by a Communist convert and staffed by Communists; a trade union system in which three quarters of the executive belonged to the Communist Party; a press set-up in which news and newsprint were freely available only to the Communist newspapers; a radio that broadcast nothing but Russian propaganda, and rationing so arranged that the easiest way to subsist was to be a Communist.[12]

Far less obvious to the newcomers was the very subtle work which the Soviet cadres had been conducting for months to control the German political scene. Unlike the Western Allies, particularly the Americans, who arrived in Germany with the perception that all Germans were Nazis or their willing followers and that the country was collectively guilty for all the crimes committed in its name, the Soviets arrived in Germany with an ideological framework for differentiating between 'good' Germans (i.e. communists) and 'bad' Germans (everyone else, who could be labelled either 'fascist' or 'capitalist' as convenient).

Even before the end of hostilities, German communists, trained in Moscow during the war years, were working systematically to take control of all self-help groups that sprang up in Germany when the existing infrastructure disintegrated. In this manner, they took over almost anything that vaguely hinted at self-government. They were aided in their work by a genuine, domestic movement in favour of communism.

The German Communist Party (KPD) had a very long and heroic history. In the last free election in Germany before the Nazi seizure of power, the KPD polled a full 17 per cent of the vote and was the third largest party in parliament after the Nazis and the Social Democrats (SPD). The first victims of Nazi oppression had been communists (and socialists), even before the Jews. The two institutions, with the highest percentage of members executed by the Nazis for opposition to the Nazi regime, were the German General Staff and the German Communist Party. For many former rank-and-file members of the German Communist Party, the arrival of the Red Army on German soil *really was* viewed as liberation.

Surviving German communists who thought their time had come at last were frightfully disappointed. The Soviets ensured that within the KPD all power went to those German communists who had been living in the Soviet Union and trained in Moscow. These cadre leaders made it equally clear that they would tolerate neither criticism nor discussion within the party. There was only one right answer to any question, and that was the answer provided by the party leadership in Moscow.

While this policy worked openly in most areas occupied by the Red Army, the returning communist leadership had clearly been briefed on the fact that the Western Allies would be in occupation of roughly two-thirds of Berlin. As a result it was decided that subtler methods were called for, and the leader of the KPD, Walther Ulbricht, openly told his close followers that the objective in Berlin was to 'appear' democratic while retaining control of all key organisations. The favoured means of doing so was to appoint a 'technocrat' – preferably an academic or intellectual with no party affiliation – to the figurehead top position in any organisation or governing body and ensure that a communist was the 'deputy' with the real power. Ulbricht specifically ordered that the mayors of the respective boroughs of the city should be known communists only in the traditional strongholds of the KPD such as

Wedding and Friedrichshain. In upper-class suburbs such as Zehlendorf, conservative politicians should be appointed mayor, while in much of the city Social Democrats should be 'allowed' to hold office.

Meanwhile, the SMAD worked diligently to ensure that the Communist Party would win the next municipal elections. This was a two-pronged attack. On the one hand the KPD was given almost limitless resources with respect to such things as paper allocations for leaflets and posters, petrol rations for functionaries and agitators to travel around the devastated country, special rations and better housing for loyal party members and – perhaps most enticing of all – jobs for their followers. On the other hand, and simultaneous with this overt political campaign, was the establishment of a covert police network. Wherever the Red Army went it brought the Soviet Secret Police, then known as the NKVD, with it. As with the Gestapo, the NKVD infiltrated into civil society with the purpose of observing, identifying and eliminating elements that looked independent, intelligent and spirited enough to cause 'trouble'. Troublemakers could be sent either to concentration camps taken over from the Nazis, such as Bautzen in Saxony, or sent to the Gulags in the Soviet Union.

Within a short time of moving into Berlin the Soviets had re-established an efficient Communist Party machine run by Soviet-trained Germans and supported by the Soviet Secret Police. They expected that between the carrot (better rations, housing, jobs) and the stick (fear of disappearing into a concentration camp or Gulag), they would be able to 'win over' the German population to communism.

Against this highly planned, well-funded and efficiently executed political programme, the West had literally nothing to offer. The policy of 'collective guilt' meant that the Americans particularly were suspicious of all Germans, while British and American democratic traditions were based on a plurality of competing parties. In short, the Western Allies were scrupulously careful not to favour one party over another, a position that was reinforced by the fact that there was a Labour government in the UK which inevitably sympathised with the SPD, while the American authorities were more conservative and almost as suspicious of the SPD as the KPD.

Given the greater resources and unabashed support of the Soviets for the KPD, it is astonishing that the German people did not simply embrace communism. But they did not, largely due to the fact that the political class in Germany had strong memories of the KPD's pre-war policies and, after their experiences with the Nazis, a healthy hatred of totalitarian parties of any colour. While the Right hated the communists as much as ever, the SPD remembered vividly the tactical swings of the KPD which had periodically treated the 'social fascist' SPD as a greater enemy than the Nazis. For the 'man on the street' the KPD was simply too obviously 'the Russian Party', and the man on the street already had good reason to hate the Russians.

The Germans were not the only people in Europe who failed to recognise the superiority of the Soviet system and embrace it with joy. In November 1945, the Hungarians elected a new parliament in which only 18 per cent of the votes went to the communists. A week later the Austrians went to the polls and the communists reaped less than 5 per cent of the vote.[13] At the same time, the NKVD in Germany must have been reporting the fact that despite all the advantages showered upon the KPD and its members, the SPD was gaining strength at the expense of the KPD. Stalin quickly concluded that the German working-class movement could no longer 'afford' to be splintered into two parties. It was time to merge the KPD and SPD into a single 'Socialist Unity Party' which could represent all 'progressive' elements in their struggle against the 'reactionary' forces of capitalism and fascism.

A bitter battle for the votes of the registered members of the SPD ensued. A KPD attempt to take over the leadership of the two parties via a coup in the respective executive committees was foiled by the secondary SPD leadership, which rebelled against their own executive. They demanded a referendum among party members and this was set for March 1946. At issue was whether the two parties should merge or not, and the referendum was hotly contested and anxiously monitored by the Occupation Powers. When the day of the referendum rolled around, it was so obvious that the vast majority of SPD members would vote against a merger of the two parties that the Soviet Union felt compelled to intervene on the side of 'progress'. 'Due to procedural errors' no voting was allowed to take place in a number of key boroughs of the Soviet Sector. In those boroughs where voting was initially allowed to proceed, Soviet troops arrived shortly after the opening of the polls, and results already registered were confiscated while those people in line to vote outside were dispersed by force.

Unable to prevent or stop voting in the Western Sectors, however, the Soviets were forced to rely on terror tactics to attempt to discourage participation in the referendum. They spread rumours that the Soviets would punish anyone who did not vote the 'right' way and threatened leading SPD figures personally and directly. Altogether these tactics worked well enough to convince almost a third of the registered SPD members that it was too dangerous to vote. Of the 23,000 SPD members who did vote in the referendum, 20,000 voted against a merger with the KPD; but the Socialist Unity Party (Sozialistische Einheitspartei Deutschland – SED) was founded anyway in the Soviet Zone/Sector. In the West there continued to be two leftist parties, the increasingly strong and self-confident SPD and the old KPD, which was now also going under the name of Socialist Unity Party (SED), and was run by Moscow.

This referendum had an impact far beyond the two leftist parties who contended it. The Soviet tactics of denying voting opportunities, confiscating results and harassing voters *of the socialist Left* was a clear alarm signal to everyone that the Soviet Union would under no circumstances tolerate other classes or parties inside the territories under its control. If the German working class in 'Red' Berlin was to be denied their right to have a say in the future of their political parties, then it was obvious to thinking voters with liberal or conservative leanings that they would be disenfranchised in any political system controlled by the Soviets. Any illusions about the tolerance of the Soviet Occupation Power for political diversity died as a result of this referendum.

The Western Powers were experiencing a less spectacular but no less profound disillusionment with Soviet policies of their own. Unlike the SED founding, which represented an open confrontation and final break between the Soviets and the democratic Left, there was no one issue which crystallised the conflict between the Soviets and the Western Powers. Instead, there was a continuous struggle over virtually every aspect of governing Germany and Berlin. Although conflicts were often individually minor, they were cumulatively vital. What the Western Powers discovered in a year of painstaking efforts at cooperation, both at the summit and the working levels, was that it was impossible to come to agreement with the Soviet Union about anything having to do with the reconstruction of Germany. Since everything had to be agreed unanimously, this meant that no progress towards the reconstruction of Germany was being made whatsoever.

At first the Soviets were energetically supported in their obstructionist tactics by the French. The French came to the Allied Control Council and Kommandatura late (only after Potsdam) and with huge chips on their shoulders about having been left out earlier. They were insecure in their place among the 'victorious powers' and no doubt acutely aware of the absolute contempt of the Germans, who remembered all too well that the French Army had been defeated soundly in just a few weeks in 1940. The French were determined to punish Germany for this humiliation and distract world attention from the fact that the bulk of the French had happily collaborated with the Germans for the better part of the war. They worked diligently to reduce Germany to a rump, agricultural state incapable of ever again being an industrial, much less military, power. They laid claim not only to Alsace-

Lorraine but the Saar and the Rheinland as well. They pursued a reparations policy that was only marginally less rapacious than the Soviet one. Indeed, the French state set about dismantling any industrial capacity that was modern and sophisticated, from watch-making to surgical equipment, not to mention factories for aircraft, automobiles and telecommunications.

Like the Soviets, it was not only the factories that were dismantled and taken away, but skilled workers as well. These were deported to France and put to work rebuilding the stolen factories. In parts of Germany entire forests were felled, destroying 500 years of careful forest management. Meanwhile, in the Control Council the French vetoed American proposals for a central German transport agency. They refused to allow the German labour unions to organise on a national basis. They prevented the establishment of national political parties in Germany. They even stopped the free movement of goods and people between Zones. In this manner they hoped to prevent Germany from ever becoming a unified nation again. What they achieved was the complete breakdown of a Four Power government and an end to the Potsdam system.

FACING UP TO REALITY

The United States was in the enviable position of not suffering from any kind of war damage and of having a powerful domestic economy. As it became increasingly evident that there was no progress being made towards postwar reconstruction, America could have turned its back on Germany and Europe and washed its hands of the whole mess. That it did not do so is to the credit of President Truman, his Secretary of State, General George Marshall, and the American Military Governor in Germany, General Lucius Clay.

Clay came to Germany with profound distrust and dislike of Germans, as he admitted openly in his memoirs, and an equal conviction that the Russians were a fine, down-to-earth people with whom he, as a soldier, would be able to get along. He saw the problems with the Soviet Union as superficial and diplomatic. Less than a year later, by May 1946, he had learned differently. He summarised the situation in a cable to the Department of State in which he wrote:

> After one year of occupation, zones represent airtight territories with almost no free exchange of commodities, persons, and ideas. Germany now consists of four small economic units which can deal with each other only through treaties, in spite of the fact that no one unit can be regarded as self-supporting, although the British and Russian zone could become so.

> Economic unity can be obtained only through free trade in Germany and
> a common policy for foreign trade designed to serve Germany as a whole. A
> common financial policy is equally essential. Runaway inflation accompanied by
> economic paralysis may develop at any moment. Drastic fiscal reforms to reduce
> currency and monetary claims, and to deal with the debt structure, are essential
> at earliest possible date. These cannot be obtained by independent actions of the
> several zones.[14]

Clay recognised that both the United States and the United Kingdom were
pouring food into their Zones in Germany, while the Soviets and French were
not only making their respective Zones subsist on their own resources, they
were also withdrawing huge quantities of raw materials, industrial capacity
and finished products. Clay concluded that the situation could not be allowed
to continue because 'it represented indirect payment' of reparations to the
French and Soviets by the US and UK, and because it would keep Germany in
poverty indefinitely, a permanent drain on the US and British treasuries.

If the American taxpayer had every reason to object to being a milk-cow
for the Soviet Union and France while being called upon to sustain Germany
in eternal poverty, the situation in Britain was graver still. At the start of the
Second World War Britain had possessed abundant gold and dollar reserves
and had carried a public debt of just £469 million; by the end of the war
Britain had no reserves and the national debt was £3.5 billion.[15] For the
average British citizen, the national debt was less disturbing than the high rate
of unemployment and the continued rationing. Due to bad harvests across the
globe, a worldwide wheat shortage had developed in early 1946 and bread
and potatoes had to be rationed in the UK, something which had not been
necessary at any time during the war. Pure self-interest dictated that British
policy favour the reconstruction of German manufacturing and agricultural
capabilities. This could only be achieved if the foundations for a self-sustaining
German economy were laid, starting with a functioning infrastructure, a sound
currency and civil government. Thus, the British government was desperate to
stop the economic haemorrhage that its Zone in Germany had become and was
growing increasingly concerned about Soviet designs on postwar Germany and
the world. And so was the US Department of State. The then Under-secretary
of State, Dean Acheson, later wrote: 'Life in Europe as an organised industrial
community had come well-nigh to a standstill and, with it, so had production
and distribution of goods of every sort.' Furthermore, agricultural production
was 'lower than at any time since the turn of the century'.[16]

Then came the winter of 1946/7. This proved to be the most severe winter
in a century. Temperatures dropped far below freezing and stayed there for

weeks on end. In Berlin the water supply froze and that meant the sewage system collapsed, as did the railway, preventing the importation of coal. Unable to provide coal for private consumption, public places from pubs and cinemas to air-raid shelters were turned into public warming halls. Schools were put on short weeks and factories were closed. Over 1,000 Berliners literally froze to death, 60 on one night alone. One Berliner who lived through the winter measured the temperature in her kitchen at −6°C and described how her bread was frozen solid. She went on to say:

> Most of the families which sold their porcelain, carpets, and furniture to get money to buy fat and meat on the black market . . . have nothing more to sell and are no longer able to buy black market food. People have no coal to heat rooms. . . . Old people are dying like flies. . . . There is no water in the houses because all is frozen.[17]

In Britain the situation was only marginally better. The frigid winter, even more unusual in the UK than in Berlin, exhausted coal reserves leading to power shortages. In December, England's largest auto plant was forced to shut down; then the Thames froze all the way from Windsor to the sea, closing London to coal barges and preventing the supply of coal to power stations. Electricity to households was reduced to 6 hours per day, 3 in the morning and 3 in the afternoon. By February, the crisis was so acute and widespread that the government ordered all non-essential factories to close for three solid weeks. Unemployment shot up to 2.3 million, welfare payments for these unemployed drained the already depleted treasury, while the government had been forced to cut food rations to below wartime levels.

The cold receded, but the mood of despondency remained. Doctors reported an increase in TB, pneumonia and other illnesses. By now most urban dwellers in Germany (and that was the majority) had not seen milk, sugar, fat or vegetables since the end of the war. Chronic under-nourishment had become a problem, causing a drop in industrial production per worker by 20 per cent. People, particularly the elderly, were dying of hunger still. A social worker summed up the situation by saying: 'The energies of the people are spent in pursuit of a loaf of bread and a pair of shoes. Hope is alien.'[18] Rations were now set at 1,275 calories per day in the US Zone (still less than half what Americans then considered normal) and at 1,040 calories in the British Zone, which was more industrial and had less agriculture than the US Zone. In the French Zone the rations were set at just 925 calories, causing the Germans to refer to it as the 'FZ' in a play on the German term for concentration camps, 'KZ'. It was now 'a vicious circle in which the Germans starved because they could not produce enough, and could not produce enough because they were starving'.[19]

But the problem was not confined to Germany, rather it *emanated from* Germany. There was a need to rebuild everywhere, but the former occupied countries, starting with the Soviets and French, demanded German reparations to enable them to start their economies. Germany, on the other hand, could not pay reparations if it did not produce anything it could sell, and it could not produce anything if it did not receive the agricultural products necessary to feed its workers or the raw materials to feed its factories.

Perhaps the most cogent example of the situation was the state of German coal production. Coal was Germany's principle postwar asset and export commodity. It was the fuel needed to fire not only its own but much of the rest of Europe's power and industrial plants. Without German coal, Europe could not recover. However, because of inadequate rations, the miners in the Ruhr produced on average just 711kg of coal per shift in 1947 rather than the 1,547kg they had produced before the war.[20] Germany could not increase coal production and exports unless its workers had enough to eat and had shoes on their feet and coats on their backs. It could also not increase coal production unless there was electricity to light the pits and keep mine equipment working; unless there was rolling stock and track, barges and lorries on which to move the coal from the pithead to the ports of export. But Germany could pay for none of that unless it could export more coal to earn hard currency with which to purchase all those things.

One of America's most brilliant diplomats, George Kennan, assessed the situation as follows: 'To talk about the recovery of Europe and to oppose the recovery of Germany is nonsense. People can have both or they can have neither.'[21] With this analysis, Kennan brought the entire State Department into a position directly opposed to the policies of two of its wartime allies, France and Russia, but fully in line with the British position. After the catastrophic winter of 1946/7, Britain was desperate to stop the haemorrhaging of scarce resources into Germany and was fully cognizant of the need to restore industrial production: the British Zone was the heartland of German heavy industry.

Both the UK and the US sent their delegates to the Council of Foreign Ministers in April 1947 determined to establish a sound framework for German recovery such as had not been attained at Potsdam. This meeting, held in Moscow, gave the US Secretary of State, George Marshall, the first opportunity to meet with Stalin personally. According to Charles Bohlen, who acted as Marshall's interpreter and adviser at the meeting, Marshall came away from the meeting convinced that Stalin was pleased with conditions in

Europe precisely because they were so bad and deteriorating. According to communist theology, the worse conditions became the more a people became ripe for communist revolution. To the pure economic imperative of fostering German economic recovery was added a political component of stopping the spread of communism. The spread of communism was feared not out of ideological bigotry as historians on the Left are wont to suggest. It was feared precisely because observers like Clay and Marshall, who had expected to work well with the Soviet Union, were appalled by what was happening in those countries which the Soviet Union occupied.

While the 'Iron Curtain' made it difficult for journalists or private citizens to see what was happening behind the lines of Soviet Occupation, diplomats and intelligence services were able to gather enough evidence of what was going on to send chills down the spines of civil servants and politicians in the US and Britain. The Gulags not only continued to exist, but it was now clear that Soviet POWs and forced labourers, who had been captured and forced to work as slaves for the Nazis, had not been repatriated to their families but rather loaded into cattle cars and sent to the Gulags as traitors. The long-suffering Soviet troops still in uniform, many of whom had not been home on leave during the entire war, were not sent home like their Western brothers either. Instead they were kept under arms in occupation of 'liberated' countries. The Soviet economy was not even turning to the production of the consumer goods of which the Soviet people were starved. Instead the production of arms continued. Across Eastern Europe people were not being given the opportunity to exercise self-determination, but were instead having 'Soviet-friendly' governments imposed on them by the weight of Soviet tanks. Soviet-sponsored 'insurgent movements' were starting to threaten the elected governments in Greece and Turkey, while Norway had also been told by the Soviets that closer 'friendship' was expected – or else. The Norwegians knew what Soviet 'friendship' meant for the Finns, and they wanted none of it.

While much of this was happening, either far away or behind an almost impenetrable 'Iron Curtain', what was happening in Germany was very visible to Western observers and the Occupation authorities alike. Not only had the Soviet authorities refused to respect the will of the SPD members, as recorded in the referendum on merging the SPD with the KPD, they were increasingly interfering in the Western Sectors of the city too. Officials appointed to office during the period of Soviet occupation, most notably the police commissioner, were with increasing frequency refusing to take orders from the Western commandants. They only carried out those orders which had been approved by SMAD. The radio station, located in the West but controlled by the Soviets, allowed the British and Americans only 1 hour of air time per day: for 22 hours of every day it broadcast what the SMAD ordered. SED activists, who accepted the opinion and wishes of no one other than their superiors, disrupted the efforts and activities of union, youth, and social welfare organisations to function as democratic organisations. Perhaps most demoralising of all, Soviet troops continued to loot and rape everywhere in the city and were not called to account by the Soviet-controlled police forces; only US and British MPs – who could not be everywhere at once – offered the population protection from uniformed Soviet predators.

In October 1946, six months after resisting the attempt by the KPD to absorb it, the SPD won a resounding victory in the first free municipal election since the war. The SPD alone polled nearly 50 per cent of the vote (48.7 per cent), while the new CDU, a party just 15 months old and lacking any support from the outside, came in a respectable second, with 22 per cent of the vote. The liberals took nearly another 10 per cent and so the non-communist parties combined had an overwhelming majority in the Berlin City Council of more than 80 per cent. They found their power, however, limited at every turn by the SMAD. On 24 June 1947, the Berlin City Council elected Ernst Reuter, a former communist turned socialist, as Lord Mayor, only to again have their choice vetoed by the Soviets in both the Kommandatura and the Control Council.

It was now crystal clear that the Soviets recognised neither the will of their own people nor that of any of the liberated peoples of Eastern Europe, much less the conquered Germans. Equally clear was that they were not willing to work together with their former allies to re-establish a viable economy throughout Europe starting in Germany. In retrospect, it could be argued that it had taken the Western Allies roughly eighteen months to discover what should have been evident at Potsdam: that the Soviet Union had stopped cooperating with and had reverted to warfare against the 'reactionary' Western Powers. It was better late than never, though, and once the US and UK had recognised this fact, the response was comparatively swift; swift for two democracies dependent on political consensus. On 1 January 1947, the American and British Zones were administratively merged into a single entity affectionately known as 'Bizonia'. Typically, the United States had offered to join up with 'any other Zone' interested in cooperating, but only the British had responded positively. Nevertheless, the move enabled at least the pooling of resources and reduced some of the burden of duplication, although it is important to note that Bizonia also lacked the agricultural resources to sustain its population of 32 million normal residents plus 7 million refugees. The need for a sound economy capable of paying for the import of raw materials remained critical.

On 5 June 1947, the US Secretary of State publicly announced the establishment of a European Recovery Program, better known to posterity as the Marshall Plan. This was a plan designed to put the vast resources of the US at the disposal of a still destitute Europe. Marshall stated very explicitly: 'Our policy is directed not against any country or doctrine, but against hunger, poverty, desperation and chaos.'[22] He said its purpose was 'the revival of a working economy in the world so as to permit the emergence of political and social conditions in which free institutions can exist'.[23] Again the offer was made to all European states, and the only prerequisite of the aid was that the European countries work together and come up with a cooperative system for allocating, administrating and distributing the aid so that the United States would not have to work bilaterally with each recipient country. As was to be expected, the Soviet Union declined to cooperate, but the French were lured out of their absolute obstructionist position. It can be said that throughout 1947, while the United States decided to do what it thought was necessary to foster European recovery, it was by no means openly confronting the Soviet Union.

When the foreign ministers met yet again in London in November 1947, the representatives of the West had lost all expectation of agreement with the Soviets. The Western Allies, however, had not given up hope. Clay and his British counterpart, General Robertson, started to move consciously towards the establishment of a West German government at least for Bizonia, regardless of the position and policies of the Soviet Union.

THE IMPERATIVE OF CURRENCY REFORM

Reluctantly, and after a year and a half of trying to work together with the Soviet Union, the West embarked on a path of economic reconstruction for Europe completely independent of the Soviet Union. Central to this policy of fostering sustained recovery for Germany was the creation of a sound banking system, a currency to replace the barter economy, and the creation of institutions capable of self-administration, i.e. the establishment of an independent and sovereign German government. The Soviet Union too had repeatedly proclaimed its interest in a currency reform, provided it had control of the currency. With respect to a new German government, the Soviets were working diligently towards this goal through their party cadres and with the help of the Secret Police. The Soviet Union was very committed to creating a German government, as long as it was controlled directly from the Kremlin without the slightest deviation or hint of independent thought or action.

The West perceived the currency question as most pressing and so turned their attentions to the subject of currency reform first. The Soviets had been asked repeatedly over the previous two years to support measures to put German finances on a sound basis, but since they were very much a part of the problem, it made it very difficult to work with them towards a solution. (It should be kept in mind that at no time in the history of the Soviet Union did it, or its satellites, ever have a freely convertible and internationally recognised currency.) In any case, in postwar Berlin, whether because Soviet ideology prevented it or Soviet policy makers simply never grasped the essentials of finance, there can be no doubt that the Soviet Union was largely responsible for the fact that the official postwar currency, the so-called 'Occupation Mark', was utterly worthless.

Even before the occupation of Germany, the Allies had agreed to print an 'occupation currency' to be used by all troops in occupation of Germany. The Soviets insisted on being given a set of plates for printing these Marks, and promised to provide a strict accounting of the notes produced on them. In the event, they not only failed to provide an accounting to the West, they apparently never bothered with such a burdensome task even for internal purposes. Instead the Marks were printed as recklessly as toilet-paper and used to pay soldiers with years of back-wages. The Soviet soldiers thus found their pockets bursting with tens of thousands of Marks which they were strictly prohibited from taking back to the Soviet Union. Uncontrollable inflation inevitably ensued.

The situation was aggravated by the fact that the official exchange rate for American soldiers was 10 Occupation Marks to a dollar and the army post exchanges were obliged to convert the worthless Marks, which the Soviets were printing by the hundreds of millions, into dollars. This meant, for example, that:

> A soldier with a gift of a crisp ten-dollar bill from home . . . had the choice of converting it to one hundred marks at the official rate of exchange or taking it to the black market, where the same ten dollars would bring one thousand marks, which could then be converted back into dollars at the official rate and sent home again in the form of a money order for one hundred dollars – a profit of 900 per cent on a simple transaction. It really was not much of a choice.[24]

The worthlessness of the 'official' currency meant that most genuine economic transactions took the form of barter, and cigarettes rapidly became the principal alternative currency. Yet, while a carton of American cigarettes, available for purchase at $0.50 could bring 1,500 Occupation

Marks or $150 on the black market, wages paid to German workers in Marks could not cover the basic necessities of life. Unskilled workers, for example, earned as little as 180 Marks (at the above rate of exchange for cigarettes, $0.06) per month. Butter cost $60 a pound (6,000–9,000 Occupation Marks), and bread $12 a loaf (12,000–18,000 Occupation Marks). Given the disparity between wages and prices, it is hardly surprising that a social worker reported to Gen Clay: 'Many people find it not worth while to work for a wage. It takes too much time away from earning a living on the black market.'[25] But people could only 'earn a living' on the black market if they had something to sell. Occupation Marks and cigarettes were in the first instance issued to the Occupation forces. In order to obtain these, the Germans had to sell something to the Occupation forces. Furthermore, since the Soviets had printed the Occupation Marks by the billion, farmers refused to accept them, so food could only be purchased in exchange for goods: a Persian carpet for a sack of potatoes, the family silver for a side of ham. Anyone without a lucky hand (and the time and connections) for successful trading on the black market got progressively poorer, while the poor, who had no Persian carpets or silver to sell in the first place, were reduced to prostitution or starvation.

Another side effect of the black market was that it drained away resources that would otherwise have been distributed through official channels as rations. It has been estimated that 'at least' 10 per cent of the imports from abroad each month failed to reach the rationed consumer, while as much as 40 per cent of the domestically produced food was 'being siphoned off into the black market'.[26]

The situation was intolerable and everyone recognised that a currency reform was long overdue, but still the Western Allies hesitated to take independent action. It was obvious that the Soviets were not going to allow currency controlled by the Western Powers to circulate in their Zone; that would have made them dependent on the West. However, if the currency could not circulate freely throughout Germany, then it would reinforce the division of the country rather than help overcome the fragmentation of the economy. With each day the delay of currency reform meant more delay in economic recovery, and once the European Recovery Program had passed through Congress in late 1947, a currency reform became imperative to enable Marshall Aid to flow into Germany.

On 1 March 1948 a central bank was established in the Western Zones and from that point forward, despite intense secrecy about the details, it was obvious to all that a new currency was coming. Consumers tried to buy up everything they could find in order to rid themselves of their soon-to-be-completely-worthless old money. Retailers and wholesalers on the other hand tried to hoard their products until they could be sold for 'real' money. When the new currency was finally introduced, it was like a purifying summer thunderstorm.

No currency reform can be completely equitable. It is impossible to ensure that people's personal savings are not wiped out without burdening industry with unrealistic debt etc. This currency reform was no exception, but for all its imperfections, the overall impact was dramatically positive. Goods, which had been held in warehouses or 'under the counter' for months, suddenly appeared in the stores. One observer claimed: 'Practically everything disappeared from the shelves and some stores closed altogether until 25 June; afterwards things that one hadn't seen in ages could be seen in the windows.'[27] More important in the long run, was an overall greater willingness on the part of workers to accept wages, and on the part of companies to invest in raw materials and productive capacity, because it was now possible to calculate both costs and returns. The confidence in the new currency grew rapidly and it laid the foundation of what was later known as the German Economic Miracle.

PROSPERITY *VERSUS* UNITY

From the day the D-Mark was introduced into the Western Zones in 1948, the economies on opposite sides of the zonal border started to diverge at an increasing rate. Within just months of the currency reform an English airman reported:

> As seen from the air, West of the East Zone border, life appeared normally civilised, re-building was taking place, there was motor traffic on the roads, and the countryside was alive. After crossing the border to the Russian Zone, the roads were empty except for the occasional horse and cart and it was apparent that none of the war damage had been repaired and reparations were being carried out by the Russians, removing as much as they could carry back to their own country. In the Russian occupied zone large buildings were decorated with pictures of 'Stalin' but there were little other signs of life.[28]

By 1989 the contrast between economic abundance in the West and economic bankruptcy in the East induced the population to revolt against their incompetent leadership. The SED was toppled in record time and without bloodshed. Seldom has there been a 'revolution' that was so clearly economically motivated.

The Economic Miracle initially passed Berlin by. This was because there was no good way to introduce currency reform in just part of a city. Trying to find a satisfactory solution was like trying to 'square the circle'. One of Berlin's City Councilmen anticipated the difficulties in January 1948, predicting:

> If you do nothing, there will be complete chaos. Berlin will become an even greater smuggling hub than it is already. But if Berlin becomes part of the Soviet currency area, then it will inevitably be absorbed both economically and politically into the Soviet Zone. If the Western Sectors use western money and the Eastern Sector uses eastern money, than the city will be torn in two – which is not sustainable in the long run.[29]

This observer proved prescient, but in the event, the chaos was even greater than anticipated. The Western Allies opted for the introduction of a Berlin Mark – separate from the Deutsche Mark in that it was marked with a large 'B' for Berlin and was only valid in Berlin – in theory in *all* of Berlin, both East and West.

The Soviets, getting wind at the last minute of the impending introduction of the B-Mark, worked fast and furiously to introduce a Berlin Mark of their own. As usual, the Soviet effort was marked by the dilettantism that characterised their monetary policy throughout their history. Rather than printing new notes, the Soviets took the worthless Occupation Marks which circulated in completely uncontrolled numbers. Then they glued by hand, with poor glue, a little sticker on the old notes to make them 'new' notes. Not only did the stickers come off easily – even without evil intent – but the stickers had no serial numbers, water marks or any other security features. They were easy to forge and could be printed up by the millions ensuring that the new currency was just as worthless as the old. It is hardly any wonder that the Berliners in 1948 – no less than the Germans in the German Democratic Republic (DDR) in 1989 – wanted the D- (or even the B-) Mark more than any other thing the West had to offer.

Having created the currency catastrophe by printing the Occupation Mark without accountability or control, and aggravated the situation by now creating a currency only good for wallpapering (the Berliners referred to it as the 'wallpaper mark' – *Tapetenmark*), the Soviet 'solution' was to simply forbid the use of the hard B-Mark throughout Berlin. The Western commandants were quick to point out that the SMAD had no authority to forbid anything whatsoever in the Western Sectors, so the Berliners had two currencies, and this led to a number of absurd situations. For example, one had to use

East Marks to purchase stamps at post offices in the East and B-Marks to purchase the identical stamps in the Western Sectors. People using the same public transport system were paying in different currencies, and workers who worked in the East but lived in the West had no money to pay for their rent, while workers who worked in the West but lived in the East were not allowed to pay their rent in the currency of their wages.

The Soviets provided a vivid display of their concept of fairness by making the rates of conversion from the old Occupation Mark to the new East Mark dependent upon loyalty to the Soviet regime. Soviet-controlled enterprises and SED organisations could convert their Occupation Marks to new East Marks at a rate of one-to-one, but the general public got a less favourable rate and 'profiteers', 'capitalists', and 'fascists' (as defined by the SMAD/SED without trial or recourse) simply were not allowed to convert money at all; their liquid assets were wiped out from one day to the next. The signal was not lost on anyone.

Despite the most diligent efforts of the SED and SMAD to portray the B-Mark as the instrument of evil which was dividing Germany in two and enslaving her people to 'Western capitalism', the Western currency remained the currency of preference to everyone in both East and West. So much so that the SMAD and SED were forced to pay at least those workers who had legitimate reasons for travel to the West (i.e. they lived or worked there, or worked on the public transport system that crossed the Sector borders) partially in Western Marks.

SED/SMAD efforts to incite opposition to the Marshall Plan were equally futile. Efforts to convince the labour unions to condemn Marshall Aid failed miserably. Responding like the creatures of Adam Smith rather than Karl Marx, Germans steadfastly refused to be convinced that offers of financial and material aid were evil, particularly not when the voice maligning the aid was responsible for robbing them of what few resources they had left.

The one issue that seemed to have sufficient emotional appeal for the SED to exploit was 'unity'. Opinion polls indicated that the Germans had a strong national identity and were opposed to the fragmentation of Germany into arbitrary Zones of Occupation as had happened at the end of the war. The Germans did not view the partition of Germany as in any way 'natural', 'legitimate', or 'fair'. The SED therefore launched a propaganda campaign which portrayed every aspect of the Western economic recovery programme as a 'subversive' campaign to tear Germany in two and so prevent it from ever again becoming a proud and sovereign country.

The Western response was uncertainty and hesitancy with regard to their plans for the creation of self-governing institutions in the Western Zones.

They feared there would be a backlash against them and the SED would gain ground. Western caution, in turn, fuelled SED confidence. Believing they were on the right track, they increased the pressure. The SED proposed a 'plebiscite' on 'unity'. The German people were to be asked if they wanted 'division' – which they clearly did not – without being asked if they preferred the alternative: economic stagnation.

The SED started circulating petitions demanding such a plebiscite. Quite aside from the issue of whether the plebiscite would have had any value in the form planned, there was good reason to fear that the mere exercise of collecting signatures would be exploited by the SED to identify their 'friends' and 'enemies'. A district leader of the SED openly announced at a mass rally that 'the time will come when the card you receive for signing must be shown in order to prove that you really stand on the side of the People'.[30] By prohibiting the plebiscite, however, the West played into the hands of the SED by appearing to fear a vote in favour of unity, i.e. to genuinely favour partition.

Despite being on the right side of an important and emotional issue, the SED failed to turn the indisputable public desire for national unity to their own advantage. They found that no amount of hysteria could mobilise people outside their own political cadre to protest Western economic actions. It proved completely impossible to organise a general strike or even the kind of mass – albeit minority – protests that had brought down the government in Prague in February 1948. The SED was undoubtedly 'the Unity Party' and the Germans undoubtedly preferred unity to partition, but not at the price of being kept in economic destitution and excluded from the 'milk and honey' now flowing from the US in the form of Marshall Aid. It was rather like choosing between half of a wonderful, thick, juicy rump steak or the leftover bones of a whole but scrawny chicken. The way to a man's vote is often through his stomach.

CONFRONTATION

Even before the introduction of the new currencies, the political tensions between East and West had been mounting. In retrospect, the failure of the fifth meeting of the Council of Foreign Ministers held in London in November–December 1947 appears to have been a signal to the Soviets that the time for more forceful tactics had come. On a political level, the most obvious manifestation of these tactics was the fact that the Soviet representatives walked out of the Allied Control Council and the Allied Kommandatura on 20 March and 16 June 1948 respectively. In both cases, the pretext for the walkout was petty and in both cases the Soviets read prepared speeches condemning the Western Allies for their stubbornness, arrogance and failure to respect the spirit of Potsdam. The insults were, by then, so routine that they wearied more than provoked the Western representatives.

If the Soviets had expected the West to respond with distress to the break-up of Four Power government, they were disappointed. All Four Powers – with the possible exception of the French – recognised that Four Power government was moribund. The official break-up of the instruments of Four Power rule was therefore more a relief than a shock. The West was moving ahead at full steam to carry out the currency reform and establish instruments for German self-government in their area of occupation and the Soviets were moving ahead at full steam with their plans for a blockade of Berlin.

In preparation for a blockade, the Soviets escalated their guerrilla tactics against the Western garrisons and their terror tactics against the German population. As far back as early 1946 there had been isolated incidents of Soviet police abducting persons from the Western Sectors; three municipal judges who had refused to render judgments desired by the Soviets had 'disappeared' from their homes, never to be seen again. In early 1948 various observers reported the increased use of abduction. An American intelligence officer based in Berlin reported that Russians, disguised as German police, were arresting German officials living in the US and British Sectors of Berlin. Police officers who were not sufficiently loyal to the SED and Soviet Union were also targeted for such actions and disappeared, but it was not only city officials who had to fear abduction. German scientists were being kidnapped from their homes and sent to work in the Soviet Union, particularly on the atomic bomb project, simply because they had skills the Soviet Union needed. Likewise, German workmen and skilled female labourers could find themselves deported on 2 hours' notice. Even the Allies were not exempt from at least short-term arrest. Gen Clay reported that ninety-three American servicemen were detained in the first half of 1948 and few of the arrests had any justification. In many instances 'the Americans were held for hours under humiliating conditions . . . '.[31]

The harassment of inter-zonal traffic also increased noticeably in 1948 and took many forms. One simple tactic of the Soviets was the sending of Russian soldiers dressed in civilian clothes to systematically rob passengers arriving at the train stations. On other occasions, Soviet soldiers openly held up buses of the public transport network at gunpoint and took what they liked without bothering to disguise themselves. More subtle but equally effective was the Soviet tactic of changing without notice the bureaucratic requirements for possession of a lorry licence. Everyone was required to possess a licence from the SMAD, but the form, shape or colour of this licence could change without warning from one day to the next. When this happened, all lorry traffic came to a virtual halt while drivers and firms scrambled to get the new documents. After paying the fees and standing in lines and collecting the signatures and stamps for the new document, the owners of such documents had no certainty that the rules would not change again the next day – and naturally such documents were completely unobtainable if one had incurred the displeasure of the SMAD in one way or another.

The Soviets also introduced new licences for moving from the Western Sector to the Western Zone, and the costs and difficulties of obtaining the licences brought such movements to a virtual standstill. The harassment of German passengers travelling between Berlin and the Western Zones escalated, so that Germans had to dread not only intrusive searches (which often ended in official and unofficial confiscations) but also arrest for alleged infractions of rules they had never heard of.

The Soviets did not shrink from challenging the Western Allies directly. One day they might try to seize locomotives from the marshalling yards in the West, on another they tore up the railway track itself – 'reparations'. The pinpricks of harassment, individually insignificant and hardly warranting reporting higher up, were increasing and the American Military Governor, Gen Clay, rightly sensed that all these little measures were part of an orchestrated campaign. He was quick to note the rising tensions, and he later worded it as follows: 'Somehow I felt instinctively that a definite change in attitude of the Russians had occurred and that something was about to happen. From Sokolovsky down there was a new attitude, faintly contemptuous, slightly arrogant and certainly assured. . . .'[32]

The Russians had at least one good reason to feel self-assured, and that was the victory they had just enjoyed in Czechoslovakia. The elected government there had been brought down by mobilising communist supporters in the streets. Given the evident inability of the SED to mobilise similar troops of militant supporters, the Soviets may in fact have planned to strike at the Allies' weakest point – their presence in Berlin – right from the start.

In January 1948, an American medical officer overheard a drunken Soviet general brag that: 'If those swines [the Americans] aren't out of Berlin by June, we'll close every access there is.'[33] It was also reported that Soviet automobiles carrying high-ranking Soviet officers frequently cruised around the Western suburbs apparently selecting their future residences. More indicative still of the change in policy was an official press release by the Soviet-controlled press in March 1948 in which the right of the Western Allies to be in Berlin was explicitly dismissed, and it was predicted that they would soon leave.

On 1 April 1948 the Soviets struck. They announced that henceforth they would board all trains passing through their Zone and 'check papers'. When the Western Allies refused to allow Soviet inspectors to board their trains, the trains were simply side-tracked and held. On the same day, the Soviets also tried to establish a road blockade within the British Sector and the following day attempted to place their own guards around the central railway station in the American Sector. Both these attempts were foiled by a show of force by the respective Allied forces, but clearly the Soviets were testing how far they could go without provoking a response stronger than they were prepared to tolerate.

On 5 April a Soviet fighter buzzed a scheduled passenger aircraft making a routine approach into Gatow. In close, aerobatic manoeuvring around the BEA airliner, the Soviet pilot apparently lost control of his aircraft and crashed into the passenger plane killing all on board. The British and Americans immediately ordered fighter escorts for their civilian aircraft. Confronted by the British commandant, Gen Robertson, Gen Sokolovsky insisted that the aggressive airliner had rammed the innocent Soviet fighter aircraft. Although the Soviet tone became even harsher in the days that followed, one thing was consistent: they insisted it had been an accident. All accounts, whether British, Russian or German support this, but the fact that the Western Allies' initial response had been to order fighter escorts – and not to ground their aircraft – may have sent a critically important signal to the Soviets. The Allies were not going to sit by and let their aircraft be shot down; they would defend their right to the air corridors with force if necessary.

On 10 April, *Der Tagesspiegel*, an independent newspaper published in the American Sector of Berlin, responded to rumours it had heard by asking Clay if the Americans would allow the Russians to control the cargoes and passengers on their aircraft by landing in the Soviet Zone while in transit between Berlin and the West. Clay replied that the West would reject any measures that restricted the freedom of air traffic between Berlin and the Western Zones. The very next day, the same newspaper reported a new and different tactic by the Soviets to restrict Allied access to Berlin. Capitalising upon the accident with the BEA airliner, the Soviets recommended 'in the interests of air safety' that *all* Allied passenger flights and all night flights to and from Berlin should be prohibited, and only 'technical' flights be allowed. The Allies rejected these proposals out of hand, but the Russians specifically reserved the right to raise them again.

On the ground, the harassment continued. On 20 April restrictions on barge traffic were introduced; a cargo manifest had to be produced and each barge was inspected individually leading to hour-long delays. On 24 April two passenger coaches were detached from an Allied train departing Berlin for the West. On 25 April new rules for documenting freight travelling to and from Berlin were introduced without warning. On 30 April a British road convoy was stopped and denied transit. Throughout the month, disruptions to mail and telephone services between Berlin and the West increased dramatically. On 20 May barge traffic was again disrupted by demands for yet another form of documentation. On 1 June, train traffic between the West and Berlin was temporarily suspended without warning or apparent reason. On 4–6 June twenty-six railroad cars full of mail from Berlin destined for the West were seized and confiscated by Soviet officials. On 10 June five coal trains for West Berlin were stopped by the Soviets for alleged deficiencies in their documentation. On 12 June Allied trains were halted because of improper 'labelling' of freight. On 15 June the autobahn bridge across the Elbe was closed indefinitely 'for repairs'. On 18 June the Soviets cancelled all internal motor-coach licences and suspended passenger trains and mail service between the West and West Berlin. On 21 June US trains were stopped and returned without explanation.

The increasing level of Soviet harassment did not go unnoticed. Clay sent a warning to Washington, which set off a mini war scare in the US. During the four days in April in which all trains had been halted, Clay had asked the USAF to bring in the most urgent supplies for the US garrison in Berlin by air. While the tonnage carried was ridiculously tiny compared to needs – and to what would later be achieved by the subsequent airlift – it did allow the USAF to learn a number of valuable lessons. First and foremost, the USAF recognised the need to have some entity in Berlin that would determine requirements and assign priorities. The USAF also identified the need to have a control agency in the Western Zones to regulate cargoes before they left for Berlin. Last, but not least, the restrictions on the movement of goods induced the European Command to start building up stocks of supplies. The amount of coal imported into Berlin jumped from just 1,541 tons in March to 10,062 in April and 10,443 in May.[34] Meanwhile, the British Army of the Rhine and RAF Transport Command made contingency plans for flying in supplies to the British garrison and flying out dependants and non-essential personnel.

While the Allies and civilians in Berlin both sensed the rising tensions and noted the increasing harassment of the Allies, no one really expected the Soviets to completely sever the lifelines of vital materiel that kept the Western Sectors of the city supplied with everything essential to mere survival. The Allies knew they were vulnerable and it was increasingly obvious that the Soviets wanted the Western Allies out of Berlin, yet no one seriously considered the possibility that the Soviets would risk starving to death a civilian population of over 2 million just for the purpose of driving the Western Allies out of Berlin.

In retrospect, the Soviets probably never thought they were threatening the survival of the West Berliners either. They probably believed in all sincerity that the chosen method of confronting the West was the one that was most 'reasonable' and *least* aggressive. After all, the blockade did not call for any outright use of force. For months the Soviets stubbornly denied that there was any blockade at all. There were simply 'technical difficulties' that simultaneously prevented the movement of goods into West (but not East) Berlin by road, rail and water. At the same time, the Soviets hinted that these purely technical difficulties could miraculously be solved simultaneously, if the Western Allies would simply withdraw the D- (and B-) Mark from circulation – at least in Berlin.

Clay himself doubted that the Soviet intent was to drive the Allies out of Berlin by threatening to starve their dependent subjects. He thought the Soviets simply intended to scare the Berliners into rejecting the Western currency. Another theory was that the Soviets wanted to stop the Western Allies from including Germany in the European Recovery Program and from creating government institutions for a new Germany. There could be no doubt, though, that the Soviets were now repeating, with monotonous consistency, their claim that the Western Allies had 'no right' to be in Berlin at all. Whatever the Soviet motives, the West had to deal with an immediate emergency: how to sustain their garrisons and a civilian population of over 2 million people in a city that was cut off from its sources of food, fuel and other necessities.

Chapter 3

SO WHAT DO WE DO NOW?

ALLIED OPTIONS

The Western Allies appeared to have just two options at the start of the blockade: retreat, i.e. give up their rights to Berlin and withdraw their garrisons, or fight back by challenging the Soviet blockade with a show of force. The French clearly favoured a retreat. They felt it was wrong to place so much emphasis on the importance of Berlin in the first place. Who wanted a unified Germany with Berlin as a capital anyway? Certainly not the French. They argued that it was patently obvious that the Allies could not sustain themselves deep inside the Soviet Zone in the long run, and so the sooner and more discreetly the Western Allies cut their losses and left, the better. The longer and louder the Allies protested and resisted, the greater the humiliation would be in the end. Why give the Russians the satisfaction of humiliating as well as defeating the West?

The British and American political leaders would not even consider the option of abandoning their rights to Berlin and retreating 'with their tail between their legs'. This dogged determination on the part of the political leadership was equally pronounced in Washington and London. When President Truman was briefed in the White House on the results of a meeting among his senior security advisers on the Berlin Crisis, he refused even to listen to the option 'abandonment'. He interrupted the briefer and stated flatly: 'There is no discussion on that point. We stay in Berlin – period.'

The British Cabinet was equally as clear on the point. The day *before* Truman made his command decision, Foreign Secretary Ernest Bevin informed American envoys that the full British Cabinet had already agreed that under no circumstances would Great Britain pull out of Berlin. Just days later, before the House of Commons, he announced: 'His Majesty's Government and our western allies can see no alternative between [remaining in Berlin] and surrender, and none of us can accept surrender.'[1] Thunderous applause from both sides of the aisle greeted this statement, while Harold Macmillan, speaking for the Opposition, added: 'We must . . . face the risk of war. The alternative policy – to shrink from the issue – involves not merely the risk, but the certainty of war.'[2] However, it was former Prime Minister Sir Winston Churchill who, as so often, voiced what they were all thinking: 'The issues are as grave as those . . . at stake in Munich 10 years ago.'[3] Clearly no one in the British government or parliament wanted to follow in Chamberlain's footsteps. Appeasement as a policy, when facing off against a totalitarian dictatorship with military dominance on the continent, had been tried once before. It had failed and been completely discredited.

There was a catch. Truman and Attlee might not be willing to consider withdrawal from Berlin, but that didn't keep over 2 million German civilians from starving to death. While the political leadership flatly refused to think about retreat, they equally emphatically refused to use armed force – as Gen Clay quickly discovered – to restore access to Berlin by land and water.

Gen Clay was fiercely committed to making a stand in Berlin. During the mini-blockade in April he had made his commitment crystal clear. When he was informed that a large number of requests had been made by officers in his command for permission to send their families home, he announced quite simply that he felt it was 'unbecoming' for an American officer to 'show signs of nervousness'. He then said that, of course, if anyone was uncomfortable with the situation he would arrange for their transfer home, but that he wanted no one with him in Berlin who had sent his family home. In effect Clay said in modern language what Shakespeare put in the mouth of Henry V:

> That he who hath no stomach to this fight,
> Let him depart; his passport shall be made,
> And crowns for convoy put into his purse:
> We would not die in that man's company
> That fears his fellowship to die with us.

Clay's wife stayed with him throughout the Airlift, and Clay did not shy away from confrontation. He strongly advocated sending a heavily armed convoy up the autobahn to Berlin 'equipped with the engineering equipment to overcome the technical difficulties which the Soviet representatives appeared unable to solve'.[4] Clay was so determined to proceed that while awaiting the go-ahead for this measure from Washington, he started organising an Allied Task Force composed of between 5,000 and 6,000 troops including armour and artillery.

Clay was not a hothead and he had more reason to fear the outbreak of war with the Soviet Union over Berlin than anyone in London or Washington – he was sitting there. Clay knew perfectly well that the armed forces of the Western Allies were hopelessly outnumbered; in Berlin, in Germany, and in Europe. In Berlin, the Allies could muster at best 8,500 troops, without heavy weapons, while the Soviets had 18,000 men stationed in East Berlin alone. The Soviet forces in Berlin could be reinforced rapidly by the 300,000 troops in occupation of the surrounding Zone, but the US did not have even 100,000 troops in all of Germany. The troops they did have were a cross between policemen and clerks, completely unsuited to the task of fighting their way to the relief of the Berlin garrison. A 19-year-old corporal in the US infantry, then stationed in Berlin, recalls being told by his company commander: 'Gentlemen . . . if the Russians decide to come in, we all have about 2 hours left to live.'[5]

The situation for the British garrison was no better. The British had demobilised almost as rapidly as the Americans, and added to the popular demand to 'bring the boys home' was the acute budget crisis of the British treasury that made it quite impossible to sustain a large standing army even if someone had wanted to. What troops Britain did have in Germany at the time were greatly outnumbered, and those who served in Germany at the time remember their apprehension vividly: 'We had no idea of Russian intentions so it is not surprising that from time to time in those few moments before sleep one would reflect that within an hour Wunstorf and other airlift bases could be over-run by Soviet tank columns.'[6]

As for the respective air forces, the US Air Forces Europe (USAFE) controlled just 275 combat aircraft. The Royal Air Force in Germany fielded 132 combat aircraft organised in four bomber and six fighter squadrons. The Soviet Air Force in Europe, in contrast, disposed over 4,000 combat aircraft, roughly two-thirds of which were stationed in Germany. In short, there was no conceivable way the Western Allies could win a clash of arms with the Soviets.

Clay, however, defended his plan precisely because he was convinced that the Russians would *not* risk war over Western rights of access to, and occupation of, Berlin. Clay wrote in his memoirs after the war:

> The care with which the Russians avoided measures which would have been resisted with force had convinced me that the Soviet Government did not want war although it believed the Western Allies would yield much of their position rather than risk war . . . I shall always believe that the convoy would have reached Berlin.[7]

No one but Clay was willing to take the chance. The British rejected the idea because they believed that Clay's convoy could be stopped *without* the resort to war. They felt that all the Soviets would need to do was blow up a few bridges or put up some manned barricades and thereby stop the convoy from reaching Berlin without actually engaging American troops and starting a war. This in turn would constitute a humiliating defeat for the West. The State Department agreed with the British assessment, arguing that 'the Soviets would just sit up on the hillside and laugh . . . '.[8] Rather than challenging the Soviets in Berlin, the State Department preferred the idea of punishing the Soviets by closing the Panama Canal to Soviet shipping or blockading Vladivostok. The Pentagon and White House both refused to consider Clay's proposal because they were not prepared to risk war, even if the risk was small.

It was therefore more by default than intention that people gradually came to see an airlift as the only possible alternative to retreat. As one British participant worded it:

> We were under duress, Berlin could not wait 6 months for a plan, no one had anything else to suggest apart from Clay's armoured column, and RAF top brass flew the first lot of UK-based transport aircraft to Germany . . . on a philosophy variously described as 'the British genius for improvisation' or 'Limey muddling through', according to one's level of politeness.[9]

In any case, after the experience of the mini-airlift in April, an airlift had been instituted almost immediately, but only as a stop-gap measure not as a policy. The possibility that an airlift could alone sustain the city of Berlin was dismissed out of hand as 'absolutely impossible' by Clay and as 'out of the question' by the British commandant in Berlin, Major-General Herbert. While Clay's reply was a spontaneous answer to a question put to him by a reporter, Herbert was responding to a suggestion brought to him by Air Commodore Waite, the Director of the Air Branch of the British Control Commission in Berlin, on 23 June – the day *before* the start of the blockade.

Fortunately for the future of the West, Air Cdre Waite was not easily discouraged. Waite went back to his office and started working out some rough calculations of cargo requirements and priorities, aircraft load-factors and the like. He came up with a detailed proposal, and on the next day he asked for just 10 minutes with the British Military Governor in Germany, Gen Sir Brian Robertson. It was 24 June. The blockade had just started. The problem of supplying the city by air was no longer theoretical, it was on the very top of the agenda. Robertson saw Waite. Even if he wasn't entirely convinced by Waite's proposal, he still liked what he saw and heard. After all, since the maximum capacity of an autobahn convoy was about 1,000 tons of supplies a day, this was all that an airlift need carry to make Clay's armed convoy superfluous. Roberston decided the idea had enough merit to share it with Gen Clay.

Some accounts claim that Clay was enthusiastic, but that would have been out of character. Clay was not a man given to displays of emotion and some hasty calculations by an RAF officer did not warrant great leaps of joy under the grave circumstances. Clay was a man who took his responsibilities not only to his superiors but to the civilian population of Berlin deadly seriously. He was prepared to do almost anything that might help – if not to end, then at least to ease – the acute crisis.

Nevertheless, Clay was not about to do anything until he was certain that the people of Berlin were indeed prepared to suffer for the abstract rights of their former enemies, which was the way it looked to him on that first day of the blockade. He took the unprecedented step of summoning the elected mayor of Berlin, Ernst Reuter, to his office. Clay then asked the mayor in very blunt language if the Berliners were prepared to go without many basic necessities, including electricity and fuel, while the Western Allies tried to support the city by air. Reuter's answer is most commonly reported as: 'You look after the airlift, and I'll take care of the Berliners.' Willy Brandt, who was later to be Chancellor of West Germany, accompanied Reuter to this historic meeting. He remembers Reuter responding with more eloquence, something along the lines of the Berliners being willing to die for their freedom. If Reuter did say something of the kind, Clay must have been a little baffled. After all, the immediate issue was one of Western Occupation and access rights to Berlin. All Germans were in a sense 'unfree' because they were under Occupation and had no political rights. The American opinion of Germans was that they did not value freedom very much or they wouldn't have elected and supported Hitler. Unfortunately for posterity, Clay makes no mention in his memoirs of the historic meeting with Reuter at all.

Reuter left the meeting impressed by Clay's determination, but by no means convinced that the city really could be supplied from the air. After he left Clay's office, he remarked to an aide: 'Clay's determination is wonderful, but I don't believe it can be done.'[10] Shortly after Mayor Reuter left, Sir Brian Robertson called on Clay to tell him that the Royal Air Force was going ahead with its efforts to fly as much materiel into the city as possible. As yet, neither general had received clearance for action from their respective governments and neither had significant air transport resources at their disposal. (Waite had 'shocked RAF headquarters in London by saying he wanted their entire worldwide fleet of transport aircraft in Germany at once'.[11]) What they were talking about was at best a tiny contribution and at worst a mere gesture. Nevertheless, Clay reached for the phone and asked for a connection to the senior US Air Force (USAF) Commander in Europe, General Curtis LeMay. The conversation is reported as follows:

Clay: Have you any planes there that can carry coal?

LeMay: Carry what?

Clay: Coal.

LeMay: We must have a bad connection. It sounds as if you were asking if we have planes for carrying coal.

Clay: Yes, that's what I said – coal.

LeMay: General, the Air Force can deliver anything. How much coal do you want us to haul?

Clay: All you can.[12]

The USAF did not, in fact, have very many transport aircraft in theatre at the time, so it is not surprising that Clay's order eventually worked its way down to a junior officer, who had the bright idea of asking for help from the only US civil airline then operating in Germany, American Overseas Airlines. Captain Jack O. Bennett described what followed:

I was working in my US airline office at the Frankfurt Airport. The US Air Force telephoned from their base on the south side of the field. 'Captain, do you have a DC-4 airplane that can fly coal to Berlin?'

My feet came off my desk to the floor with a bang, 'Wha— What? Coal?'

'Yes, sir, Captain,' and with a chuckle, 'I said coal!'

'You're kidding! Coal dust would ruin our passenger cabins. We're carrying people on our airline. Doesn't the Air Force have freighters over there?'

'No, surprisingly we don't. We have only two DC-4s in Europe, and they're not in Germany, sir. You could take out your seats and we could pack the coal in sacks, and . . . '

I cut him short, 'Forget it, no way. What's going on? Have the Russkys closed down the autobahn again?'

The Soviets had been playing cat and mouse with the autobahns, trains and waterways into Berlin, shutting them down for hours at a time.

'Yes, Captain, Helmstedt has been closed all day. Intelligence says this might be permanent. We may have to supply Berlin by air. Now how about flying potatoes in sacks?'

I thought a moment. 'Well, I suppose I can, but I'll have to find a co-pilot and an engineer. How soon can you sack the potatoes?'

While Clay and Robertson were doing what they could to improvise and buy time for decisions to be taken at a higher level, and while the political leadership was very quick to back the spontaneous decisions of their commanders on the ground by refusing to back down, many experts and senior officials remained completely unconvinced that the Allied position in Berlin was tenable and thought that an airlift was doomed to failure.

These experts had history on their side: the Allies had managed to provide vitally needed supplies to the China theatre by flying them in across the Himalayas. As much as 550,000 tons of all kinds of cargo was flown over this dangerous route, and – significantly – the operation was, by the end, highly regimented and professional with aircraft taking off every 2½ minutes. It had not always been so, however, and the cost had been great. In the early months, casualties were so high that it was literally safer to fly a bomber deep into Germany than to fly a transport plane across 'the Hump'. At the peak of the operation, when over 200 C-54s were flying the route, the average daily capacity was less than 2,400 tons, yet early calculations suggested that this was only a little more than half of the daily airfreight required to sustain the city of Berlin. Furthermore, the USAF didn't have two C-54s in Germany, much less 200.

Another airlift precedent with many similarities to the situation in Berlin was even more discouraging. This was the attempt by the Luftwaffe to sustain the 6th Army at Stalingrad after it had been encircled by the Red Army in November 1942. The Luftwaffe at that time had already successfully demonstrated its ability to supply roughly 100,000 besieged troops from the air at Demjansk during the previous winter. Although twice as many men were trapped in Stalingrad, the Luftwaffe still had a large fleet of aircraft at its disposal. What was more, they flew supplies to the city from three different airfields, the farthest of which was just 220km (132 miles) and the nearest of which was just 50km (30 miles) away from the besieged city. These distances meant that aircraft could make more than one round-trip journey into Stalingrad in a 24-hour period. Last, but not least, the German Army calculated that they needed just 550 tons of food, clothing, equipment and munitions each day to sustain the 6th Army. Despite all the positive factors, the reality was that the largest tonnage ever delivered on a single day was 290 tons while the average was just 140 tons in December and a mere 60 tons in January.[13] The German 6th Army gradually starved and froze to death. Instances of cannibalism were reported. On 2 February 1943 the remnants of the 6th Army surrendered. The Luftwaffe's largest and most important airlift had failed miserably.

Thus, it is not necessarily to their discredit, that some of the greatest sceptics of the airlift were to be found among the most senior officers of the American armed forces, men who had fought in the Second World War. They were reinforced in their views by intelligence reports which warned that if the Soviets cut off the access routes, it would be 'impossible' to supply the city by air alone. A US Army general staff study from January 1948 had come to this conclusion, so it is not surprising that the key senior officers in the Pentagon, Army Chief of Staff, General Omar Bradley, the Air Force Chief of Staff, General Hoyt Vandenberg, and the US Army's Director of Plans and Operations, General Albert Wedemeyer, *all* believed that no airlift could support a city of 2 million people. They were backed up by America's senior diplomats, who spent more of their time bickering about who was responsible for the failure to have written agreements with the Russians about the access routes than looking for a solution to the problem.

Since both the Pentagon and State Department were equally opposed to a war over Berlin, they were anxious to start preparing for an orderly withdrawal – in unison with their Allies, of course. Gen Wedemeyer was sent to London by Bradley for the purpose of discussing with the British the best means of evacuating the Western garrisons from Berlin gracefully. Wedemeyer met with Ernest Bevin and outlined in detail all the difficulties associated with staying in Berlin and supplying it from the air. His words did not have the expected effect. The British Foreign Secretary responded bluntly: 'General, I am deeply disappointed. I never expected to hear the Head of the American Air Force explain that the American Air Force couldn't do what the Royal Air Force is already doing.'[14] Sir Frank Roberts, who was private secretary to Ernest Bevin at the time, reports further that: 'I took Wedemeyer out and he shook his head – rather like a Labrador, you know, coming out of a pond – and he said, "I suppose that means we've got to do it." I said, "That was the message."'[15]

THE REQUIREMENTS

As the political leadership would not even consider backing down or fighting, and because an airlift de facto already existed, it became the Allied strategy. Admittedly, not a long-term strategy, but an ad hoc strategy for weathering the immediate crisis until a diplomatic solution could be attained that would reopen the surface access routes. The problem was, of course, that since no one had ever contemplated an airlift on this scale, nobody had the faintest idea of what was needed.

The very first task was to make an accurate assessment of what the population needed to survive. The second step would then be to calculate the resources necessary to meet those requirements. Lastly, the resources to meet those requirements would have to be found – if possible.

The Allies knew that prior to the blockade 15,500 tons of supplies had been imported into the city every day simply to sustain a meagre standard of living and an anaemic level of industrial production. There was clearly very little 'fat' in the supply chain. Also prior to the blockade, electricity – and the coal to power the electric power plants – came from the East, along with other vital goods such as fresh milk, fruit and vegetables. Even though some of the 15,000 daily tons previously imported from the West might have been superfluous, other things such as coal, fresh vegetables and milk, which had previously been provided by the surrounding Eastern Zone, would now have to come from the West and that meant they would have to be flown in by air. To calculate minimum requirements, the West had to work from the bottom up, deciding how much of what materials were absolutely necessary for the city to survive for an indefinite period.

Just how much grain, butter, salt, meat, and milk did the city need to keep from starving? How much coal and petrol were necessary to keep the electricity turned on and public transport operating? How much coal was needed to keep people from freezing in the winter? How much detergent, soap, toilet paper and toothpaste, and how many sanitary products and babies' nappies were indispensable to keep the population healthy? Could hospitals keep functioning without medicine, bandages and disinfectant? For how long and what might be the consequences? What about raw materials to keep Berlin's factories working, and if factories closed, how would the unemployed workers respond? Would they riot or start supporting the SED? What about clothes and shoes? Or newspapers to keep people informed of events? What *was* 'absolutely essential' and what were luxuries?

Calculating food needs was probably the easiest (as well as the most urgent) task facing the Allied governments. They now had long experience in working out caloric requirements for various categories of workers in order to establish rations both at home and in Occupied Germany. All that needed to be done was to convert calories into units of weight and multiply by the number of mouths to be fed. Within a relatively short period of time, it was decided that the most essential food requirements in short tons per day were:[16]

Potatoes	900	Meat/fish	106
Flour	641	Other cereals	105
Vegetables	165	Sugar	51

Salt	38	Coffee	10
Fat	32	Cheese	10
Milk	20	Yeast	3

Altogether these daily requirements amounted to round about 2,000 short tons of food which needed to be airlifted into the city each day. These early calculations, however, did not yet take into account the fact that it was more efficient to carry dried goods than goods with water content (for example dehydrated potatoes would later save the lift 780 tons a day). By boning meat before transport, the weight could be reduced by a quarter. Despite the costs of heating baking ovens (in terms of coal that needed to be flown in), it was later calculated that it made more sense to fly in wheat rather than bread etc. These savings evolved over time.

The other commodity that was relatively easy to calculate and was of equal importance was coal – as was demonstrated by Clay's first telephone call. The thing about coal was that it was needed not just for heating homes, schools, factories and offices, but as a fuel for the electric power plants. Electricity powered public transport, public lighting, water and sewage systems and industry. Without electricity the city could not function. The initial British estimate of coal requirements for their sector alone was 1,200 tons of coal per day – or 400 Dakota loads. This exceeded the freight capacity of the RAF even if it flew nothing else.

Since the latter was impossible, the British decided that they needed to reduce coal consumption by improving the efficiency of the power plant capacity in their Sector. In addition to flying in as many generators as they could lay their hands on, they revived plans, which had pre-existed the blockade, to rebuild the major power plant which had once served the Western Sectors of Berlin but had been dismantled by the Russians prior to the arrival of the Western Allies. The new-built plant would be as modern as possible and so would save coal. The catch-22 was that to rebuild this power plant during the blockade meant that virtually all the component parts – most notably the turbines and boilers and the 11m-long steel girders, not to mention concrete and construction equipment – would have to be flown in by aircraft. Another unexpected side effect was that the more efficient burning of coal would mean less coke as a by-product. Many of Berlin's central heating plants, particularly in administrative and public buildings, were coke-fired, so these would have to be converted to oil-burning plants. Of course, the oil too would have to be flown in via the Airlift. . . .

Until the new power plant was built, however, the existing power plants had to be fed with coal, and there had to be coal for at least some domestic heating, coal to fire baking ovens for bread and coal to keep factory furnaces working and more. All in all, the Allies came up with a minimum daily requirement of between 2,500 and 3,000 short tons. At the end of the Airlift, it was possible to look back and see that two out of every three aircraft flying the Airlift would be 'hauling coal'. Not that the Allies didn't try to be creative about delivering the coal. An attempt was made to 'airdrop' coal from low-flying bombers. Unfortunately, the coal pulverised on impact and was of no further use to anyone. There was nothing for it but to pack it in sacks and load it onto aircraft which dutifully landed and offloaded it at the other end.

Where, though, were all those coal sacks supposed to come from? The traditional coal sack, made of jute, lasted only three trips. The US Air Force discovered that duffle bags lasted more than three times as long, around ten trips, but these were more expensive and wore out at a rate of 850,000 duffle bags a month. It was soon costing the US government $250,000 per month just for the sacks in which the coal was transported.

Coal sacks were only one of hundreds of items required to deliver the cargoes needed to sustain the city. Once it had been determined that the city would need between 4,000 and 5,000 tons of goods delivered each day, the Allies had to calculate just how many aircraft would be required in order to haul that much cargo. The number of aircraft, naturally, depended on the cargo capacity of the respective aircraft to be employed and these varied widely. The ageing, but still common, C-47 Dakota (known to the civil airline industry as the DC-3) could carry just 3 tons, while America's largest transport in operation, C-74 Globemaster, had a capacity of 25 tons. Between these extremes were the principal workhorses of the Airlift fleet, the C-54 Skymaster (civil designation DC-4) with a capacity of between 9 and 10 tons, and the RAF freighters the Avro York (9 tons), the Handley Page Hastings (8½ tons), the Handley Page Halton (6 tons) and the Avro Lancastrians and Tudors (both 5½ tons). For the transport of some awkward cargoes (bulldozers and turbines, etc.) aircraft with special loading features or cargo-room configuration were needed, while for the transport of liquid fuels, tankers were required. Notably, the aircraft that was to carry the greatest amount of cargo on the Airlift, the Skymaster, had never been designed as a freighter but as a long-distance passenger aircraft. During the Airlift it was to prove its value in a role exactly opposite to that for which it had been designed: rather than carrying light loads long distances, it was to carry heavy loads short distances, and with remarkable success.

Another type of requirement, needed to keep a fleet of aircraft flying around the clock, was aviation fuel. That fuel had to be transported across the Atlantic by tanker and transported by rail to the Airlift departure airfields in West Germany. Twenty-five tankers were needed to maintain the Airlift, and at the start of the blockade tankers had to be diverted at sea from their scheduled destinations. Later US Navy tankers were used. As an example of the quantities of petrol required, Rhein-Main airfield alone required 820,000 litres of aviation fuel per day when the Airlift was at its peak. The demand for fuel was to increase throughout the Airlift from the 82,000 barrels a month of July 1948 to 291,000 barrels a month one year later. Altogether the Airlift would consume 100 million gallons of aviation fuel.

Aircraft do not run on fuel alone. They have many parts that wear out and need to be replaced at regular intervals. In the normal course of events, those intervals are dictated by the number of hours flown. The aircraft on the Airlift had been designed and used as long-distance transport planes. Nobody knew what the impact of frequent short-haul flights (with a correspondingly higher number of take-offs and landings per hour of flying) would have on the requirements for spare parts – or on engine serviceability or metal fatigue. The fact that the aircraft were initially operating from grass fields or pierced steel plate (PSP) runways (a type of temporary runway surfacing) complicated matters further. Tyres and brakes wore out at astronomical rates; mechanics were soon reconditioning 60,000 spark plugs each month; six months' supply of windscreen wipers was consumed in just twelve days. The list is endless. Likewise, the fleet of vehicles needed to load and unload the aircraft were provided by the army and, for the most part already war-weary and rundown. They too broke down and required maintenance and spare parts.

Aircraft do not fly themselves and both aircrew and ground crew were needed to fly the aircraft and keep them flying. Since the aircraft were expected to fly round the clock, more than one crew was needed per machine and maintenance facilities had to be in operation 24 hours every day with successive shifts of maintenance personnel. The motor pools doing the loading and unloading likewise had to work 24 hours a day, and again there was a need for trained personnel to maintain them. To support the air and ground crews there had to be messes and canteens, laundries, barber shops and post exchanges, not to mention air traffic control and meteorological support. These services also had to work 24 hours a day, 7 days a week, to support the men working both the day and night shifts. Last, but not least, people were also needed to load and offload the aircraft and maintain the runways and motor transport and run all aspects of cargo-handling operations. The Airlift manpower requirements were estimated by one US source[17] at:

45,000 German cargo loaders and airfield workers
3,000 displaced (mostly Baltic) cargo loaders and workers
12,000 USAF staff
2,000 US Army Airfield support staff
800 US Navy staff
8,000 RAF and Commonwealth staff

This list, however, appears to ignore entirely the role played by the Royal Engineers and the Royal Army Service Corps (RASC). German sources put the number of permanent German workers a good 5,000 higher, while the list appears to overlook the construction workers at the airfields, notably Tegel. This list must be viewed as conservative at best, but even so, it gives a manpower requirement of 70,000 men, 20,000 of which needed to be highly skilled and trained.

Bringing all these various factors together, calculating the needs, converting raw needs into concrete orders, getting the orders placed, the goods purchased, packed and transported to the departure airfields, and then ensuring that cargoes got loaded according to both priority of need and optimal safe use of aircraft capacity required planning and organisation. Likewise, keeping aircraft flying around the clock, with fresh crews and proper maintenance, ensuring that spare parts were where they were needed and that crews got enough sleep and enough food but not too much alcohol, required effective command structures. As one German observer wrote: 'More than a miracle, the Airlift was the result of hard, extremely detailed work.'[18]

SHORTFALLS

The exact figures of what would be needed were inconceivable at the start of the Airlift. No one involved at the very start ever contemplated or imagined the dimensions that the Airlift would eventually assume. All that they knew was that they needed 'a lot' of everything, or as Clay had put it, 'all they could haul'. RAF instructions were equally vague. The political leadership told the RAF – who it knew perfectly well was under-funded, under-staffed and short of aircraft – 'to do their best'. As one of the RAF staff officers charged with organising the operation remarked: '"Something at once" and "do your best" hardly appeared the most well considered instructions issued at the start of a military operation.'[19]

The most glaring deficiency at the start of the Airlift was of aircraft. The French were fully engaged in Indochina and sent their regrets from the start. The American transport fleet in Europe consisted on paper of 102 of the twin-engine C-47s, affectionately know to USAF aircrew as 'Gooney Birds', with a 3-ton cargo capacity and only two of the larger C-54s, which could carry 10 tons. In fact, the number of transport aircraft available for the lift was even smaller than the paper strength. One of the two carrier groups allegedly assigned to USAFE, the 60th, was in fact deployed in support of American commitments in the Mediterranean and Near East. When the Airlift started, aircraft and crews were scattered all over the Middle East and they had to be returned to Europe before they could join the lift. This meant that as on 24 June, the USAFE could commit only 37 Dakotas. All of these were at least 5 years old and had a minimum of 2,000 flying hours already clocked. The prospect of keeping them flying around the clock was a maintenance nightmare and it was predictable from the start that there was going to be a high rate of unserviceability in the fleet.

The situation for the RAF was similar. Defence expenditure in Britain had been capped months prior to the start of the Airlift and RAF Transport Command (never a glamour item in the defence budget) was undergoing severe contraction. When the blockade started, the RAF had only a single squadron of Dakotas in Germany. On the evening of 24 June a second squadron of Dakotas was sent to Germany to reinforce it. Thereafter, the transport fleet in theatre was reinforced with virtually everything Transport Command could spare from around the world. In a comparatively short period of time a large and diverse fleet of aircraft of different types, from Dakotas to Sunderland flying boats, was collected in Germany. Some of these aircraft were very old, some required American spare parts (which had to be bought with US dollars which Britain could ill-afford), and almost all were poorly designed for carrying cargo. Problems ranged from small doors and the lack of internal loading lifts and hoists, to tail-wheels, which meant that while on the ground the floor sloped, making it very difficult to stack cargo. As will be seen, however, this motley fleet was to do a magnificent job.

The USAF and the RAF did not possess any tanker aircraft whatsoever. This fact probably more than any other induced the British government to decide to charter aircraft from civil companies. Roughly one month into the Airlift, the British started contracting civil airfreight companies to carry cargoes to Berlin. This brought in the vitally needed tanker aircraft plus a wild mixture of other aircraft (and aircrew) as well. The charter airlines ranged from established and highly organised public airlines such as the British Overseas Airways Corporation (BOAC) to tiny operations run by wartime pilots with a couple of ageing, converted bombers. Nothing whatsoever was standardised about this hodgepodge fleet of aircraft. All that these companies had in common was that they were *not* authorised to carry the same loads and were *not* outfitted with the same landing and navigation aids or radio frequencies as the RAF. Some of them were even operating with only a single crew and flew to Germany without any maintenance or administrative personnel. Few could afford navigators, and the training, skills and dedication of the pilots was very uneven. On the other hand, one thing must be said to their credit: the civil fleet provided some of the most colourful characters of the Airlift.

They could not, however, make up for all the shortfalls. To keep the RAF's own fleet flying, the RAF needed more trained aircrew than they had. This had a negative impact on utilisation rates, despite the fact that RAF ground crews were superb, highly rated and performed by all accounts magnificently under very difficult circumstances. For the USAF the situation was reversed. They could draw on a huge reserve of pilots, but suffered from an acute shortage of properly trained ground crews. Lack of experienced mechanics caused serious maintenance delays even for routine checks, which could take up to three times as long as when a properly trained ground crew did the work. The shortage of trained personnel did not stop with air and ground crews either. There was also a shortage of meteorological staff and so inadequate weather data, and perhaps most serious of all, both the USAF and the RAF had a shortage of trained air traffic controllers. The situation was so bad that one USAF general claimed military air traffic control had become 'a lost art' by 1948.[20] What controllers there were worked to their very limits, and sometimes beyond.

Among all these sundry shortfalls, one stood out above all others the minute planners got serious about the Airlift: airfield capacity. It did no good to collect mountains of food and coal and assemble a huge fleet of aircraft with their air and ground crews, if there were no suitable airfields from which to fly to Berlin, or if the airfields in West Berlin could not receive the incoming traffic.

At the start of the lift, the USAFE operated from two airfields: Rhein-Main (near Frankfurt am Main) and Wiesbaden. The main RAF airfield was located at Wunstorf, near Hannover, near the end of the shortest of the three air corridors. The air corridors were the routes, according to an agreement reached in the Allied Control Council on 30 November 1945, which the Western Allies had to use when flying in and out of Berlin. (Note: the agreement applied only to *Allied* aircraft, which excluded, for example, aid from other interested parties such as Holland that very much to its credit, had offered aircraft for the Airlift.) The agreement had been reached in response to Soviet complaints about risks to air traffic safety caused by the fact that Allied pilots had up until then simply flown where and when they liked. Since there were no navigational aids in the Soviet Zone, Allied pilots got lost readily and it had indeed been dangerous flying under these conditions. The Western Allies had consequently welcomed the Soviet initiative for regulation of air traffic in the interests of air safety. The agreement provided three corridors, each 20 miles wide and 10,000ft high, running to Berlin from roughly Frankfurt/M, Hannover and Hamburg.

Frankfurt/M lay in the American Zone and the corridor connecting it to Berlin could be served by the two USAF bases, Rhein-Main and Wiesbaden. Rhein-Main had been rebuilt after the war into the USAF hub for all of Europe and it boasted a 6,000ft concrete runway and most of the facilities necessary for air transport operations. A proper loading dock, however, was not built until near the end of the Airlift. Wiesbaden was a former Luftwaffe fighter base, but it too had been modernised by the USAF, including construction of a 5,500ft concrete runway, and a loading dock. Furthermore, it had mechanical loading equipment such as fork-loaders. Of course, neither of these airfields had been conceived or re-modelled with the scale of operations which would develop in the Airlift in mind. More important, they were more than half as far away again from Berlin as airfields in the British Zone, plus the corridor originating in the Frankfurt/M area crossed hilly countryside with a correspondingly higher risk of accidents than the routes to Hannover and Hamburg over flatlands.

The RAF began the Airlift by pouring all available transport aircraft into Wunstorf, the airfield closest to Berlin. Unfortunately, the arrival of large numbers of aircraft and crew coincided with several days of heavy rain 'which highlighted . . . the need for extensive development work including hard standings, to fit West German airfields for intensive air transport operations'.[21] Even after a massive expansion programme, including the clearance of 5 acres of forest, the laying down of 180,000sq. yd of PSP hard standings and the building of 5 miles of railway sidings, Wunstorf was clearly not going to be able to bear the burden of the British airlift alone.

The Allies needed more departure airfields if they were going to fly enough supplies into Berlin to sustain the city, and they needed to locate these airfields near to the shorter and safer northern corridors ending at Hannover and Hamburg respectively. The advantages of the northern corridor can be illustrated by a simple example: the distance from Fassberg to Berlin was just 145 miles compared to 280 miles from Rhein-Main to Berlin. This meant that two planes based at Fassberg could do the work of three based at Rhein-Main, or that planes based in Fassberg could make five round trips a day as opposed to just three and a half from Rhein-Main. The use of Fassberg therefore offered a savings not only in terms of aircraft but also with regard to aviation fuel. Fortunately, in addition to Fassberg, there were a large number of other 'embryo' airfields left behind by the Luftwaffe scattered across the British Zone which could, with good planning and hard work, be turned into efficient departure airfields for the Airlift.

The situation in Berlin was considerably more critical given that it was a built-up city, but things could have been much worse. There were two fully operational airfields in West Berlin at the start of the Airlift, one in the British Sector (Gatow) and one in the American Sector (Tempelhof). Both had their advantages and disadvantages. Gatow was located on the very outer south-west fringe of Berlin, surrounded on three sides by rural landscape, making approaches to the field easy and safe – except that all those fields were in the Soviet Zone and occupied by Soviet troops. The nearby Soviet military airfield at Stakow could easily mislead a partially lost pilot into landing in 'enemy' territory and, equally unpleasant, the Soviets could use the field for harassment. It was from this field that the Soviet fighter which collided with the BEA airliner had flown.

When the British took control of the airfield it had no runways at all; it was a grass field. The British put down a PSP runway almost at once and added a concrete runway shortly afterwards, so that at the start of the Airlift there were two runways at Gatow, the concrete and the PSP one. Neither, however, was constructed for the volume or kind of traffic that the Airlift would bring. There were no perimeter tracks and the aprons at Gatow were of concrete blocks which soon proved inadequate for the demands made of them in the Airlift. At least one more runway and a better perimeter track, aprons and hardstandings were needed at Gatow. Likewise, facilities for offloading liquid fuel were required if Gatow was to be used for receiving tankers.

The situation at Tempelhof was worse. The airport was located in the middle of the city and the field was surrounded by five-storey buildings, the upper stories of which were residential. Just what this meant for flying is well described by Pilot Bill Martin of the USAF, who described his first landing at Tempelhof as follows:

> When I broke out [of the cloud] it seemed like I was in a crab and I was looking into somebody's window. There were lights on in there, and I could see these people sitting around a table, eating their dinner. I had heard about how narrow that corridor was . . . but that was my first experience. To eyeball it that close – those people eating dinner while I'm flying an airplane right by them![22]

The US Army Corps of Engineers required airfields to be built so that approaching aircraft could come in on a 'glide path' with a slope of 1:40, i.e. an aircraft was supposed to travel forward 40ft for every foot of altitude it gave up. At Tempelhof the glide angle on the principle runway was 1:16 and on the shorter, secondary runway 1:10. An aircraft on approach to Tempelhof came within less than 100ft of the roofs of the surrounding buildings, and this proved a serious psychological handicap to many Airlift pilots. Controllers had to 'coax' pilots down against their instincts, and no less than three aircraft crashed because they put down too late; none ever wrecked because they put down too soon! In short, aircraft swooped down at steep angles to land on improvised runways of PSP because Tempelhof didn't have even one concrete runway at the start of the Airlift.

The PSP runways started to disintegrate almost at once and teams of roughly a hundred men, equipped with shovels, landing mats, sand and asphalt, were stationed beside the runways. Their job was to do repairs by lifting (or replacing) a steel plank, pouring in a mixture of asphalt and sand from the wheelbarrows they had with them, and then re-welding the steel plates together – all between landings. 'As soon as a plane roared by, they'd jump out and make what repairs they could, then jump back out of the way when the next plane came by.'[23] The experts concluded they needed *two* new runways at Tempelhof.

Even if there were new concrete runways in place at both Gatow and Tempelhof, the Allies calculated they would not together have sufficient capacity to receive the number of aircraft that would be needed to supply Berlin. This was because there was the ever present possibility of an accident closing down either Gatow or Tempelhof completely for an indefinite period. Everyone agreed that what was needed was a whole new airfield.

Fortunately, there was a suitable field, formerly a manoeuvre and training area for the Luftwaffe's anti-aircraft (flak) divisions, in Tegel in the French Sector. The area was large and relatively flat and far enough away from the other fields to enable comparatively safe air traffic control. The problem was that in all of Berlin there were only six bulldozers and a single scraper. More were clearly needed – particularly since all this construction (the additions at Gatow and Tempelhof and the new construction at Tegel) had to take place more or less simultaneously. The construction of runways would also require cement mixers, steamrollers, graders, tractors and dump trucks, the bulk of which did not exist in the Western Sectors of Berlin because they had already been removed as 'reparations' by the Soviets.

The airfields, whether in Berlin or the Western Zones, all lacked adequate de-icing and snow-removal equipment, as the winter would prove, and more immediately had insufficient lighting and air traffic control for night and blind flying. Berlin had only one radio set for Ground Controlled Approach (GCA) and one for corridor control. While Rhein-Main and Wiesbaden were better equipped, they were by no means adequately prepared for the envisaged volume of traffic. There were no navigational aids in the Soviet Zone, so control at both ends of the corridors had to be especially good, but the real challenge lay in the fact the airfields in Berlin were close together and the approach and landing patterns intersected so that very competent and disciplined air traffic control would be necessary to avoid collisions the minute traffic increased. General Tunner, former Commander of the airlift across the 'Hump' and soon to be appointed Combined Airlift Task Force (CALTF) Commander felt at the time that 'the Berlin airspace present[ed] the trickiest traffic problem that aviation ha[d] yet produced'.[24]

Group Captain Noel Hyde, appointed Officer Commanding at Wunstorf, 29 June 1948, kept a diary providing a glimpse into the chaotic situation that faced the Airlift commanders. He recorded for example:

P[etrol] and F[uel] section completely overworked and in a muddle.

Yorks going to be difficult to handle with present congestion on airfield.

Insufficient oil and petrol bowsers.

It appears that night flying under present conditions costs us more than we gain because of difficulties loading, servicing etc.

Army cannot cope with both Yorks and Daks.

Wing-Commander Tech[nical] says we cannot with present manpower cope with 10-minute intervals between take-offs. Marshalling and refuelling are the difficulties.

Yet perhaps the greatest shortfall of all was the lack of a unified command and control structure. Although in close consultation with one another, the British and Americans each launched their own operation. The British had initially activated an existing plan, code-named 'Knicker' to support the British garrison in Berlin, and then officially expanded it to include support of the civilian population of Berlin two days later. They changed the name of the operation first to 'Carter-Paterson' and then, for psychological reasons,[25] to 'Plainfare' on 19 July 1948. Meanwhile, the USAF officially launched its Airlift under the code-name 'Vittels' on 26 June. Despite close cooperation at the political level, the two air forces were in effect running their own independent operations.

Within the separate air forces there was considerable confusion about who was in charge. The USAFE, headed by Gen Curtis LeMay thought it was their show, but the officers at USAFE were all combat fliers, not transport specialists. There was not one American Air Force officer in the European theatre who had airlift expertise. All the air transport experts of the USAF were stationed in the US. In the RAF the situation was similar. The British Air Forces of Occupation (BAFO) believed the Airlift was their operation because it was in their theatre, while RAF Transport Command (which was providing the aircraft, the aircrews and the expertise) felt that they ought to have overall control of the Airlift even if their HQ was in the UK.

So the largest and most ambitious airlift in history grew out of a combination of military improvisation at the local level and political determination at the highest level. It was launched not knowing how much of what the Berliners needed in order to survive – much less how much these supplies weighed. It was launched without knowing how many aircraft and aircrews were needed to get that tonnage of freight to Berlin, or how those aircraft were to be maintained and by whom. It was launched despite an almost complete absence of aircraft and aircrew resources in theatre and despite the serious inadequacies in airfields and air traffic control. It was launched without airlift expertise in theatre and without a unified command structure. But once it took wing, it flew and turned into something that not even its originators and advocators had ever imagined or expected.

Chapter 4

HUMBLE EXPECTATIONS

Regardless of one's role in the crisis, everyone impacted by the Airlift – Western Allies, Soviets and Berliners – shared the fundamental expectation of failure. Or, put another way, no one believed that an airlift could sustain a city of 2 million people indefinitely. Where the parties differed was with regard to what the end result would be, i.e., how the Airlift would affect the long-term situation of the Allies in Berlin and German progress towards economic and political independence.

When the Allies settled upon the idea of trying to sustain Berlin from the air, the decision was based on two vitally important assumptions. First and foremost, that the Airlift itself would not provoke a war with the Soviet Union and, secondly, that a diplomatic solution could and would be found with the Soviets 'soon'.

The Allies based their expectation of Soviet passive reaction to the Airlift on the fact that they had written agreements about the air corridors and, perhaps more important, that stopping the Airlift would require active aggression from them. The rules of the game at the time appeared to entail a constant probing by the Soviets of the West's determination to hold on to certain 'rights'. The Soviets appeared to want to find out just how far they could go by 'peaceful' means, and very vigorous reactions by the West consistently caused the Soviets to back down. This is the reason Clay believed an armed convoy would have been successful. Although Washington was not willing to risk the convoy, the game continued to be played 'by the rules' in the context of the Airlift.

It has been pointed out many times that the Soviets *could* have closed down the Airlift any time they wanted. They could have either shot down aircraft, or they could have put barrage balloons in the corridors. After the air accident, which had induced the British and Americans to provide fighter escorts for their aircraft, it was clear to the Soviets that any interference with air traffic would be met by a sharp reaction on the part of the West. This made them think that hostile actions against aircraft would be met by a more vigorous response than closing the autobahn, canals and rails. These the Soviets had repeatedly interdicted with a variety of transparent excuses and the response from the West had been nothing worse than verbal protests. The very fact that the Soviets did not *try* to close the air corridors is *ipso facto* proof that the Soviet Union did not want to risk outright war with the West at this time.

It can be said with certainty that despite the head-on clash of wills over developments in Berlin and Germany, *neither* side wanted the crisis in Berlin to escalate into a real war. This led to truly bizarre situations throughout the Airlift. One of the most ridiculous was that electric power for Gatow airfield came from the Soviet Sector. On one occasion the Russians did try to turn off the lights at Gatow, but the British only had to remind them that the source of power for their own airfield at Stakow came from the British Sector; the power at Gatow came back on within hours. The Soviets also remained members of the Air Safety Centre. Although pilots were warned that if they strayed out of the corridors they would be shot down, unsuspecting pilots – such as one pilot of the civil airlift, who had never even heard of the corridors – did fly through Russian airspace on their way to or from Berlin with impunity. That civil pilot, incidentally, had flown from an airfield in England to Berlin by 'the most direct route' without the slightest regard for the corridors, but was at no time even intercepted by Soviet fighters, much less attacked.

Another reason why the Soviets 'played by the rules' was simply that they did not think there was any point in provoking the West into violent reactions because it was so obvious to them that the Airlift would fail. Throughout 1948, the Red Army in Germany, and particularly in Berlin, had shown increasing contempt for the Western Allies in a variety of small ways – from insults in the Allied Control Council to ignoring Western speed limits and road blocks. In their own circles they celebrated the start of the blockade. Despite maintaining the fiction of 'technical difficulties' and denying the very existence of a blockade at the UN and in the press, the Soviet Military Governor told his British counterpart face to face on 3 July 1948, that the blockade would continue until the West abandoned its efforts to set up a German government. This was significant because it made it clear that even the currency reform, which many in Washington continued to view as the issue which had provoked the blockade, was a secondary concern for the Soviets right from the start.

The Soviets confidently believed they could achieve with the Blockade of Berlin what they had failed to achieve in three years of Foreign Ministers' conferences and in the Allied Control Council: Western acceptance of a communist

Germany. The strategy was not without merit based on the assumption that it was impossible to support a city of over 2 million people by air. The reasoning was that either the Allies would recognise the futility of the situation from the start – or very soon – and so concede defeat, or they would be forced out of the city by an outraged population. Either outcome was satisfactory from the Soviet perspective since either way the Western Allies would be out of Berlin and so out of the Soviet Zone. The second scenario was probably preferable because it had the added benefit of humiliating and discrediting the West, thereby bolstering the Soviet image as the rising power in Europe and the shape of things to come. The second scenario assumed that since the city could not be supported by air, factories would close, public transport would come to a standstill and people would have neither work, nor food, nor electricity, nor heat. The people in the Western Sectors would start to riot, demanding the withdrawal of the Western Allies. The Western Allies would then either have to use force against the starving population, completely discrediting themselves around the world, or withdraw with their tail between their legs. One way or the other, the ties between the West and the Germans would be so shaken, that it would be easy for the Soviet Union to move into the power vacuum and set up a German state that could be controlled from Moscow. In such a scenario, it would not just be the Germans who would be expected to turn to the 'benevolent' Soviet protectors. Around the world, from Paris to Athens, the Soviets expected that if the West used force to suppress riots in Berlin, then the image of the West – greatly profiting at that time from the launch of the European Recovery Program – would be tarnished. However, even if the West simply accepted defeat and withdrew from Berlin in humiliation, this retreat would demonstrate to the whole world Western weakness. The defeat in Berlin would show up the Western capitalist countries as paper tigers incapable of defending their own interests, let alone those of Europe.

It was this supreme confidence on the part of the Soviets, that the Allied Airlift would fail, that made the second expectation of the Allies, a rapid diplomatic solution, unobtainable. The Soviets had absolutely no interest in negotiating with the Allies until they had been brought to their knees by the failure of the Airlift. If they were surprised that the Allies tried an airlift at all, they were not really disturbed by it. They felt certain that they had time on their side and, of course, one of Russia's most powerful allies at all times: winter. The Allies, they calculated, might be able to keep Berlin supplied with bare necessities as long as the weather was good and no one needed coal for heating, but as soon as the fog closed in and the days got short, reducing the number of flights at the very same time as demand increased, the whole Airlift would collapse.

Allied assessments on this point were really not that different. Even that most dogged defender of the Airlift, Foreign Secretary Bevin, was reported to have remarked: 'It will never work in the long term . . . you could never feed two and a half [sic] million people by air. But it's well worth trying . . . even if it fails entirely, you know, it will give us all time to negotiate.'[1] This was the key assumption that brought His Majesty's Cabinet and parliament behind the extravagant and expensive measure: the blockade would need to last only a few weeks. After that a diplomatic solution would be found. The British Military Governor, Gen Robertson, likewise thought in terms of 'a few weeks'.[2]

In the United States, where scepticism was greater from the start, it seemed obvious to everyone – except Truman himself – that an Airlift could not be sustained for long and so would inevitably fail. As late as 22 July 1948, Clay found himself still fighting significant resistance to the Airlift from both the Pentagon and State Department. In both ministries the opinion still reigned that Berlin was 'indefensible' and the Airlift was too expensive. Furthermore, by this time Clay's staff had worked out that they needed 160 of the large (10-ton cargo capacity) C-54s (in addition to the UK contribution) in order to sustain Berlin in the long term. The Chief of Staff of the Air Force was appalled by the request, protesting that to provide that number of transports for Berlin would denude the rest of the world of aircraft. Truman again came down decisively on Clay's side, stating: 'If we move out of Berlin . . . we shall lose everything we are fighting for.' Truman emphatically insisted that somehow Berlin would have to be sustained 'even if it takes every Piper Cub in the United States' – but only 'until the diplomatic deadlock is broken'.

These were the optimists.

The pessimists were far greater in number. Public opinion held that it would not be possible to supply a city of millions for more than one week. The Berlin City Council thought they had just three weeks before the shortages in the city would be so acute that the Soviets would have no need to stage riots – they would break out on their own and from genuine anger and despair. Two weeks into the Airlift the situation was rapidly deteriorating: rations had been cut, electricity for private households had been reduced to just 4 hours per day and on a rotation system that meant a household might have electricity only in the middle of the night. The underground, street-cars and commuter train networks were restricted to 12 hours of service from 6 a.m. to 6 p.m. There were absolutely no newspapers in circulation in the West and equally no electricity for radio broadcasts, creating an environment in which the wildest rumours spread. At the same time, USAF pilots transferred to the Airlift were being briefed that their tour of duty on the blockade wouldn't last more than twenty-five days. After that, there would 'have to be' a political solution.

Compared to these assessments, the British Berlin commandant appears rather positive when arguing that the Allies could hold out in Berlin until October. By then, he expected (just like the Russians) that due to deteriorating weather and increasing demand for coal the Airlift would break down entirely and unrest would force the Allies to concede defeat. The Air Staff in Washington agreed, and the National Security Council decided that since an Airlift was unsustainable in the winter no one should make any plans to keep it going past October. Why bother transferring all those aircraft Clay wanted? Better to face the fact that if no diplomatic solution to the crisis had been found by then, then it might be time to reconsider Clay's armed convoy idea after all – i.e. to risk escalation – if that was what the president wanted.

Two common themes ran through Allied doubts about the Airlift. On the one hand was the near certainty that an Airlift was technically impossible in the long run, particularly in the winter, and on the other was the assumption that since the Airlift would eventually break down, bringing fewer and fewer of the needed goods to the city, that the Berliners would choose communism. There was talk of massive unemployment, paralysed public transport, widespread hunger and cold, all of which would inevitably lead to civil unrest and riots – against the Western Allies for staying in the city rather than against the Soviets for imposing the blockade.

The most fascinating facet of these Allied expectations is the degree to which they are the mirror image of Berlin expectations. They reveal a complete misreading of the mentality of Berliners at the time. To be sure, the Berliners shared the Allied doubts about the technical feasibility of supplying a city by air. Stalingrad was a more painful and vivid memory to Berliners (many of whom had lost sons and brothers there) than to Allied generals. If the Luftwaffe could not keep even 200,000 men alive through one winter, how could the Americans and British keep ten times that many people alive indefinitely? Many people believed there simply were not enough aircraft 'in the whole world' to sustain a city of 2 million.

While Berliners initially shared Allied scepticism about whether an Airlift would work, their deeper doubt was whether the Allies would bother trying. Why should the Western Allies go to any trouble or expense on account of their former enemies? Why should they risk a war with the Soviets? The consensus was that one 'had to be a fool' to expect the Allies to even try.

Chapter 5

BERLINERS, EAST AND WEST

THE WESTERN POWERS AND THE BERLINERS

The Germans have an expression when everything is perfect – and it is almost always sarcastic: they say that everything is just 'peace, happiness and apple pie'.[1] In June 1948, the relationship between the Berliners and the Western Occupation Powers was anything but 'peace, happiness and apple pie'.

There were a number of reasons for the tensions between the civilian population and the Western Powers, not the least of which was the legacy of the war itself. It was only a little more than three years since the last Allied air raid on the city. The heavy bombing campaign against Berlin had started after the Casablanca Conference in response to Stalin's demand for a Second Front – which the Western Allies were not yet ready to open. Instead, starting on 10 June 1943, the Royal Air Force opened an intensive night-bombing campaign directed against the German capital. From early 1944 until the end of the war, the United States Air Force complimented this campaign with daylight raids. In total over 350 air raids were carried out against Berlin and roughly 75,000 tons of explosives were dropped on the city, killing an estimated 50,000 people.

By no means were the wounds left by that bombing healed at the start of the Airlift. The physical scars still had the power to shock Airlift pilots. 'Nothing I had read, heard or seen, prepared me for the desolate, ravaged sight below,' wrote one Airlift pilot.[2] 'The gaunt, broken outlines of once majestic buildings struggling towards the sky, supported by piles of rubble at their base, irregularly stretched from one end of the city to the other – a mottled mass of total destruction.'[3] Flying into Berlin for the first time, the engineer of an Airlift C-54 asked in disbelief: 'Where in the world do two million people live?'[4] On closer inspection they were no less shocked, and an RAF airman remembers visiting a German family who:

. . . were living in a partly demolished block of flats damaged during the war. The whole family were living in one room, eight of them, grandfather, grandmother, father, mother and four children. They cooked on an oil stove which also provided the heating. The lighting was by oil lamp, plus two beds and a wash basin, all crammed into the one room. Their only luxury appeared to be a radio set, of which the father was extremely proud and showed us that he could tune into English stations.[5]

Less visible than the physical scars were the psychological scars – scars which the Soviets subtly but persistently sought to reopen and aggravate. Right up until the Berlin Wall came down in 1989, plaques throughout East Berlin marked the places where historical and architectural monuments had been 'destroyed in Anglo-American air raids'; in East German history books, the Red Army 'liberated' Germany after the 'Anglo-American air forces' had destroyed its cultural treasures and countless innocent (in as much as they were working-class) civilians.

At least one RAF airman remembers being advised not to wear RAF uniform when off duty because of the hostility it aroused in the civilian population. Another RAF pilot recalls walking into the local pub in uniform and bringing all conversation to an instant halt; the German patrons then pointedly walked out rather than drink in the same bar as he and his crew.

If the Germans found it difficult to forgive and forget the bombing, the Western Allies were equally unable to forgive and forget the atrocities committed by the Germans. The liberation of the concentration camps by both British and American forces in the closing months of the war had for the first time exposed the genocide perpetrated by the Nazi regime. As one member of the German Resistance pointed out forcefully, all subsequent generations have been raised in the knowledge of the holocaust and Stalin's atrocities, and Pol Pot's and the actions of the Lord's Resistance Army etc.;[6] ordinary British and American soldiers stumbling upon Hitler's concentration camps in the spring of 1945 were utterly unprepared for what they found. The shock produced a revulsion greater than cynical modern observers experience at the revelation of new crimes. Furthermore, modern media made the images available to those who had not personally been present. The images of Dachau and Bergen Belsen haunted the Allied soldiers in Occupation of Germany, and made it difficult in the early years to view the Germans as normal humans.

The situation was aggravated by the fact that many early occupiers in Germany and Berlin were offended to discover that the Germans did not appear to have any sense of *guilt*. Clay, generously, suggests that the Germans had been kept in ignorance of the crimes committed in their name and therefore stressed the importance of the Nuremburg Trials in educating the Germans about their guilt. Other observers were less kind, finding the Germans politically naive and dim-witted. The Germans were viewed by many Americans and British as incapable of thinking for themselves and easily manipulated. One American officer felt that Germans had so complacently accepted their racial superiority that they 'were confused and bitter about their humiliating defeat and hadn't begun to sort out fact from fiction'.[7] Viewing the Germans collectively as thick-headed criminals was clearly not the best basis for building a relationship of trust and mutual respect.

The Germans on the other hand were deeply offended by the fact that the Allies, particularly the Americans, were indiscriminating, and treated all Germans as equally guilty. They found it frustrating that the Americans appeared incapable of comprehending the variety of factors which had led to Hitler's rise to power or the complex nature of totalitarian society which mixed incentives with terror and extracted compromises even from bitter opponents. Many Germans felt that it was the Americans who were politically naive, and lacking in sophistication, subtlety and depth.

This frustration and sense of misunderstanding did not extend to the same degree to the French and British. The French–German relationship was characterised more by antipathy, bordering on hatred on the one hand and contempt on the other. The British–German relationship in contrast was one of wary respect. Britain and Germany were the only two adversaries who had fought from start to finish in the long war. The British knew just how hard it had been to defeat the Germans, and the Germans respected British tenacity and conceded that they had, with sacrifice and persistence, won the right to be a victorious power.

In the first years of Occupation these attitudes led to a curious situation in which the Americans and Russians seemed to have a greater affinity for one another at the personal rather than governmental level, than the Americans and the British. An intelligence officer described the situation as follows:

We Americans were drawn like magnets toward the Russian troops . . . we liked the Russians most of the occupying forces. Their country had exercised unexpected and decisive military power, and in their willingness to try anything, they more closely resembled Americans than the gentlemanly French and British. No French or British officer would ever help repair a vehicle. Russians were different, Russian officers would pitch in and act like other ranks. They laughed a lot, were jolly, and responded to Americans with great curiosity.[8]

On the other hand, as an RAF pilot reported candidly, the British often felt closer to the Germans than the Americans. He pointed out that both Britain and Germany were bankrupt, and that:

> Brits could not afford to keep up with Americans, who found us stand-offish as a result. We still had rationing. The British diet was also being kept down by the London government to what the civilians were getting at home, and when US crews landed at UK controlled airfields there were sometimes near riots. Our relationship was closer with the Germans actually – we'd *both* been bombed![9]

By the time the Airlift started, the salient feature of Berlin–Western Powers relations was a profound disillusionment with the Western Allies on the part of the Berliners. Some of the disappointment was caused by the unsavoury behaviour of the Allied soldiers, particularly the American passion for the black market. Americans all over the world love a flea market – and a bargain. They also love to think of themselves as extremely clever traders and businessmen. Given the fact that American GIs received the highest salaries and free allocations of the unofficial currencies (cigarettes and chocolate), it was inevitable that even the simplest soldier became a self-proclaimed 'master' of the black market. It was rare that the GIs understood the implications of their actions for the Berliners. Decades later, an American officer's wife complained that her husband had not let her buy all the wonderful things that were being offered for sale at bargain prices. She insisted, 'after all, people needed the money for food; I would have been doing them a favour'. Her husband replied: 'If they were hungry then you should have given them food – not buy their treasures for a pittance.'[10] Her husband was an exceptional man.

The British were not inherently more virtuous, they simply had fewer of the coveted goods to trade. According to one veteran of the Airlift with nearly 150 Airlift sorties in his log-book, 'all' the Airlift pilots traded on the black market, despite the limited opportunities and the fact that it was heavily penalised. Being illegal only ensured that all dealings were conducted 'out of sight – usually in the aircraft – to avoid detection'. The rationalisation, like that of the American officer's wife, was simplistic: 'What harm was there? All we were doing was taking a little more food into Berlin in exchange for souvenirs. The food was in the shape of packets of cocoa and the souvenirs I favoured were beer steins.'[11]

Blithe exploitation of the situation by Western military personnel was the rule more than the exception and the papers were filled with scandals involving even relatively high-ranking officers who enriched themselves with stolen works of art and other valuables. The papers also recorded cases of rape, murder, assault and drug dealing by members of the Western Occupation forces. A year after the end of the war, the rates of venereal disease in the US Army in Germany was running at nearly one in every three soldiers, while 'assaults on women by American soldiers were so frequent that American women attached to the occupation took to wearing armbands to identify themselves as Americans to prevent being harassed'.[12]

One young Berliner summarised the feelings of his countrymen as follows: 'Actually I didn't have a very good opinion of the American soldiers. After they marched into the city in July 1945 we set great store by them. But then came the first instances of offences and theft against civilians . . . and we lost our faith.'[13]

Some of the disappointment was also economic. Rations continued to be inadequately low, unemployment unacceptably high. Reconstruction was not taking place to any significant degree or at a noticeable rate, and it was clear to virtually everyone that there could be no real economic recovery until there was a stable currency. But the West again and again failed to take the necessary measures. German politicians started to see this as at best incompetence and at worse policy. In a speech before the Party Congress of the CSU, the leading economic expert of the fledgling conservative party raged:

> Today we could almost say that 1945 was a Golden Age. Everyone in the world knows that it is impossible to live on 1,500 calories a day. . . . Everyone knows that we now, 3 years after the end of the war, are sliding into famine. . . . They have sent us corn and chicken feed. And nothing is given freely. We have to pay for everything in dollars earned with German labour and we're supposed to be thankful for it! It is time for German politicians to stop saying 'thank you!'[14]

The German politicians did not find much to like in the initial 'road map' put forward by the Allies in June 1948 for the return to sovereignty either. They felt they were being given very little by way of self-determination because far too much was already 'dictated' to them. They were directed, for example, to set up a two-chamber legislature and to establish a federal system of government. Worse still, the Western Allies insisted that there would still be an 'Occupation Statute' and that certain powers would be reserved to the occupiers. In short, the Germans felt they were not being offered independence or sovereignty at all.

The greatest disillusionment of all had to do with the perception that the West had failed to stand up to the Soviet Union. In part this attitude stemmed from the old notion that the West and particularly Britain was the 'natural ally' of Germany. Many Germans did not understand why the Western Allies had not made common cause with them against the 'real' enemy, the Soviet Union and communism at the end of the war. Even those who accepted their own defeat and guilt, still saw the West, particularly America, as being weak and indecisive in the power struggle that was obviously unfolding. One member of the Berlin City Council summarised it: 'Russia acts. The Governors horse-trade. The Western Powers retreat and sell us down the river.'[15]

Western weakness was seen in the fact that the Western Powers never fully insisted on their own rights. For example, they left the Soviets in control of the radio station although it was located in the British Sector, and then allowed the Soviets to spew forth anti-Western propaganda from that radio station 22 hours out of every 24. Weakness was also perceived in the fact that the West appeared to make no protest and take no action against the increasing number of kidnappings, many of which were carried out by the communist-controlled police. In the eyes of most Berliners, Western spinelessness was further demonstrated by the fact that the West allowed the Soviets to stop the elected Mayor of Berlin, Ernst Reuter, from taking office. When the Soviets started turning up the pressure on the access roads, targeting particularly German civilians travelling on Allied trains, the fact that the British governor decided to stop taking German civilians on British trains altogether looked to Germans like a complete sell-out. These increasing signs of 'craven submission' to Soviet demands caused the Berliners to lose all faith in the Western Powers. A public opinion poll taken in January 1948 showed that the Berliners increasingly believed the Western Allies would pull out of Berlin. The most optimistic of them thought that the Allies would not go willingly, they might resist or protest – but only in a language that was too 'lily-livered' to impress the Soviets or force them to any concessions.

THE SOVIETS AND THE BERLINERS

As the latter point of friction suggests, if the Berliners were less than enamoured with their Western occupiers, their relations with the Eastern occupiers were even more strained. It is fair to say that relations with the West were in large part – at least in the early years – a by-product of relations with the Soviets. It was because the Berliners detested the Russians as much as they did that they first looked to the West for salvation and protection. When the West failed to live up to expectations, their continued hatred of the Soviet Union dictated disappointment and disillusionment in face of the West's failure to stand up to the Soviets at the local, national and international levels.

German hatred of the Soviets pre-dated the end of the war. There were the years of Nazi propaganda against communism, and four bitter years of exceptionally vicious warfare on the Eastern Front which had consumed German lives by the division. Still, the major problems began when Soviet troops crossed into Germany. They were soon expelled again, so the German media had ample evidence of the atrocities committed and the fear of the advancing Red Army was fed and intentionally magnified. Many sophisticated and educated Germans believed that Goebel's propaganda machine was exaggerating Russian excesses wildly and that things couldn't and wouldn't be as bad as German media reports. In fact, they were worse.

In the final assault on Berlin, an estimated 100,000 civilians lost their lives. That was twice the number killed in all the air raids of the previous three years, but that was war. What profoundly and undisputedly altered fear into an inexorable and bitter hatred was the behaviour of the Soviet troops *after* they had achieved their victory.

It has been estimated that the Red Army raped as many as 1 million German women – that is the number of victims, not the number of rapes. Due to the high number of gang or multiple rapes, their number may well have exceeded 2 million. Gang rapes were particularly common in the early days, frequently occurring before the eyes of young children or ageing parents. Ursula Koster, a mother of 6-year-old twins and a 7-month-old boy, was raped by four Soviet soldiers one night. The following morning, while nursing her infant, she was raped again by two more soldiers. Another Berliner reported how she had been raped 'seven times in a row. Like animals'. Eighteen-year-old Inge Zaun was raped sixty times. Russian officers reported arriving in homes and finding only the limp and battered corpses of young girls draped over pieces of furniture – not shot, simply but literally raped to death. More mature women who resisted – and many who didn't – were shot or had their throats slit. Thousands of others committed suicide, before or after the abuse.

These excesses were not a short-lived phenomenon, a perverse kind of 'victory celebration' lasting a few days and then ending in the restoration of order. On the contrary, they appear to have been a deliberate policy or at least so benevolently condoned at the highest levels of the Soviet military and political hierarchies that the excesses continued for months after the end of the war and even after the arrival of the Western Allies in the city. The American commandant of Berlin reported that during the first week of US Occupation 'two hundred Soviet officers and men came into Kreuzberg, in the American sector, and began looting and raping in a large apartment house. Not even a jeepload of American MPs could get them to leave.'[16] One hospital in the American Sector reported treating 250 rape cases in a single day. Note: that is only the *reported* cases in *one* hospital on *one* night *after* the arrival of the Americans.

In a city inhabited almost exclusively by women, the epidemic scale and brutality of the rapine committed by Soviet troops traumatised all those who survived this sexual reign of terror, whether they had personally been victims or only witnesses to the ravishment of others. Interviews with women resident in Berlin in 1945/6 to this day call forth a raw and unrelenting revulsion towards all things Russian. As the historians Ann and John Tusa worded it: 'The Red Army lost Berlin politically at the moment it captured it militarily.'[17]

If the orgy of rape was the most repulsive and emotionally devastating of the Soviet policies, it was by no means the only way in which the Soviet Union systematically outraged the population. Their wild and indiscriminate vandalism and obsessive plundering also earned them a kind of hatred that is devoid of respect. The fact that Russian soldiers, ignorant about the workings of electricity and plumbing, carried away light-bulbs and toilet seats with the expectation of having light and flushing toilets wherever they took their trophies contributed to an image of the Russian 'Ivan' as not only brutal but idiotic as well. The machine-gunning of the supplies stored in the International Red Cross warehouses, destroying invaluable medical supplies, many of which the Red Army itself lacked, branded the Russians as sheer barbarians. At Tempelhof, a civilian airfield never used for military air operations and so largely undamaged by Anglo-American air raids, the Soviet troops smashed the pumps and piping that kept the cellars dry and so flooded the complex in an act of senseless destruction of no use to anyone.

Soviet behaviour was best epitomised by an incident recorded by Col Howley in which a car full of Soviet soldiers passed a young girl on her bicycle and noticed she was wearing a wrist watch. They stopped her and demanded the watch. The girl refused. The Soviets got out of the car and one of them shot the girl dead. Then they removed the watch, got back in their car and drove away. She was probably lucky not to have been gang raped *before* being shot and robbed; presumably the Soviets were in a hurry.

Historians, and many modern readers, are familiar with the depth of the Soviet regime's contempt for its own people. Arguably, it was because Soviet soldiers had seen their own friends and family cut down casually and without greater cause that they could not conjure up any sympathy or even pity for their former enemies. War barbarises men and total war barbarises them totally. The individual Soviet soldier had on average been subjected to the demoralising influences of brutal warfare far longer and under far more gruesome circumstances than his British, much less American, comrades. Perhaps it was impossible to infuse humanity into troops that had been fighting for so long, especially troops raised in a merciless, totalitarian regime that engaged in the wholesale slaughter of its own citizens and employed induced famine as a weapon against its own people. Whatever the reason, the behaviour of Soviet troops was not designed to win friends and influence people. The same goes for the Soviet reparations policy.

As touched on earlier, Soviet economic policy called for Germany to pay reparations not from production or earned income but in raw materials, industrial goods and – most significantly – capital goods. It has been estimated that 85 per cent of the industrial capacity of the Western Sectors of Berlin was dismantled and transported to the East. No matter how justified Soviet reparation claims were, the means chosen to fulfil them were calculated to cause resentment as not only did Germans see their country being stripped of virtually everything that hadn't been destroyed in the war, but it left them unemployed and so with no hope for the future. It is bad enough to see the fruits of your labour taken away from you, but when the very means of producing are taken away as well, the effect is doubly demoralising.

Again, that too might have been tolerable at some level if the Soviets had not also started taking the workers too. At 3.30 in the morning on 22 October 1946, for example, hundreds of skilled workers at a factory producing high frequency radio equipment and their families were rounded up, loaded onto trucks and deported to the Soviet Union. Skilled workers from a variety of other factories such as AEG-Kabelwerk and Askania were also subjected to the same treatment. In all, thousands of technicians and skilled workers, filling ninety-two trains, were dragged involuntarily from their homes and sent to work in the Soviet Union. True, the Germans had done such things too, but Nazi Germany didn't claim that its slave labourers were the 'ruling class' in a worker's paradise.

Then there were the kidnappings. As soon as the Soviets arrived in Berlin, people started disappearing. The sight familiar from the days of the Gestapo, of cars driving up, strong men jumping out and seizing someone, forcing them into the back of a car and disappearing forever, continued. Unlike the rape, the looting and the reparations, the incidents of kidnapping rose as time went on. Col Howley estimated that there had been a total of 2,000 politically motivated kidnappings in Berlin since the arrival of American troops and more than half of them occurred in the first half of 1948.

Some dissidents, the lucky ones, didn't disappear entirely, they were simply sent to 're-education' centres. The Soviets were fortunate not to need to build facilities for their re-socialisation efforts. They found the former concentration camps of Buchenwald and Sachsenhausen eminently suitable for their purposes. Between 1945 and 1950, no less than 200,000 people from the Russian Zone (and some captured from the Western Zones) were sent for 're-education' in these camps; one-third of them died there.[18]

Meanwhile, another form of re-education was being exercised at the only major university in Berlin. Communist ideology was now a compulsory subject and all lectures had to be submitted to party ideologues in advance to ensure conformity with the party line as dictated from Moscow. To ensure that alternative perspectives could not develop, propaganda broadcasts were piped into the cafeteria to inhibit discussion among students. *Still* the university was a hot-bed of 'reactionary' thinking forcing the Soviet authorities to arrest 2,000 students in 1948 alone, 600 of which were found to be in such dire need of serious re-education that they had to be sent to Buchenwald or Sachsenhausen.

Even if a Berliner could avoid having skills useful to the Soviets or having thoughts subversive to communism, he/she still faced a degree of harassment and intimidation unknown in the West or under the Nazis. Namely, his/her freedom of movement was severely restricted by a variety of bureaucratic measures that made it necessary to ask permission for almost anything. On top of that, he/she was subjected to arbitrary search and the 'confiscation' of 'illegal' goods whenever he/she tried to move about the city or travel between Berlin and the surrounding countryside. It is hardly surprising that most Berliners viewed the 'confiscations' as a continuation of the plundering of the early days of the Occupation.

It was humiliating for the Allies to have their trains and convoys stopped, but they never had to live in fear of deportation or disappearing into a re-treaded Nazi concentration camp. The Western Allies were being harassed and humiliated with regard to their rights and prerogatives, Berliners were being threatened in their very existence. While the Americans fretted about whether the Berliners could be expected to suffer hardships for the sake of Western Allied rights, the Berliners were despairing that the Americans would ever grasp the fact that the Soviets were inherently untrustworthy, congenitally aggressive and fundamentally evil. It is notable that at no time leading up to the crisis did the free press in West Berlin perceive the growing crisis as one of *Allied* rights. For the Berliners the issue was always one of *their own* freedom.

Berliners had hoped and expected the Western Powers to put an end to Soviet offences from the day they arrived in the city; they had not. They had hoped that the Western Powers would restore the currency and the economy; they had not. They had hoped the Western Powers would defend democracy;

they had not. After so many disappointments, the Berliners didn't expect much of the West any more. They had their complaints against their greed and licentious behaviour too, but they were still so very obviously the *lesser* of the two evils that Berliners were prepared to make a stand if only for the sake of dignity and without any hope of success. Asked by a cynical West German why Berlin was enduring the blockade and if the West Berliners really thought they were going to be thanked for 'fighting for freedom', a Berliner retorted: 'Do you expect to be thanked for breathing?' Baffled, the West German admitted that of course he didn't expect that. The Berliner then asked him why he bothered to breathe. It was as simple as that to Berliners. They did not expect the West to hold up and they did not believe that an Airlift could sustain them, but surrendering to the detested Soviets was not an option.

When the Airlift started, the Allies had little love for and only limited expectations with regard to the stamina and commitment of the Berliners, and the Berliners had even less love and lower expectations for the will-power and political insight of the Western Powers, but both felt that they had no choice. The Soviets had pushed them too far once too often. It became a case, on both parts, of: Here I stand. I cannot do otherwise.

Chapter 6

THE AIRLIFT BEGINS

'We'll Fill the Air with Eagles,
We'll Fill the Clouds with Men'[1]

AIRCRAFT AND AIRCREW FOR THE AIRLIFT

Into the middle of this bungled international crisis and tense political environment the Airlift aircrews and their support forces started pouring in, literally by the hundred. The USAF 60th Troop Carrier Group, with assets scattered across the continent and the Middle East, started recalling its aircraft to Wiesbaden. In addition, C-47s from other bases in Europe were concentrated at Wiesbaden and Rhein-Main, bringing together a fleet of 102 of these small cargo aircraft for the short term. More important, President Truman personally mandated the redeployment of the larger C-54s from the four corners of the earth, and on 28 June orders went out to the first four squadrons; crews in Alaska and Hawaii, Texas and Panama got orders to report to Germany 'at once'.

Instances of just 30 minutes' notice to pilots were not uncommon. They rarely had time to fill out pay-allotment forms for dependants left behind, so wives were left without pay for weeks until all the paperwork could be sorted out. Meanwhile, their husbands flew the heavy four-engine transport aircraft halfway around the world with stops only for refuelling and weather briefings. They arrived in Germany still in the kit they had been given for their point of departure, whether that was Alaska or Hawaii.

Individuals, not just units, were caught up in the frenzy to provide the necessary men and machines for the Airlift. A USAF pilot with thirty-five missions over Europe in a B-17 was on his way to an assignment in the Pacific when the clerk at a stopover base in San Francisco asked him how many hours he had in his four-engine aircraft. The following dialogue ensued:

'At least 1,700 hours,' [the pilot] answered without even looking at his log book.

'Good. You're going to the Berlin Airlift.'

'No, I'm not. I've got orders for the Pacific.'

'That's what you think,' said the clerk, rubber-stamping [his] orders with a large, black "CANCELLED".[2]

So he went to Berlin instead.

The situation for the RAF was similar. Although the distances involved were comparatively short, the sense of urgency was the same. No. 30 Squadron took off from Schleswigland airfield in northern Germany on 25 June, flew a salute sweep over their favourite holiday resort, the Island of Sylt, and then headed home for England at the end of their routine tour of duty. Two hours later they put down at RAF Oakington and, before they had even cleared the runway, Flying Control was calling the squadron leader to report to the station commander. 'Good heavens,' Sqn Ldr Johnston thought, 'what have I done now?' What awaited him wasn't (as the good squadron leader expected) a rocket for some regulation he had broken but rather a question: 'How soon can you go back to Germany?'

No. 77 Squadron reported to work as usual the same day, only to be told the whole squadron including ground crew would be flying to Wunstorf in Germany that same morning. Since the whole operation would only last 'a couple of days', the ground crews were instructed to take 'only their tool kits' and light clothing with them.[3]

Another RAF pilot remembers his introduction to the Airlift as follows:

Poor Wunstorf, it hardly knew what hit it. From being a rather cosy single fighter squadron station it was suddenly descended upon by eight Dakota squadrons complete with servicing personnel, equipment and the necessary loading and movements organization. It was a permanent ex-Luftwaffe station with a fine Officers' Mess [but] . . . by the time we got there all the beds had been taken. I slept on an armchair in the anteroom the first night, and I remember there being bodies all over the place, even on the billiard table.[4]

As rapidly as possible, the RAF pulled together a transport fleet. By the end of July 1948, the RAF had dedicated a total of 48 Dakotas and 40 Yorks to the Airlift and was already meeting their cargo target of flying 3,000 tons a day into Berlin; and the British build-up was not yet over. In addition to the Dakotas and Yorks, the British contributed to the Airlift RAF Sunderlands (5 July), civil Lancastrians (27 July), Haltons, Liberators, Hythe flying boats

(4 August), Tudors, (3 September), Bristol Wayfarers (18 September), Vikings (23 September) and finally RAF Hastings aircraft, the latter making their appearance on the Airlift routes on 1 November 1948. Altogether, eight squadrons of Dakotas and eight squadrons of Yorks took part in the Airlift as well as three squadrons of Hastings and two Sunderland squadrons. With the civilian aircraft, more than 150 British aircraft were flying on the Airlift by the time it reached its peak half a year later.

By then, the Americans had converted almost entirely to the larger C-54s, building up the fleet to a maximum of 312 of these four-engine workhorses. The USAF also committed a single C-74 Globemaster to the Airlift, but it was too dangerous to land this large aircraft at Tempelhof with the steep glide-paths, and so it could only land at Gatow. Even there, where the runway was sufficient, it was too wide for the newly constructed taxiways and the edges started to break up under its weight. So the flight remained a single, unrepeated gesture although the Globemaster did good service for the Airlift by flying awkward and heavy cargoes across the Atlantic to maintain the C-54s. Last, but not least, there were five C-82 Packets assigned to the Airlift to carry particularly unwieldy cargo. These twin-engine, twin-boom aircraft were especially suited to Airlift operations because of their hangar-like cargo compartment and their clamshell rear-loading doors. Unfortunately, they were not available in great numbers.

None of these aircraft elicited quite the same popular response or affection as the flying boats of the RAF, the Sunderlands. Nos 201 and 230 Squadrons were in Northern Ireland preparing for a joint manoeuvre with the Royal Navy when at 8 p.m. on 2 July the call to the Airlift came – in the middle of a Friday-night dance. Sqn Ldr Payn of No. 230 Squadron regretfully interrupted the entertainment and announced that they had just 30 minutes to load up their aircraft and return to base. At the time, they did not even know where they were heading. At a little after 9 a.m. the following morning they had their orders to take part in the Berlin Airlift and were headed for the old Blohm and Voss shipyard basin on the River Elbe. Here they were astonished to find that the words Operation Plainfare worked like a magic incantation to produce anything they needed by way of equipment and supplies. On Monday morning, No. 230 Squadron set off for Berlin with its first 'Plainfare' cargo.

Payn's Sunderland bored down the Hamburg corridor, skimming 100ft above the pine forests and the silver vein of the Elbe. . . . From Russian fields all along the route planes of every shape and description from the MiGs to R-1 spotter planes, their observers armed with cameras, rose up to focus on them. Then, as the flying boat, carrying its first token load of 3½ tons of spam, hit the Havel

'like a pelican landing on a puddle', Payn and his crew were astonished by the
city's reaction: paddling toward them like a Hawaiian war party came scores of
canoes steered by lustily singing Berliners, bearing garlands of summer flowers.[5]

Not only were the aircraft of the Airlift fleet diverse, the 'house flags' that
they carried were also varied. Obviously, the two air forces bore the burden
of the operation. More Airlift aircraft bore the USAF star than any other
symbol, while the RAF roundel graced the second largest number of Airlift
aircraft, with a total of twenty-one squadrons flying on the Airlift at one
stage or another. What is often forgotten, however, is that from the very first
day (when the USAF found out it didn't have even one C-54 where it needed
it), civilians were also involved. Various US airlines played an indirect role in
the Airlift by flying the transatlantic route with vitally needed supplies and
spare parts for the Airlift fleet, as well as the coveted 'Care Packages' for the
civilian population. American Overseas Airlines, which had been operating a
passenger service out of Frankfurt since mid-1946, contributed to the Airlift
from start to finish. By far the biggest civil contribution, however, came from
British civilian air charter companies. These played a vital role by providing
not only added capacity but specialised services, most notably liquid fuel
tankers. Altogether no less than 25 British civilian companies took part in the
Airlift with 103 aircraft.

The men flying this polyglot fleet of aircraft were equally diverse. In
addition to the USAF pilots from every State of the Union and British RAF
pilots, the Commonwealth contributed aircrew from Australia, New Zealand
and South Africa. With such a diverse group, it was inevitable that levels
of training, not to mention experience, varied greatly. Only RAF Transport
Command had given their pilots any training in flying 'in streams', and
this training had only been introduced in September 1947 and consisted of
a two-week course. While RAF pilots assigned to the Airlift had to be fully
categorised and instrument rated, this was by no means the case for the
civilians. USAF pilots as a rule had less experience in flying close formation *at
night* than their RAF colleagues and were used to flying long distances, much
of it on auto-pilot – although not necessarily as some RAF pilots imagined
'with a big cigar lighted, a cup of coffee in one hand and their feet on the
dashboard'.[6]

Still, what these crews – British and American, civilian and military – had
in common was more important than what differentiated them, and that was
wartime experience. Although the USAF pilots initially deployed on the Airlift
came from Air Transport Command and were professional transport pilots,
as the Airlift grew and the need for pilots far outstripped the supply, the

USAF started deploying all active pilots and recalling reservists with multi-engine experience, and that meant the bomber boys. By the closing days of the Airlift, it was predominantly former B-17 and B-24 pilots, often from the US 8th Air Force, who were again flying over Germany. Tunner's own staff included a former 8th Air Force B-17 group commander, who had led the most costly operation of the USAAF in the entire war: the Schweinfurt–Regensburg raid of 17 August 1943.

The RAF pilots of the first wave were also professional transport pilots; the whole resources of RAF Transport Command were committed to the Airlift, but many of these had served in Bomber Command during the war years. Operation Plainfare found among its aircrew many men with truly distinguished wartime careers behind them. For example, flying in the peacetime rank of flight lieutenant was a former wing commander of Coastal Command with DSO and Bar, DFC and Bar, AFC (Flt Lt Ensor).[7] Flt Lt Thompson was the recipient of the Military Cross and DFC, and had been a Pathfinder pilot.[8] There were many others also.

The civilian airlines chartered to assist the RAF were manned almost exclusively with former Bomber Command aircrew. Although the skills and above all the reliability of the civilian pilots were to prove uneven, the civilian companies did not lack for stars. At Lancashire Aircraft Corporation, for example, the chief pilot was Capt Wallace Lashbrook DFC, AFC, DFM. He was a former Halton apprentice, who had earned his wings in 1936, flown with Bomber Command throughout the war and, in one incident, was shot down and evaded capture to return to active service via Gibraltar.

Most famous at the time was the former wartime Air Officer Commanding (AOC) of the RAF's elite No. 8 Pathfinder Group, Bomber Command, Air Vice-Marshal Donald Bennett. Bennett had written the textbook on air navigation before the war, *The Complete Air Navigator*, a book that was still in use at the time of the Airlift. He held the world long-distance seaplane record, set in the autumn of 1938, on a flight from Scotland to South Africa. He was shot down in an attack on the German battleship *Tirpitz*, but evaded capture and escaped via Norway. As an air commodore, he became the first (and only) commander of the RAF's newly formed Pathfinder Force, No. 8 Group, in 1942. On his first Airlift trip to Berlin, Bennett did a sightseeing tour for his somewhat embarrassed RASC passenger, apparently proudly pointing out all the damage he had done to the city just a few years earlier. He had had his share of misfortune too, however. While serving as managing director of British South American Airways (BSAA) after the war, an Avro Tudor of the airline was lost between the Azores and Bermuda with twenty-six passengers and a crew of six on board. Bennett lost his job and the Tudors were grounded, no longer approved for passenger travel. Bennett used his severance pay to snap up the unwanted aircraft for his new company, Airflight, and then match the jinxed aircraft with the most dangerous of cargoes – liquid fuels. Not that Bennett left the flying of such a dangerous mix to others. Quite the contrary, he was the only qualified night pilot in his company and carried the burden of twice-nightly flights alone for two full months. During the days, he worked alongside the ground crews overhauling the engines of his Tudors.

Another personality of the civil airlift was Freddie Laker. He was anything but famous at the time and without a distinguished rank, a collection of gongs, or the right accent, but he left an impression on those who met him. J.O. Bennett of American Overseas Airlines remembers:

> Melodramatic was the arrival at Tempelhof of Freddie Laker's old English Halifax bomber, converted to carry cargo. Courageous Freddie was flying his single, tattered war surplus airplane on contract to the Royal Air Force. The bent and ancient craft looked as though it could not survive another flight. After each landing, and just as the hurried unloading crews would spring on the airplane, Freddie, in oily coveralls, would rush to put the pieces of his flying wreck back together again.[9]

Freddie Laker built his fleet up to twelve second-hand bombers and soon turned a profit, so that in retrospect he viewed the Airlift as his first great piece of luck.

FLYING THE AIRLIFT

Wherever they came from or whatever national or corporate symbol decorated the fuselage of their aircraft, the pilots of the Airlift were thrown into a situation that was unprecedented. They might be first-rate combat or airline pilots, their courage tested, their experience extensive and the number of hours flown impressive, but none of them had ever flown in quite the same circumstances as they now found themselves. Nowhere else in the world did aircraft have to fly in very narrow corridors over distances of 100 miles or more and in effect have to follow along behind one another like cars on a motorway, maintaining a safe distance and as much as possible the same speeds.

Initially aircraft flying to and from Berlin had to share the same narrow corridors just 20 miles wide and 10,000ft high. To reduce the risk of collisions it was soon decided to pour aircraft into Berlin on the northern

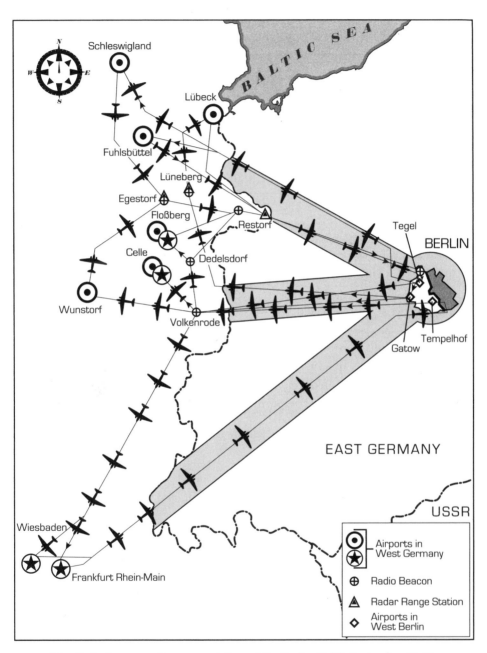

Map 2: A diagrammatic representation of the Berlin Airlift, September 1948.

(Hamburg) and southern (Frankfurt) corridors but fly them out again on the central (Hannover) corridor. This helped somewhat, but could not solve the problem posed by different aircraft types having different optimal cruising speeds. To reduce the risks associated with faster aircraft overtaking slower aircraft in the corridors, it was decided that the various types of aircraft had to fly at different altitudes. On the northern corridor the vertical separation between aircraft of different types was 500ft and on the southern corridor the separation was 1,000ft.

In bad weather and poor visibility it was surprisingly easy to stray – or get blown – out of these corridors and sometimes aircraft did not discover their error until they were confronted with evidence in the form of Soviet MiGs or the like. An RAF flight engineer remembers:

> Going in [to Gatow] we must have been well off the glide path as when we broke cloud we were just above a Russian camp and facing us was a water tower with a large painting of Stalin on the top. We returned to Wunstorf as there was no way we could go around again and have another try, as we would have interfered with the rest of the wave trying to get in.[10]

That was the next problem. Regardless of which of the two corridors they came from, or what height and speed they flew in those corridors, all these various aircraft had to take off and land at the same airfields in Berlin. Gen Tunner made the following comparison:

> Back on the Hump we had thirteen bases in India feeding planes into six bases in China, practically all of Southeast Asia to manoeuvre in, and little interference from the enemy. But here in Berlin all planes had to land at two airfields. . . . They were only 4 minutes apart by air, and they lay in the midst of a checkerboard of Soviet fields.[11]

Another means of reducing the dangers of so many aircraft with different speeds flying in such close proximity was to concentrate the aircraft at the departure airfields by type and to fly them in 'blocks' or batches to Berlin. That is, a squadron of Dakotas would take off, one behind the other at 3-minute intervals, and set out for Berlin. Then a squadron of C-54s from another airfield would take off and feed into the corridor at a different altitude. Then a squadron of Yorks etc.

These precautions could only prevent collisions if the pilots flew at very precise heights and speeds. The precautions also presumed that there would be no mechanical or other emergency that would inhibit the ability of an aircraft to fly at the prescribed speed and altitude. One American Airlift veteran remembers the following 'bad moment': when making an approach into Gatow on three engines he was advised by the tower that a civil Lancastrian without radio communication was 'hedge-hopping' in directly beneath them. The USAF C-54 aborted its landing and headed back for base, only to promptly lose a second engine. Tech Sgt William Michaels, the flight engineer, felt it was little short of a miracle that they landed back at Celle with a full load of coal.

It must be noted that British aircraft flew with highly trained navigators (capable still of celestial navigation) and very sophisticated on-board navigation systems (e.g. Rebecca Eureka, Gee, and BABS). This enabled them to maintain their position in the stream and *vis-à-vis* the ground even without ground navigation aids. The USAF, on the other hand, had no navigators and their aircraft had been designed and their crews trained to receive frequent position fixes from ground-based navigation infrastructures; it had not been anticipated that *cargo* aircraft would be flying over 'enemy' territory. Flying to Berlin meant flying over a stretch roughly 95 miles long on the northern (Hamburg) corridor, 177 miles long on the central (Hannover) and 216 miles long on the southern (Frankfurt) corridors in which there was neither radio nor other navigational aids. This meant that USAF aircraft had to fly on these stretches by dead reckoning alone. It was easy for USAF aircraft to get blown off course (i.e., get blown just a mile or two outside the corridor) or to start rushing the aircraft ahead in tailwinds or lagging behind in headwinds. In consequence, the Americans were never as punctual or precise as the British when flying, and this meant that more space between the blocks of US aircraft was needed than between the British aircraft.

For all these precautions, the risk of collision, particularly at night or in bad visibility, was high. It is little short of a miracle that there was only one mid-air collision during the Airlift. On 24 August 1948 two C-47s of the USAF both returning empty from Berlin and en route to Rhein-Main airfield were involved in a crash just shortly before reaching their destination. Apparently, one of the aircraft rammed the other in poor visibility, but since all aircrew were lost in the crash the details were never ascertained.

There were many near misses. One pilot remembers flying on one 'nasty night' and suddenly seeing a red navigation light flash past his window so close that he could clearly read the aircraft number – no more than 8in high – on the tail. It was 411. We will never know how many other pilots experienced similar near misses which were never reported.

Another source of worry and risk was the extent to which the aircraft were flying overloaded. As Sqn Ldr Robinson remembers it:

We were authorised to fly the aircraft 4,000lbs overweight for the Airlift operation, so the occasional engine failure became a major problem, particularly during or shortly after take-off. One good friend, Flt Lt Thomson and his crew were killed taking off from Wunstorf with a heavy load of coal, as they were unable to control the aircraft during the subsequent engine failure.[12]

The problems did not end when the aircraft landed. Different aircraft had different cargo capacities and so different loading and offloading times. Initially it took just 45 minutes to turn around a Dakota at its home base while Yorks took fully 2½ hours to refuel and reload. Thus the timing of the blocks of aircraft had to take into account turn-around times as well as different rates of flying, thereby complicating schedules.

At least the aircraft could be in continuous use, as long as they were serviceable; crews could not be used in the same manner. Aircrews worked in shifts, and these varied depending on the organisation for which they worked and the number of pilots in their unit/company with the instrument qualifications necessary for night or bad-weather flying. One RAF pilot remembers:

The first few days were rather hectic as we were doing three trips a day into Gatow which took about 14 hours overall, and whilst alternative days we did morning shifts then late afternoons it did not leave time for other pastimes. I recall at first I did not get much sleep and never managed to get my socks off for a few nights.[13]

Another recalls simply:

I personally flew four sorties on that first day and into the night, catnapping between flights until, after 22 hours on duty, I was released with my crew to go to bed. . . . We continued like this for a few more days: flying, eating between flights and catnapping until, when reporting as ready, there was not an aeroplane immediately available which was both serviceable and loaded; we were then sent off to bed.[14]

Another account of the work is slightly different:

Crews were working six 12-hour shifts (with inevitable fluctuations). First, three day shifts, then 24 hours off. Then three night shifts followed by 48 hours off. This went on for three weeks, when the crew went back to the UK for about a week's leave. Men could, but preferred not to, spend their 'breaks' in former German luxury hotels converted into 'rest homes'.[15]

One RAF pilot even reported: 'For relief from Airlift routine, pilots of the RAF were sometimes given a short spell flying regular passenger service between Bückeberg, Germany and Northolt in England. . . . This was pleasant because it was always daylight and the food was provided by BEA instead of RAF.'[16]

The civil aviation companies each had their own routine based, to a certain extent, on how many aircrew and aircraft they had – and their own inclination to fly. In the beginning, some of the smaller civilian companies didn't even have ground crews or managers in Germany. Others had only one crew per aircraft. By preference, or due to inadequate training and experience, many civilian aircrews could not or did not want to operate at night, so the RAF had to adjust its own schedules to give the civilians the coveted daytime slots in the stream of aircraft and take the night slots themselves.

Under the circumstances, it is perhaps not surprising that some of the civilians taking part in the early days of the Airlift found the lifestyle eminently civilised. The only two pilots flying for one particular charter company decided between them, for example, that it was 'pleasant' to make two trips a day to Berlin. Admittedly, it was sometimes difficult persuading someone to load their aircraft, but eventually it would get done and then a morning flight could be made to Gatow, lunch taken there, and then back to West Germany for a second flight in the afternoon. One of these pilots reported that, during these early days, he 'thoroughly enjoyed himself' because 'it was all carefree flying' and as far as he could see 'there was no organisation at all'.[17]

Most pilots did not find things quite so relaxing. Capt Roy Day, who flew 143 sorties on the Airlift with BSAA, remembers being on duty for 12 hours and off for 24, alternating the day with the night shift. Airlift veteran Flt Lt Rusty Waughman reports: 'To give you an idea of the pressures, on the 26th of August 1948 I flew some 10 hours and 20 minutes, 6 hours and 5 minutes by day and 4 hours and 15 minutes by night. That was an exceptionally long day. I had sandwiches brought out to the aircraft for my lunch and tea.'[18]

J.O. Bennett reports that his pilots were flying many more hours than the Federal Aviation Administration (FAA) officially allowed; his own log-book recorded an average of 128 hours per month compared to the regulation 85 hours. He reports:

Arriving in Berlin, I would go to our operations office while my airplane was being unloaded and sleep on the floor for a few minutes, under a desk. To sleep on top of the desk was to be annoyed by the bustle in the office. . . . Now that the airlift is history, it can be revealed: there was considerable sleeping done in flight. It was the only way to stay rested. After take-off the captain and co-pilot would take turns snoozing on the cockpit floor. Some crews played a game of seeing whether the pilot flying could land so smoothly that the sleeping colleague would not be wakened.[19]

A pilot's work did not end on the ground either. In these early days both USAF and RAF aircrew recall helping service their own aircraft, particularly in Berlin. This was necessary because, as a USAF pilot remembers: 'We naturally flew with mechanical conditions that under normal flight operations would have caused a delay or cancellation of the flight.'[20] The RAF was no different. Air Marshal Sir John Curtiss stresses that: 'To keep the aircraft flying we were prepared to fly with a number of items unserviceable; in fact we flew provided we had four engines, a compass and a radio. Aircraft that had engine trouble in Berlin were brought back empty on only three engines.'[21] It was clearly in the interests of aircrew to do what they could to maintain their aircraft as best they could.

Working outside in all weathers, Airlift veteran pilot Sqn Ldr Robinson reports that many pilots 'flew trip after trip soaked to the skin, many suffering from humiliating complaints such as haemorrhoids and fibrositis through sitting in wet clothes on wet aircraft seats'.[22] Another remembers flying the Airlift as:

> . . . cold aircraft, with dust from the cargo blowing into the cockpit, dodging German lorry drivers on the tarmac who seemed bent on running you down, flying through bad weather in the winter with the flight path just in the rain cloud height, waiting for the unloading without a crew room, plus the perils of aircraft in the wrong pattern or the wrong height – I wasn't excited, only pleased when the pay cheque went in the bank![23]

The cargoes the Airlift pilots were expected to fly contributed to their adversity. If the load was flour the aircrew 'returned looking like the conventional Dusty Miller' but if it was coal they debarked looking like coal miners. Coal dust was particularly insidious. It covered not only the occupants with its soot but also worked its way into the instruments and corroded electrical wiring. Both coal and flour dust swirled around the inside of an aircraft during flight and both could be explosive under the right conditions. Various methods for cleaning out the aircraft were experimented with – including trying to blow/suck the dust out while in flight – but nothing ever proved satisfactory.

Aircrews flying liquid fuels faced other difficulties. Whether petrol, diesel or paraffin, it was too dangerous to use the cabin heating on Tudor tankers and so the aircrews of Flight Refuelling had to fly without any heating regardless of outside air temperature. As one veteran reported, despite RAF flying suits and sheepskin flying boots, 'the cold could at times be unbearable'.[24]

Sunderland crews never had to carry liquid fuel and only rarely had to carry coal or flour, but they faced a plethora of other problems unique to flying boats. The problems started with not having proper rubber moorings and so having to tie up to cast-iron battleship moorings; these were themselves a serious hazard to the thin-skinned flying boats, and collisions with their own moorings in bad weather, darkness or heavy seas could damage the flying boats severely. Next, refuelling had to be carried out by hand-pumping from 55-gallon drums brought out to the flying boats on barges. The Sunderlands had to fly without on-board radar and had to land without a flare path or ground-controlled approach on the waters of the Havel. The only thing they had by way of a 'tower' or 'control' was a couple of RAF flight lieutenants with two-way radios watching from the British side of the Havel. Once on the water of the Havel, unloading took an inordinate amount of time as there was no jetty. Offloading was done by a rag-tag collection of barges, tugs, converted luxury cruisers and army pontoons. Then, since turn-around times were so terrible anyway, it was decided that the Sunderlands would carry a larger share of return cargoes than other aircraft types. This meant the Sunderlands had to wait for industrial products produced in Berlin, or passengers, before setting out on their return journey. By that time it was likely to be getting dark or the weather might have turned bad somewhere along the route. Most dangerous of all, however, were the uncharted wrecks of ships that littered the bottom of the Elbe and the floating surface debris on both the Elbe and Havel. This debris – that no one had time to clear at such a moment in history – could be deadly during landing or take-off and so the Sunderlands were permitted no night flying at all. Nevertheless, by the time the Sunderland aircraft were taken off the Airlift because of the risk of icing on the rivers, the Sunderland pilots were completely exhausted.

'TODAY WE WILL HAVE WEATHER AS USUAL'

The weather on the Airlift was so notoriously bad that it was the subject of a variety of jokes remembered to this day. The American comedian Bob Hope did his round of Airlift bases in December 1948, opening his shows with variations on the line that, 'flying in soup is one thing, but this stuff has noodles in it!' Another of his jokes was that 'you need instruments just to walk along the street'. The cartoonist of the USAF *Task Force Times* produced a cartoon showing two pilots approaching 'The Weather Office' with one remarking to the other, 'Oh, Oh! The weather must be really bad today.' Through the milky glass of the office window the shadow of a man hanging from a noose can just be deciphered.

The problem with European weather was mostly that it was extremely localised and changeable. On the positive side, this meant that by having a variety of departure fields, it was often possible to keep the Airlift going, albeit at reduced levels, even if weather closed down one or more of them. On the other hand, the localised nature of European weather meant that not only could the weather conditions be very different at the departure and landing fields, despite the relatively short distances involved, but that conditions could actually be good at both ends of the corridor and still deplorable in the middle. The conditions that could be encountered within a very short space of time on a single flight could be anything from sunshine to thunderstorms, and could quickly include fog, freezing rain, low cloud and high, gusting winds. Many US Military Air Transport Service (MATS) pilots were used to weather conditions in the US, where there is usually ample warning of changes and more freedom to fly around bad weather. They found it extremely difficult to cope with flying *through* weather that was far below military minimums. On the whole, the British pilots, both military and civilian, were better prepared for the weather conditions simply from having so much experience with British weather.

Even RAF pilots, however, found themselves caught out by the rapid changes in weather on the Airlift. Sqn Ldr Ray Paul remembers the following two incidents:

At Christmas Eve I was detailed to fly from our base at Lübeck to Hamburg to provide a back-up service for the BEA schedule which had gone unserviceable. The rest of the Squadron was stood down because of persistent fog over the North German Plain, which restricted the airlift to the 'Heavy' boys from Wünstorf. I returned to Lübeck in the evening to find most of the Squadron sipping soft drinks in the bar in view of an impending 0400 take off on Christmas Day. I was plied with questions regarding the weather and reported the unanimous opinions of the 'Met' men at both Berlin and Hamburg that there was no chance of flying the following day. Soft drinks rapidly changed to something more festive whilst I and my crew repaired to bed after a hard day's work.

Well – as you can guess, the 'Met' men got it wrong and the fog cleared in the night. So early calls were given at 0200 hours and a sick and sorry lot of [No.] 30 Squadron crews took off at 0400 on Christmas morning for two lifts to Berlin. One crew was reasonably bright eyed and bushy tailed and I was not the most popular chap on the Squadron that day!

A similar incident occurred over the New Year. The Squadron was on a late detail on New Year's Eve and arrived at Gatow in the early evening to be told that fog, which still persisted, had clamped down, closing all the bases in Western Germany. We were to stand by at Gatow TFN, together with most of Transport Command which had arrived in successive waves. Picture the Mess at Gatow – hundreds of stranded aircrew; New Year's Eve; and a bar with duty-free prices! At about 2300 Andrew Johnstone 'phoned the airlift HQ at Bückeburg to plead for a stand-down. Rather to our surprise this was granted and the crews all headed for the bar to make up for lost time; never (well – hardly ever!) was so much drunk by so few in such a short time! Once again the 'Met' men got it wrong. The fog cleared in the early morning and the order was given for all aircraft to return to base ASAP. With no clear billeting plan, individual crew members were dragged out of bed or from under tables, chairs, etc. formed into scratch crews, detailed to the first available aircraft, and dispatched to the west. It took two days to recover everyone and sort out the crews and aircraft. It says much for the stamina and skills of the aircrew that happily there were no accidents or incidents.[25]

Sometimes the abrupt changes in weather came once aircraft were already in the air. A high percentage of the accidents on the Airlift took place in bad weather. Depending on age, experience and temperament, some pilots were better able to cope with it. Some pilots, by nature probably, are able to make the best of any situation. One RAF pilot remembers flying in a cargo of very high priority that warranted taking a few extra risks. He reports:

The weather was bad at Gatow with rain and a cloud base of 300ft. There was no radar. . . . At the last reporting point before calling Gatow I lost VHF contact, which was not healthy. However, I saw a break in the cloud, and promptly let down until I was below the worst of the cloud and then crawled towards Gatow, found the lake and got the York in position to do a low circuit. I still couldn't see the airfield and so flew around the lake until the tower was able to direct me in. Undercarriage down, half flap, steep left turn and then I suddenly saw the runway. Full flap, cut engines, and a rapid landing; I felt like a fighter pilot.[26]

The solution for the average pilot was to insist that pilots fly instruments regardless of weather or time of day. This policy had its own drawbacks, however. An experienced airline captain felt that:

It was criminal to expect military pilots trained for different missions to engage in an all-weather airline operation. Flying relaxed on instruments, without being able to see out of the airplane for many hours, requires years of training just to get rid of mind-boggling claustrophobia. Moreover, the winter weather in Europe probably is the foulest in the world.[27]

The Airlift experienced one snowstorm with wind-speeds of 140km/h in which the heavy transport aircraft had to be tethered with heavy cables to keep them from being blown across the tarmac and wrecking. Visibility was zero – which was often the case – but icing on the runway made it necessary to completely close down Berlin's airfields for a day.

It was not just the winters that were bad. The first three weeks of the Airlift produced severe thunderstorms, driving rain, low cloud and even snow. Some American pilots reported icing conditions so bad that they had to maintain full power just to stay in the air. Tempelhof was unusable for hours at a stretch due to low cloud and violent winds. RAF plans calling for 160 trips to Berlin in each 24-hour period had to be discarded because Gatow had to be closed repeatedly while sheets of water were swept (by hand, of course) off the runway. Even when not actually closed, Gatow could only accept aircraft every 15 minutes rather than the (then) normal average of every 6 minutes.

Conditions were just as bad at the main USAF airfield in West Germany. Here the USAF was awaiting the arrival of the first of two US Navy squadrons to join the Airlift. Gen Tunner describes the scene:

They were not only the Navy, but they represented the very cream of the Navy. They came with the obvious resolution that they were going to show naval superiority, and I welcomed their spirit wholeheartedly. What a reception! The entire field was covered with water; at the hard stand where I awaited them, the water was up to my knees. As one of the mechanics pointed out to me, 'This is the only place in the world where you can be up to your knees in water and have dust blow in your face at the same time.'

The first R-5D, naval nomenclature for the C-54, landed in that sea of water, sending spray and spume high into the air. It splashed its way over to where I was standing, and came to a stop. The door opened, and its crew looked out. I'll never know who looked more ludicrous to the other. What I saw was a small group of men in navy blue uniforms with highly polished shoes preparing to step out into the winter mud and rain. . . . What they saw was a two-star general standing in water up to his knees trying to look dignified. Finally, we all started laughing. There wasn't much else to do.

'General, sir,' one of the natty young men in blue sang out, 'just tell me one thing: are we at land or at sea?'

'Why we ordered this just for you,' I said. 'We wanted the Navy to feel at home.'[28]

As the rain persisted, the damp started to penetrate the electrical systems of the aircraft. On 2 July, twenty-six Dakotas at Wunstorf were unserviceable due to electrical problems. The rain also created vast fields of mud because there were insufficient hardstandings and taxiways. One RAF York pilot reported that in order to taxi out of the mud, he found he had to rev all four engines at half power. On hitting the paved perimeter track, he had to throttle back sharply and stamp on the brakes, otherwise he would overshoot and land in the mud on the other side of the taxiway. The tale of woe continued:

> When the mud dried, it was in huge valleys and ridges which, the airfield staff soon discovered, had to be levelled by bulldozers. These, however, turned the mud to dust so that 'every time an engine started – and someone was always starting an engine – the whole flight line disappeared in a gigantic cloud of dust. The dust settled on the windscreen of the aircraft and when they flew into rain it turned back to mud. . . . [When] pilots turned on the windshield wipers . . . the gritty particles scratched the plastic screens. At night the runway flare paths turned the scratches into parabolas of blinding light.[29]

Flying-boat captains reported being marooned in their aircraft after a dangerous and nerve-racking sortie because the boat crew sent to collect them from their mooring could not locate them in the fog. The Sunderland crews had to worry about tides and the wrong combination of tide and wind could result in unpleasant, unexpected obstacles. One Sunderland pilot reported:

> I remember the morning we arrived on the jetty in Hamburg and found all our aircraft sitting on the mud. . . . During the night there had been a unique coincidence of a very strong east wind and a very low tide, which had practically emptied the Elbe River. This same low water also revealed in our mooring area the remains of an American Flying Fortress and its crew. . . . [30]

This was disagreeable but on the whole manageable, yet sometimes the weather could get so bad that it was extremely dangerous – and it threatened to wreck the entire effort. Things came to a climax on 'Black Friday', 13 August 1948:

Weather conditions were not too bad at Wiesbaden as we took off for Berlin, but as we gained altitude to clear the Harz Mountains we soon ran into those heavy, thick German clouds. . . . We were not alone in the sky . . . we knew that some twenty other C-54s were flying the same route ahead of us, each 3 minutes apart on the nose, each proceeding at 180 miles per hour. Ahead they stretched out like figures on a conveyor belt; behind we could hear each addition to the club as he passed over Fulda and gave us his time, loud and clear. . . . [But] at that very moment everything was going completely to hell in Berlin. The ceiling suddenly dropped to the tops of the apartment buildings surrounding the field, and then they gave way in a cloudburst that obscured the runway from the tower. The radar could not penetrate the sheets of rain. Apparently both tower operators and ground-control approach operators lost control of the situation. One C-54 overshot the runway, crashed into a ditch at the end of the field, and caught fire; the crew got out alive. Another big Skymaster, coming in with a maximum load of coal, landed too far down the runway. To avoid piling into the fire ahead, the pilot had to brake with all he had; both tyres blew. Another pilot, coming in over the housetops, saw what seemed to be a runway and let down. Too late he discovered that he'd picked an auxiliary runway that was still under construction, and he slithered and slipped in the rubber base for several precarious moments, then ground-looped.

With all that confusion on the ground, the traffic-control people began stacking up the planes coming in – and they were coming in at three-minute intervals. By the time we came in, the stack was packed from three thousand to twelve thousand feet. . . . As their planes bucked around like gray monsters in the murk, the pilots filled the air with chatter, calling in constantly in near-panic to find out what was going on.

On the ground, a traffic jam was building up as planes came off the unloading line to climb on the homeward-bound three-minute conveyor belt, but were refused permission to take off for fear of collision with the planes milling around overhead. . . .

Usually, when it's necessary to stack up planes, the tower sends them to a prearranged area 50 to 100 miles away from the field to fly their monotonous circles in the great open spaces. Here we had no such spaces, just the twenty-mile circle over the island of Berlin, a city surrounded by Soviet-Controlled East Germany. If we got out of the small circle over the city proper we could well attract Russian fighters or anti-aircraft fire. So we were stuck.[31]

Not only were these aircraft confined to the airspace over Berlin, but they shared that airspace with the aircraft being funnelled into Gatow – and the RAF was continuing to land aircraft there – at reduced rates but without accidents. It was simple: the RAF aircraft had navigators on board and these were trained to use BABS (Blind Approach Beacon System), but it was impossible to train up navigators fast enough to man US aircraft for the Airlift and so it is fortunate that the pilot reporting the above chaos was none other than Gen Tunner, the US airlift Commander. As a result of this incident, Tunner made a number of significant changes to the flying patterns in Berlin as will be seen later.

SOVIET HARASSMENT

No description of the flying conditions during the Airlift would be complete without mention of the many instances of Soviet harassment. The Airlift was the first battle in the Cold War, and while it is true that the Soviets could have done far more to interfere with – or even completely shut down – the Airlift, the fact remains that they were far from inactive. The Soviets had filed an official demand with the West that all flights in the corridors be registered with them in advance, including aircraft, pilot's name, take-off time, cargo etc. Although the Allies rejected the request out of hand, they remained worried that failure to comply would serve the Soviets as a pretext for more vigorous interference – and it was bad enough as it was.

One obvious Soviet harassment tactic was to try to interfere with Airlift aircraft navigation. Many pilots reported the jamming of the radio frequencies used for the vital ground-to-air communications, either by the blast of a monotone sound over the air waves that blocked out other transmissions or by the sound of ceaseless Russian chatter. Fortunately there were many frequencies that could be used and pilots knew how to switch rapidly. Less frequent was the use by the Soviets of devices that confused radio compasses. These were particularly dangerous according to some Airlift pilots but apparently not well developed because the use of the tactic was sporadic and not consistent.

A more common Soviet tactic was the attempt to distract aircraft with flares, particularly at night. More frequent still were efforts to blind Airlift pilots with searchlights. These were often switched on just as an aircraft turned on to final approach. Gatow was particularly susceptible to this kind of harassment since the Soviets controlled the territory immediately surrounding it. The British considered the tactic 'amateurish' since all their pilots could fly on instruments, and one could simply pull down the blinds and ignore the outside lights altogether.

More serious were the frequent incidents of Soviet 'manoeuvres' being held in the vicinity of the corridors. These resulted in both ground-to-ground and ground-to-air weapons being fired within the corridors themselves, often directly in front of Airlift aircraft. No less than fifty-five Airlift aircraft recorded hits by Soviet ground fire. Of course, 'manoeuvres' gave the Red Air Force an excuse to fly through and over the air corridors as well. A favourite practice was for pairs of Soviet fighters to circle high above the corridor and then dive down towards their firing range or 'targets' through the stream of transport aircraft on their 'conveyor belt' in the air. Gen Tunner sympathised with his pilots: 'It's a helpless feeling when, as you're grinding along in a cargo plane, a MiG suddenly screams down out of nowhere to miss you by a few feet, but there was nothing we could do but sit there and feel helpless.'[32]

Some Soviet fighters took the game a little further. With or without orders they either formatted on the transport aircraft, or more commonly, made mock attacks on them, often from head-on. This entailed speeding down the air corridors in the opposite direction to the stream of transport aircraft and then pulling up at the very last minute. Given the fact that an over-confident Soviet fighter engaged in such antics had caused the crash of a BEA airliner in early April, it was clear that such 'games' – even if not aimed at actually downing aircraft and possibly not sanctioned by the Soviet authorities – were dangerous.

These manoeuvres required a high degree of skill on the part of the Soviet fighter pilots and as such added an extra thrill to their exercises and flying, which they undoubtedly enjoyed. Their pleasure was likely enhanced by the thought of discomfiting the 'warmongering capitalists' in their insidious effort to undermine Soviet peace efforts. In the latter regard, however, they would have been disappointed. To former bomber crews, used to flying in formation and holding course and speed on a bomb-run while being targeted by flak and fighters, the Soviet harassment was not all that intimidating. As one former RAF pilot, flying with a civilian carrier during the Airlift, put it:

We were aware of the possible dangers and most of us experienced in various degrees the harassing tactics of the Soviet aircraft which, contrary to corridor rules, formatted on Airlift aircraft or manoeuvred in the corridor. [But] for the most part I think we were hardened to losses by our wartime experiences which had instilled us with a 'it will not happen to me' attitude.[33]

In any case, as Tunner had said, the Airlift pilots had no choice but to take it – and so again they often pulled down the blinds on the cockpit windows and flew by instrument.

The British do not appear to have kept records of these incidents, perhaps because there was no central office to report them to, given the large number of civil companies involved. The Americans, however, recorded the following incidents of Soviet harassment between August 1948 and August 1949:[34]

Search lights	103	Chemicals/smoke	54
Close flying	96	Air to ground firing	42
Radio interference	82	Ground explosions	39
Buzzing	77	Bombing	36
Flares	59	Air to air firing	14
Ground-fire hits	55	Balloons	11
Flak	54	Rockets	4

To be fair, the Western Allies did not *always* fly by the book themselves. Due to navigation problems, a fair number of USAF aircraft did stray out of the corridors and fly in Soviet-Zone airspace. In poor conditions in the congested air over Berlin, RAF pilots even encountered C-54s flying the wrong way in the middle of their own approach pattern. There are also legends of pilots enjoying a detour at low level over the Unter den Linden, and 'many a crew cheered itself up on a dreary return journey at night by picking on a Russian barracks, throttling down and dropping to 300ft or less, then opening up the engines hard to climb again and make sure everyone was woken up . . . '.[35]

MADNESS AND MORALE

The early days of the Airlift were characterised not just by improvisation and a 'total lack of organisation' but by a sense of excitement as well. Responding to orders that said 'at once' conveyed urgency – and importance. Arriving at surprised bases to find that the words Operation Plainfare or Vittles could cut through normal red-tape and bureaucracy only heightened that sense of being part of something 'big'. This attitude was reinforced in theatre by the commanders. At RAF Lübeck, if they ran short of aircrew, 'promptly every man available from off-duty controllers to Ops Room clerks, formed into a scratch crew and took off in any plane available'.[36] Gen LeMay, the senior USAF officer in theatre, was also calling on all his fliers, regardless of official duties, to fly 'whenever they could'. Nobody seemed to care which unit one belonged to. Aircrews were thrown together from available personnel and told to fly the next plane that was ready. If loaded aircraft were waiting and there didn't appear to be any aircrew assigned, staff officers or visitors would jump into the breach – just for a chance to be part of it all. The only thing that mattered was keeping things flowing into Berlin, so pilots flew when they could and slept when they could, snatching snacks of coffee and doughnuts 'on the fly'.

Non-flying staff officers were also infected with the spirit of urgency and importance. An RAF electrician remembers:

One night I was presented with a group of non-technical officers. . . . They wanted to help so I couldn't very well turn them away, after all, they were officers and I didn't know who had sent them. It was such short notice that I didn't know exactly what to do with them at first. I decided the safest thing to do was to keep them as far away from the aircraft as possible, under the circumstances, so I spent the whole night teaching them how to marshal an aeroplane.

I have often thought about them since and wondered just how they felt, being thrust into the middle of an airfield apron, surrounded by dozens of whirling propellers for the first time and wondering which is going to be the best way to run when it all goes wrong. I couldn't watch them all the time but there were no major collisions that night, so my fears of seeing an officer (and a gentleman) being chased by a rogue aircraft didn't materialise.

I have to say though, that although working with us was not really suitable for them, at least they took it upon themselves to volunteer to help and were prepared to work through the night, which they did, even after doing their own work through the day.[37]

The ground crews were no better:

Fired by the belief that within a few days this glorious adventure would have ended, scores of RAF fitters and mechanics, armed with no more than a tool kit and a change of underwear, thumbed a ride out of England on the first Wunstorf-bound plane – without checking out of their parent stations or even booking in on arrival. It took . . . weeks to locate who had ended up where.[38]

The pervasive sense of urgency led now and then to mistakes. One party of VIPs bound for Berlin in a DC-3 passenger aircraft (known as the C-47 in its military version) stopped in Wiesbaden for lunch. When they returned to their Dakota to continue the journey, they found it filled to the gills with flour.[39] Getting cargoes to Berlin had priority over VIPs – particularly those who had time to stop for lunch. On another occasion, the crew of a C-54 aircraft returning from their snack and stretch in Berlin saw the main compartment was empty, the offloading apparently complete, and so they closed the hatch and took off immediately, completely forgetting there was a second compartment below the cockpit. When they landed in Wiesbaden, they discovered they had taken a (one imagines rather distressed) Berliner along with them. He was returned by the next flight and finally finished offloading the aircraft in Berlin 4 hours after he had started.[40] Another unwilling passenger was Sgt Robert Van Dervort. He had crawled up into the so-called 'hell hole' under the fuselage floor of a C-54 to replace an inoperable ARN-7 radio compass while the aircraft was loaded with coal. The crew, not realising he was there, took off with him still in this crawl space, and he flew all the way to Berlin in this highly uncomfortable and bitterly cold compartment. Looking back on the atmosphere of these early days of the Airlift after nearly sixty years, a former RAF fitter reflected:

> I wonder how we coped. Youth, of course, was on our side. Plenty of work, but much humour. The Allied aircrew, although hollow-eyed with fatigue could still crack a joke with ground staff, who endeavoured to turn their aircraft around speedily . . . [so] the crew could return to their bases for a few hours rest.[41]

Joking between aircrew and ground crew was a feature remembered by many British participants. One RAF airman recalls:

> A Dakota arrived with a technical fault. This RAF aircraft was filthy, oil streaked and coal-dust covered. The poor thing looked sad and dishevelled. We opened the side door and fitted the alighting steps. What appeared in the doorway was an equally dishevelled pilot with a coal-dust streaked face and coal-dust swirling around him.
>
> Inevitably someone amongst our dismayed group spoke up: 'Twenty bags of your best coal, coalman, and you're a day late with the order.' An angry look appeared on the pilot's face which then turned to a white-toothed grin. 'By God,' he said, 'I thought I had landed in England being greeted with that request.'
>
> We all dissolved into laughter and one of the ground staff jumped into our Land Rover and drove the crew up to the Mess for a well-earned meal and bath.[42]

In retrospect, all this excitement was the stuff of adventure, and Airlift veterans tend to look back on the Airlift nostalgically: 'My memory will always retain the sounds and sights of rain, snow, C-54 engines, red hot exhaust and the labour and strain of lifting heavy loads into the air.'[43]

An RAF airman, working on the refuelling gang remembers:

I loved the work, the bustle and the excitement of the continuous aircraft movement. I remember . . . the roar of aircraft engines making music in my ears, always the possibility of seeing a previously unknown type of aircraft, combined with the feeling of doing something really worthwhile.[44]

This was a critical component of morale: the Airlift was not a controversial cause. The 'Russkies' had cut off food and fuel to more than 2 million *civilians*. They had stopped the deliveries of milk to babies and cut off supplies of medicine to the sick. One didn't have to support one particular political party or be a rabid anti-communist to be in favour of this operation. One did not even have to comfort oneself with assurances that those 'in power' must know more than one knew oneself. This was a very straight-forward humanitarian mission and history has shown repeatedly that men are happier and more ready to sacrifice themselves for a 'good' cause than a questionable one. As one USAF pilot put it: 'It wasn't any party. The hours were long, the food was bad, and there were so many take-offs and landings that it became tiresome. [But] we were helping people survive, and everyone realised that much.'[45]

Even if RAF and USAF aircrew had been completely convinced of the necessity of bombing Berlin just three years earlier, they *preferred* the prospect of bringing food and supplies now. A former B-17 pilot who had lost aircrew in combat over Germany summarised the feelings of many: 'I don't like to see people bullied, when defenceless women and children are involved, it cancels out a lot of the past . . . I didn't feel good about dropping the bombs. Now maybe I can do something about the food.'[46]

Even the most motivated of men eventually start to get tired, however, and for the Airlift crews that was bound to happen sooner rather than later because their orders were 'indefinite'. There *were* no replacements for RAF crews, so they could not be rotated out. USAF replacements were too far away or not yet reactivated, so that men sent out to Berlin on thirty days 'temporary duty' found that their duty extended, thirty days by thirty days, again and again, into apparent infinity. Airlift jokes started to circulate about men still being on 'temporary Airlift duty' when retired decades in the future.

The civilian pilots posed a slightly different problem. No one could hold them to any particular schedule, and since they weren't under acute orders the sense of urgency was also lacking. Yes, undoubtedly it was a good cause, but most of these fliers were a bit cynical by now, having fought in a good cause for a long time not all that long ago. They were – in a non-pejorative sense – mercenaries.

They were ex-RAF crews who had been released from the Service and had gone back to jobs as clerks or labourers or whatever it was. Suddenly, they had been presented with the chance to get their hands on a four-engine aeroplane and draw about £1,000 a year. This was really too good to be true, and they were out to make the most of it while it lasted.[47]

They were flying the Airlift for the money not the glory, and if they worked hard they also played hard. The fliers with the civilian charter companies became notorious for being very heavy drinkers, and for engaging in many very wild activities when drunk. As Flight Refuelling grew from a company with just 4 flight crews and 35 maintenance men to a company with 1,000 ground crew, they had to employ 150 aircrew just to ensure that on any one day 32 of them would be sober enough to fly. Even then they were often of questionable quality. Flt Lt Denis Moore, a former RAF navigator, serving as a navigator with Flight Refuelling during the Airlift, describes the following experience during the early days of the Airlift with that aviation company:

I was crewed up with a very experienced ex-Air Lingus pilot and it was not until later that I learned he had been sacked for being drunk in flight. . . . On one occasion whilst flying into Gatow I saw him climb out of his seat and then push past me and go to the back of the aircraft. I thought it would be a good idea to go forward and keep an eye on the instruments to make sure 'George' [the autopilot] was doing his job properly. To my consternation I saw that the aircraft was trimmed into a shallow dive (perhaps to counter his moving to the toilet at the rear of the aircraft) and there was no sign of [the pilot] returning to his seat. When we descended below 1,000ft I decided to get in his seat and was absolutely astounded to discover that the autopilot was not even engaged. I climbed it back to the proper height and called the wireless operator to go back and look for [the pilot]. He reported back that [the pilot] was 'out cold' on one of the seats at the back and he could not get him to register that he was needed! At this point we were committed to carry on towards Gatow as we were in the air corridor in the Russian Zone so I decided that I would make up some story to overfly Gatow and hope that by the time we got back to Wunstorf [the pilot] might have surfaced.

In the event, just as we approached the Beacon to start letting down to land [the pilot] pushed up to the front and demanded to know why I was in the pilot's seat. We swapped over and I pointed out that he had not put 'George' in when he went back and his reaction was to happily say 'these aircraft fly themselves!' and then carried on to a perfect landing.[48]

The RAF seemed better able to cope with the stress than either the civilians or the USAF. This was undoubtedly in part the result of the accessibility of England. Aircrews not only got home on a regular basis (one week every month), they also flew aircraft due for routine or emergency maintenance back to maintenance units in the UK. Furthermore in a pinch or some personal emergency, they could easily hitch a ride home and be in England in a couple of hours.

Admittedly, there were those who found the proximity to England a disadvantage. The worst of it, according to one pilot, was that one's 'wife or girlfriend, who probably worked at [the home airfield], got to know all about it before [one] had recovered from the hang-over'.[49] On the whole, however, the proximity to England was beneficial for morale.

Another positive morale factor mentioned by RAF veterans was the presence of British women in theatre. An RAF airman remembers:

> In early July 1948 the wives of officers . . . rallied round and helped serving refreshments and tea breaks. . . . At the time, to a nineteen-year-old, they seemed 'elderly'. On reflection I suppose they were 5 or 10 years our senior and had in all probability been in the services themselves during the war and knew how much their support meant.[50]

There was also a significant number of the Women's Auxiliary Air Force (WAAF) stationed in Germany and in Berlin itself. They worked in a variety of trades including air traffic control and aircraft maintenance. Perhaps it was the presence of British women – or the traditions of the colonies – that encouraged the men stationed in Germany to form bands that performed at the Navy Army Air Force Institute (NAAFI), Malcolm Club, and various messes and Service clubs. Whatever the reason, there is ample evidence that the personnel at RAF stations were very good at entertaining themselves.

Another morale-building factor for the RAF was the retention of squadron cohesion and identification. An RAF pilot stresses that: 'throughout the lift we flew as crews, in squadrons. This built up a wonderful esprit de corps because we always knew who was in front of and behind us at the same height. It also meant we had time off as a squadron, with the inevitable end-of-shift parties.'[51]

Yet the biggest positive morale factor for the RAF may simply have been the fact that not only did they have an important job to do, but they were getting it done with a minimum of red tape. Norman Hurst put it this way:

There was no administrative 'fat' in the British contingent. At airfield level there was a tremendous esprit – RAF and Army personnel working as one. For once the complete success of an operation was not due to high command but to the airmen and private soldiers working long hours under difficult conditions whose grit and determination to sustain their counterparts in Berlin won the day.[52]

The USAF pilots in contrast were stuck far away from home without their womenfolk or any prospects of rotating out. Aside from homesickness, Tunner suggests that the Soviets intentionally spread rumours or sent poison pen letters to airmen, suggesting that wives were unfaithful or hinting at other trouble at home. Short-term, the USAF Airlift fliers were also confronted by quite unjust discrepancies in their own accommodations and food compared to their comrades in the Occupation forces. All these factors undoubtedly and gradually undermined morale; but that was still in the future.

In the early days, weeks and even months, the Airlift was, as Gen Tunner worded it, 'a real cowboy operation'. It was an adrenaline-driven operation with lots of leeway for individualism and room for wild antics between the heroic testing of one's limits, all in the service of a good cause. It was wonderfully romantic, but as the professionals soon realised it was also unsustainable.

Chapter 7

DEDICATION WITHOUT GLORY

It has been argued by a participant of both the Allied Strategic Air Offensive in the Second World War and the Berlin Airlift that 'organising the relief of Berlin was far more complex than mounting the massive bombing raids carried out by the Allied bombers between 1942 and 1945'.[1] As with the bombing raids, the aircraft and aircrews were only the very tip of the iceberg of the organisation, sometimes called the 'sharp end' of a long spear of which the vast length of the weapon consists of various kinds of support units. It is time to look at that long 'tail' supporting the 'teeth' of the Airlift. This included everything from truck drivers to cooks, from air traffic controllers to weathermen, from supply clerks to medical orderlies, from police to radio technicians. Although it is impossible to describe the duties of the entire army of 'worker ants' who supported the Airlift, it is important to look at some of the key trades vital to the success of the operation.

MAINTENANCE

Aircraft maintenance and other kinds of support services are the forgotten step-children of all great aviation achievements. Although it is a truism that no pilot could ever set a record for distance, speed or height and no combat aircraft could ever engage the enemy without a fully serviceable machine, the huge amount of labour, time and dedication that goes into keeping aircraft serviceable is forgotten, overlooked or ignored in most accounts of great aviation deeds. The comparative ratio of ground crew to aircrew ought to underline the importance of the former. One example is that during the Airlift, every squadron of 9 transport aircraft in the USAF required just 27 aircrew, but a support staff 148 strong; that is roughly 5½ ground crew for each member of aircrew.

The USAF orders that sent the first C-54s to Europe from as far away as Hawaii – in a typical example of neglect and under-appreciation – made no comparable provision for ground crews. They were expected to follow, by sea. So, unlike the RAF, where ground crews flew with their squadrons or simply flew across to Germany on their own initiative, the USAF started the Airlift with too few ground crews and what crews they did have were trained on combat rather than transport aircraft.

As if that wasn't bad enough, these inexperienced ground crews were expected to work under extremely adverse conditions. For a start the airfields where they were working had not been built with a major airlift in mind, they lacked the necessary hangers and hardstandings, scaffolding and indeed every other infrastructure component associated with aircraft maintenance. Thus, for example, although work had to be performed 24 hours a day, there was no adequate lighting for night work.

Although on the whole RAF squadrons had their crews with them, the shortfalls with regard to infrastructure for maintenance work once in Germany at the start of the Airlift was a problem for the RAF as well. One AC1 remembers: 'Night work was the worst; many checks had to be made by torch light and fuel had to be checked with dip sticks. In the dark and cold of night, it was difficult to get a true reading, and doing a pre-flight check under such conditions was challenging, indeed.'[2]

In addition, the maintenance crews of both the RAF and USAF had to build their own scaffolding to even reach the engines of the aircraft they were servicing; and they had to work in all weathers. That weather, as discussed above, was often appalling even in summer. If pilots got drenched doing quick repairs, the ground crews were never dry. Things would have been better if there had been adequate housing and warm food for the ground crews, but in the early days these too were often lacking, particularly for the USAF. The entire build-up took place too fast, and it was months before the infrastructure to support the men was in place.

As the bulk of the aircraft had to be parked outside, the aircraft themselves required more maintenance. In cold weather, for example, it could take half an hour just to de-ice a fully serviceable aircraft, and in the rain electrical faults developed where none would have been had the aircraft been kept in a hangar.

Another problem for ground crews was the block system. While the system made flying safer, it had the undesired side effect of creating completely uneven work-flow patterns for maintenance crews. Either all aircraft of a squadron were on the airfield and needed to be turned around at once, or there were no aircraft to be serviced at all. An RAF aircraft mechanic remembers: 'Our crew-room was a wooden hut on the edge of the apron, furnished only by an old bed – no mattress; laying on it was about as comfortable as laying on a gorse bush, and yet sometimes you couldn't see the bed for bodies, flaked out with exhaustion and covered with grime and coal dust.'[3]

Since on average up to 80 per cent of all aircraft returned to base with some defect or another, the workload was completely incompatible with the incessant demand to 'keep 'em flying'. Ground crews had no choice but to perform a kind of 'triage' and fix what was essential first, sending many aircraft back to Berlin in conditions that normally would have grounded them, even in wartime.

Meanwhile, the problems for the crews were multiplying. They were multiplying because the aircraft were flying so continuously. It has been estimated that the aircraft on the Airlift used up roughly a normal year's worth of flying hours in just one month. Worse still, the aircraft were being used in ways for which they had never been designed. They were taking off and landing more frequently than their specifications called for and carrying heavier freights than legally allowed. That meant not only broken cargo floors and damaged doors, but also strained engines and overtaxed landing gear. They were landing on glide paths far steeper than recommended and putting down on PSP rather than concrete. All of which added up to aircraft pushing both engines and airframes to the limit – and wearing out their tyres and brakes at incredible rates. Coal cargoes were taking a toll too, corroding wiring and controls, forcing these items to be replaced more frequently than the hours flown would normally have indicated.

All this excessive wear and tear on the aircraft required years' worth of the necessary spare parts to be in theatre to meet the maintenance demands; but in the early months of the Airlift, they were not. There were, for example, absolutely no spares at Gatow, and if an aircraft was grounded there, then spares had to be flown in to fix it. In a number of cases the reverse happened: rather than receiving the needed spares, the aircraft was turned into a spare parts depot and cannibalised until it was nothing but a scrap heap. Later, limited supplies of essential components – nose tyres, the means to repair ruptured hydraulic lines and the like – were maintained in Berlin, but always with the goal of performing only emergency repairs and sending the aircraft back to its home base for proper maintenance. To this purpose, the Americans also assigned maintenance crews tasked with carrying out emergency repairs just good enough to make an aircraft serviceable for one flight to its home base. The flying was done by two 'suicide crews' – flight crews who flew into Berlin and took over any aircraft the regular crews refused or could not be expected to handle. The most common problems were hydraulic failure or more than one dead engine. The maintenance crews were housed at Tempelhof and bussed over to Gatow as needed.

The overall maintenance problem was complicated for the RAF by the fact that they were flying a variety of aircraft types, all requiring different sorts of spare parts. The USAF had first one type of aircraft (C-47s) and then another (C-54s) and this simplified the spare parts problem, but did not solve it. The fact is: there were not enough spare parts in theatre and the only way to get them there in time was to fly them in, but neither air force had the capacity to do so.

Rather than try to ship all the spare parts into Germany, both the Americans and the British chose to fly the aircraft back to centralised maintenance depots for major checks. What this meant in practice is that for the USAF, only the 50-hour checks, and for the RAF, daily inspections, were performed at Airlift departure bases. USAF 200-hour checks on the C-47s took place at Oberpfaffenhofen, and on C-54s at the major wartime maintenance depot at Burtonwood, Cheshire, which was reactivated especially to support the Airlift in the autumn of 1948. The 1,000-hour checks for USAF aircraft took place back in the United States, while the RAF sent aircraft for maintenance checks to Transport Command's major maintenance base at RAF Honington in Suffolk.

With aircraft usage averaging 8–10 hours a day, these checks came up rapidly, and they were time-consuming. The 50-hour checks took at least 5 hours with an experienced ground crew and longer when the maintenance crew was unfamiliar with the aircraft type, as was so often the case in the early weeks of US participation in the Airlift. The 200-hour checks took days. The 1,000-hour checks, weeks. The result was that at the peak of the Airlift, when the USAF had committed no less than 354 C-54s to the effort, only 128 of them were ever operational on any one day. The rest were in maintenance or awaiting spare parts, or flying one way or the other across the Channel or Atlantic on their way to or from 200- or 1,000-hour checks.

Conditions at Oberpfaffenhofen were anything but ideal. There was not adequate hanger space for the abrupt increase in aircraft passing through. Aircraft were washed down with a mixture of water and kerosene on open-air ramps. The personnel was completely overwhelmed by the workload and worked in shifts around the clock. In fact, the personnel shortages were so acute in the early days of the lift that the German cleaning personnel were conscripted to help. Walter Rölz, hired to sweep out the hangars, recalls that the Americans took a practical approach to things and regardless of regulations entrusted him with changing the spark-plugs on the C-47s during 50-hour checks; as he remembers it, there were twelve per engine. He was also asked to stand by with a fire extinguisher when the engines were tested after maintenance. 'To my frightened question as to what I should do if a fire broke out, I received the answer that I was just a dummy to meet regulations. The Goony Bird never had fires in its engines.'[4]

The maintenance situation at the civilian companies was even worse. Most had come out to Germany without any provision for regular maintenance at all. This meant that regular and serious maintenance had to be done at their home base in England, removing the aircraft from Airlift service for days on end. For minor repairs and daily maintenance, however, the companies generally 'improvised'. In practice, this meant that – since the companies generally lacked both spares and cash (and almost all personnel was ex-RAF anyway) – there was a tendency to borrow parts needed from the RAF, providing the RAF still stocked them. Unfortunately for many civilians, the civil companies were often flying types of aircraft that had either never been in RAF inventory or had already been mustered out of it, so it was not always easy to get what they needed. Under such circumstances, they had to find other ways to solve their spare parts problem. Lancashire Aircraft Corporation, which operated a total of thirteen Halifax bombers-turned-tankers on the Airlift, kept them flying by buying other decommissioned Halifaxes and cannibalising them piece by piece. They were stripped of everything, from engine parts to control surfaces, and then the airframes were chopped up and melted down into ingots of aluminium that could be sold for cash.

One universal problem for the civilian air companies was the fact that none of the civilian aircraft had the same sophisticated navigation equipment as the RAF nor could their radios tune into the same frequencies. The RAF had no choice but to send motorcycle dispatch riders out to scour bases and warehouses across Germany for the necessary radio crystals to enable frequencies to be changed. The weak financial position of many of the companies and their generally inadequate levels of staffing, however, meant that serviceability remained comparatively low. If civilian aircraft were scratched from the schedule, the RAF had to scramble to fill the gap.

Of the major players in the Berlin Airlift, the RAF was undoubtedly the best served in terms of aircraft maintenance and serviceability. This was a function of two key factors. On the one hand, the fully operational, well-organised and well-stocked maintenance units supporting Transport Command were only a short flight away, and on the other hand RAF technical personnel were probably the best trained in the world at that time; but that is not to say that there were no problems at the start of the Airlift.

As with everyone else, the speed of the build-up meant that units deployed to Germany arrived without adequate spares and the block system meant that the workload for the RAF was as impossibly uneven as for the USAF.

Initially, wartime habits of widely dispersed aircraft, the lack of fixed parking places and the absence of adequate hardstandings, scaffolding and lighting hampered RAF maintenance units just as it did their USAF colleagues; but remedies were soon found, starting with very simple things like assigning parking place numbers to enable ground crews to rapidly find the aircraft they were sent to work on and providing floodlights for working at night. Another important innovation was to divide the work up among self-sufficient units and to group the aircraft around the stores and workshops of each unit, shortening distances and increasing team spirit and competition.

Working conditions also improved with the inevitable increase in personnel. One RAF electrician stationed at Gatow remembers that in the early days of the Airlift, his Electrical Section worked 12-hour shifts, 8 a.m. to 8 p.m. or 8 p.m. to 8 a.m. Within weeks, however, enough additional electricians had been assigned to Gatow to enable the establishment of a 3-watch, 8-hour shift system. This worked as follows: everyone worked for 3 days on the 6 a.m. to 2 p.m. shift, then had 24 hours off, then worked for 3 days on the 10 p.m. to 6 a.m., then another 24 hours off before working the 2 p.m. to 10 p.m. shift followed by 8 hours off and then restarting the cycle.

One problem was unique to the RAF and may have been of its own making. Namely, the RAF has been accused of 'over-servicing' aircraft. Some of this was undoubtedly due to an ingrained predilection for repair over replacement. While the USAF was both culturally inclined to and financially capable of throwing away damaged or malfunctioning parts, the RAF preferred to repair parts because this was more cost-effective. The drawback was that repair generally took more time than replacement. Furthermore, to catch problems before they became irreparable and avoid the costs of replacement, the RAF called for more frequent inspections. Thus RAF aircraft were required to undergo daily inspections, while USAF aircraft were only inspected after 50 hours' flying – which could be every five or six days even on the Airlift. The next major RAF inspection was after 150 hours' flying; the USAF waited until 200 hours had been clocked. Even more dramatic was that Yorks had to undergo airframe inspections after just 1,200 hours' flying; the C-54 did not have to submit to a similar comprehensive maintenance check until it had flown 4,500 hours. In addition to these high standards for routine checks, the RAF grounded aircraft more rapidly than the USAF. While the USAF tolerated as many as 350 minor problems before grounding an aircraft, the RAF allowed only 36.

Given the safety record on the Airlift, the USAF policy appears to have been vindicated, but one can nevertheless sympathise with the RAF position. It has been said, after all, that in the USAF 'pilot after pilot experienced sweating fear of engines that balked and fell away, of planes that rode inexplicably heavy, of landing gear that malfunctioned'.[5] The following is just one example of the kind of USAF attitude to serviceability. A passenger aboard a USAF C-54 with an unserviceable port outer engine had the following harrowing experience:

> The pilot had difficulty starting the starboard inner engine, and eventually he broke the hand-starting toggle. So he called the tower and asked for permission to try to start the engine by air pressure on the propeller.
>
> Permission was granted, and the pilot slammed his C-54 down the runway with two engines roaring, one airscrew feathered and one stationary. At about seventy knots, the starboard inner airscrew turned, the engine burst into life, and the pilot immediately throttled everything back and braked hard. The C-54 shuddered towards the end of the runway, and he narrowly managed to swing her on to the taxi-track. Grinning happily, he turned back on to the runway and took off on three engines, knowing he had one unit completely out of action, and a second that was suspect.

It was not entirely unknown for British aircraft to receive less than perfect servicing. Leading Aircraftman (LAC) Charles Armstrong claims that in the early days at Wunstorf, when completely overwhelmed by the sudden build-up and the demands for delivering the tonnage, servicing could be very hasty indeed – including patching up the tyres ripped by PSP with a tube of Bostik by the light of a torch.[6] The routine of daily inspections (DIs) and more frequent hourly inspections thereafter certainly reduced the probability that hasty or shoddy work would go unnoticed for long or that it would cause a serious problem or accident.

Last, but not least, the quality of RAF ground crews must be emphasised. In contrast to the USAF, which had only gained its independence from the US Army after the Second World War and shortly before the start of the Airlift, the RAF had been an independent Service since 1918. The importance of this can hardly be overstated, particularly with respect to technical trades and training. While the tradition of any army is that other ranks are cannon fodder who should, please, think as little as possible, an air force has no cannon fodder whatsoever. Instead, air forces have highly skilled specialists who work either on the ground or in the air.

The RAF had the finest tradition of recruiting and training ground crews going back to the First World War, and institutionalised in 1920 at RAF Halton with the Aircraft Apprentice Scheme. This meant not only that the RAF actively recruited quality personnel but that successful candidates felt very proud of their jobs. Almost as important, the high quality of RAF ground crew was recognised by the fliers, and the relations between air and ground crews were exceptionally good in comparison to other air forces; particularly the USAF, whose ground crews were universally viewed as 'underpaid and under-appreciated'.

Whereas American personnel tended to be trained in only one craft and would specialise in that area, RAF aircraftmen assigned to maintenance duties were expected to be able to fill in for their colleagues if necessary and so had much broader and more comprehensive training. The same was true of the civilian companies with their more limited staffs drawn almost exclusively from the ranks of former RAF personnel. As one radio engineer of Lancashire Aircraft Corporation remembers it: 'During the night shift the waves of aircraft were maintained by a three man crew: an engine fitter, an airframe rigger, and a radio engineer. . . . It was an unwritten rule that if a returning aircraft had no snags requiring the attention of a particular tradesman, that man would help out with anything else.'[7]

The result was that throughout the Airlift, RAF ground crews proved more efficient and effective at keeping their aircraft flying than did their colleagues in the USAF, and ordinary RAF tradesmen, when loaned to USAF units, were viewed as exceptional, earning praise and commendations.

AIR TRAFFIC CONTROL AND OTHER SUPPORT SERVICES

Arguably, air traffic control was even more important to the success of the Airlift than either flying or maintenance. At a minimum it can be said that given the confined airspace over Berlin and the fact that three airfields in close proximity had to handle continuous streams of incoming traffic, the absence of centralised, precise and professional air traffic control would have doomed many individuals, if not the Airlift itself.

As with flying the Airlift, air traffic control on the Airlift was not like air traffic controlling anyone had ever done anywhere in the world previously. Aircraft had to be guided in over long distances and then threaded through one another to different airfields, all without space for 'holding patterns' since anything that took aircraft outside the congested corridors or Berlin airspace necessarily took them over Soviet Zone airspace. The fact that aircraft did occasionally wander into Soviet Zone airspace without serious consequences was no justification for assuming that there would be none, and at a minimum harassment and interference could be expected. All in all, Gen Tunner called it the 'trickiest' aviation controlling he had ever faced up until that time.

To make matters worse, the military establishment asked to take over these tricky air traffic problems was seriously lacking in expertise. The postwar demobilisation of the wartime establishment had hit air traffic controllers no less than pilots and mechanics, but unlike pilots and aircraft mechanics, the civilian market for controllers was more favourable, as civil aviation was expanding across the US. The solution was to call up former military controllers who were still reservists, and in response to an urgent request from the US Airlift Commander, twenty reservists with experience from the Second World War were recalled to the colours and sent to Berlin within four days of the request. Likewise, the Royal Navy was asked to contribute trained personnel and did so to the extent possible. The WAAF also contributed some of the controllers for the Airlift.

Berlin, necessarily, had centralised air traffic control, and this was based at Tempelhof. All incoming and outgoing traffic from Berlin's two (later three) airfields was tracked from this centre. This enabled control to send incoming traffic to whichever airfield was less congested – unless there were special cargo considerations. The control room and tower were manned 7 days a week, 24 hours a day, and the challenge was to sort out all the aircraft pouring into Berlin from two corridors so that they could land rapidly and safely at two (later three) airports without accident or delay. Since aircraft often appeared on the screens at the same time and often very nearly abreast of one another, controllers had to rapidly identify which blip on the screen belonged to which aircraft and to then give different instructions to each. Incredible as it seems, 'the only method available for positive identification was to ask [an aircraft] to make a turn and to observe which blip on the radar scope changed course as prescribed'.[8]

Inevitably, errors happened. One Airlift veteran remembers a dark night at Tegel:

> . . . as we munched our hot dogs and rolls from the PX van . . . a Hastings aircraft taxied in and parked. The crew came over to join us. I said to them: 'I didn't know you were operating into Tegel.' Five flying figures froze. 'This isn't Gatow?' Acting on landing instructions from Gatow they had slotted into the ninety-second gap between movements. Our Controller hadn't even time to fire his big red Very pistol.[9]

Aside from getting the right aircraft into the right airfield, was the problem of spacing and timing. Even the most precise flying could not ensure the 90-second interval needed for landing, so it was the controller's job to slow down some aircraft and speed up others. A Royal Navy controller describes the problem:

[Dakotas] were so slow that the [controllers] were always worried that the following wave of speedy Skymasters might overtake them. It was often necessary to direct Dakotas to cut corners from the flight plan and even break the corridor restrictions. One had to be careful too, when bringing in other types behind them. It was quite possible, in a moment of forgetfulness, while bringing in a Dakota, to ask a York which was following it to reduce revs until it was dangerously near stalling speed.[10]

Another problem for controllers was setting priorities if one airfield closed down abruptly due to weather or an accident. Airlift priorities meant that generally the largest aircraft with the most cargo for Berlin would be given precedence for landing even if this meant that blocks of smaller aircraft were sent home with their cargo still in their holds. Likewise, if aircraft developed technical difficulties, the controllers had to ensure that the pilots 'took their problems someplace else' rather than coaching them in as would have been standard procedure under another set of circumstances – unless, of course, it really was a matter of life and death for the crew.

The final approach to the airfields was then handled by the Ground Controlled Approach (GCA) controllers. These operated from trucks parked beside the actual runways, working from radar screens that showed the height, bearing and distance of all aircraft within 40 miles. Pilots could be directed by radio to adjust their course, speed or altitude to ensure separation and regular arrival at the airfield. In poor weather, the GCA controllers talked the pilots right down to the ground. 'GCA was more than equipment; it was a process that required steady nerves and mutual confidence both on the ground and in the air.'[11]

Humans being humans, sometimes it went wrong. A civilian flight engineer from Air Services remembers an unpleasant incident during a GCA into Gatow in wretched weather: 'It got a bit sweaty if you got down to 200ft and still couldn't see anything. We were, the GCA man said, "lined up nicely, a half-mile from the runway threshold". Right about then we broke into the clear and were flying straight between the factory chimneys at Spandau.'[12]

On the whole, however, as one RAF flight engineer put it, 'Those [GCA] chaps did an excellent job talking us down in bad visibility right to the end of the runway. They were calm and most accurate with their instructions and gave us a lot of confidence.'[13]

Most USAF pilots also had positive experiences and one claimed: 'The clam, soothing, deliberate voice of that final controller was the best high-blood-pressure antidote ever devised for such an occasion. . . . What a feeling – on a stormy night when you're worn to a frazzle – to have a crew like that put you at ease and guide you to the end of the runway.'[14]

Yet even the best controllers in the world could not overcome certain technical difficulties. Bob George, a draughtsman of the RAF construction wing at Gatow remembers the following incident:

> One very cold and frosty Sunday morning there was a hammering at the door and there was a representative from BAFO headquarters who said something had gone badly wrong with the Ground Controls, and planes were landing at an angle to the runway in bad visibility. . . .
>
> I quickly dressed, pulled on a warm leather jacket and grabbed my surveying equipment. When we arrived at the scene, sure enough there was chaos. Planes had been running off the runway and getting bogged down in the sand alongside. It took a little while to readjust the line of the GCA control equipment, but eventually all was well again.[15]

Notably, this occurred at Gatow, whose GCA was the 'envy' of the Americans at the time. According to a USAF pilot 'they landed me at Gatow [several times] when Tempelhof was closed due to less precise radio range landing aids'.[16]

Another service of vital importance to the Airlift was meteorology. As the Airlift aircraft had to fly in very narrow, low corridors at specific heights, the Airlift fleet could not fly around bad weather, and because the entire success of the Airlift depended on delivering more cargo to Berlin than anyone really thought possible, Airlift aircraft could not delay for bad weather either. The fact was, the Airlift had to keep operating regardless of the weather, but predicting it as accurately as possible was vital to reducing accidents and improving performance.

Perhaps the greatest contribution of meteorology to the Airlift was the fact that it aided the decision to maintain airfields in southern Germany despite the longer distances involved. A study of the weather patterns in Germany showed Airlift planners that there was often good flying weather in one half of the country while poor weather dominated the other. If all aircraft were moved to one Zone (e.g. the British), then potentially they could all be grounded at once. By keeping a large portion of the fleet in the American Zone, however, the Airlift planners ensured that there were very few days when no aircraft could get into Berlin at all.

Given the rapid changes in weather, it was vital that weather reports be as accurate as possible. Since aircraft flying in the corridors were often stacked up and flying in streams above and below each other, they could not on their own initiative simply go up or down a few thousand feet to try to find better flying conditions. It was crucial that entire streams of aircraft could be directed to different heights if necessary. This entailed knowing conditions to within 50ft and ¼ mile. This kind of weather forecasting depended less on accurate long-range forecasts (such as could be developed through reports from weather aircraft and meteorological stations in the Atlantic) than on short-term, local forecasting. This forecasting was carried out predominantly by German civilian meteorologists employed by the Airlift authorities. An American technical sergeant working at Tempelhof remembers that the German staff was 'exceptionally clever . . . at forecasting stratus cloud'. He reports: 'They could pin it down to within 15 minutes of formation over the airfield, and could tell to within a hundred feet where it would form.' They all held college degrees and several were PhDs.

INFRASTRUCTURE

The importance of infrastructure is demonstrated by a simple statistic: at the start of the Airlift there were just two airports in Berlin and three in the Western Zones involved in the effort; at the end there were three airports in Berlin and nine airfields in the Western Zones. This simple fact does not, however, convey the immense effort involved in creating that infrastructure.

The only airfield in the American Sector of Berlin was Tempelhof, and this airfield was obviously incapable of handling the demands about to be placed on it based on the state it was in at the start of the Airlift. Already by the end of June, less than two weeks after the start of the lift, the main runway was starting to break down under the constant C-47 traffic. It was clear that the arrival of the heavier C-54s would in fact put it entirely out of commission unless 'something' was done immediately.

The first thought was to get a second runway down fast, so the construction of an asphalt and pierced steel plate runway was approved and construction started on a runway south of the main runway on 8 July. By early August, it was obvious that this was not enough, and so on 20 August a third, parallel runway, this one north of the original, was started; capacity at Tempelhof was tripled in the first three months of the Airlift.

Another priority at Tempelhof was lighting. As the field was surrounded by five-storey apartment blocks it was doubly important that the flare-path was very visible from as far away as possible. It was, for the same reason, almost impossible to locate it. After careful surveying it became apparent that the only way to provide a properly lit approach path into Tempelhof was by putting the lights up in a cemetery on the edge of the field. In order to do this, several graves would have to be disturbed. The Soviets tried to make propaganda capital out of the appalling disrespect for the dead, but the Berlin City Council knew that their first duty was to the living. Likewise the congregation of a church, whose spire blocked out several lights, readily agreed to remove the spire and replace it with a flat roof that did not interfere with this vital visual aid to flyers.

At Gatow, the only airfield in the British Sector of Berlin, the situation was similar. The British had recognised the need for improvements to the airfield even before the Airlift commenced. An RAF construction unit was already stationed at Gatow and working 'normal hours' along with a team of highly trained German civilian draughtsmen and 'an excellent German engineer' to make improvements to the airfield facilities.[17] With the start of the Airlift, activities went into high gear. In addition to the work already planned, adjustments had to be made to handle a far higher volume of traffic. In fact, because Gatow had excellent Ground Controlled Approach from the start and fewer surrounding obstacles, Gatow ended up taking the largest volume of Airlift traffic, and indeed became the busiest airfield in the entire world, carrying three times the traffic of La Guardia Airport in New York – then the busiest civilian airport in the world.

At the start of the Airlift, the only concrete runway at Gatow airfield had been designed to take a few Dakotas a week. This had to be strengthened without disrupting the flow of traffic and, as at Tempelhof, this could only be achieved by keeping a force of German workers ready to rush out and carry out repairs on the runway surface between blocks of aircraft. But this could only serve as a stop-gap measure. What was really needed, just as at Tempelhof, were additional runways. Furthermore, Gatow needed taxiways, extensive hardstandings, airfield lighting, airfield drainage and ancillary buildings to house and feed the increased staff that came with the Airlift. This was beyond the capacity of the RAF construction unit in place and so help was brought in from the Royal Engineers in the form of Lt Col R.C. Graham. '[T]he pressure to get the work finished before October was intense, as we knew the rainy season would start by then, and . . . the whole enterprise could gob down in a muddy quagmire.'[18]

Working now under 'wartime-like' conditions, the RAF construction team undertook an accurate survey over a large area of land as a first step to improvement:

To minimise the danger my assistant and I lay flat on the ground to make the readings with planes' landing wheels only a few feet above us. On one occasion

I stood up during a lull and absorbed in my figures did not notice the next plane was almost on me. I made the fastest dive to the ground ever.[19]

After the survey and plans were finished, the actual construction started, but in blockaded Berlin this was anything but routine. There was no modern construction equipment in Berlin, and no construction materials either. Lt Col Graham solved the problem of construction material by opting to collect the bedding on railways from which the Soviets had long since ripped up the tracks. As for the surface, he calculated that a large part of the bitumen required could be recovered by melting down the surface paving off streets in war-devastated parts of the city where traffic was sparse. Some of the bitumen was also provided clandestinely from a factory in the Russian Sector located very near the Sector border. 'Mysteriously' barrels of bitumen were rolled across that border into the British Sector every night. When all was said and done, only 5 per cent of the total tar and bitumen used on the runway surface had to be flown in from the West.

For construction equipment, Graham was forced to scratch together an odd collection of outdated machinery. The fleet included bulldozers to prepare the ground, obsolete boilers to melt down the bitumen, crushers to pulverise the rubble and steamrollers to flatten it. One steamroller arrived completely unexpectedly. It 'came trundling on to the airfield' driven all the way from Leipzig by a German driver who 'had simply driven through miles of Russian-controlled territory to offer his services'.[20] The assembled equipment was all very old so it frequently broke down, and there were, naturally, no spares to be found in Berlin, so the RAF construction unit had to use their talent for improvisation to either make parts or otherwise effect repairs. Finally, with a team of roughly 1,500 German workers, the new runway was laid down using a large moving gantry on rails with lorries feeding all the materials in as they crawled alongside. 'The whole assembly moved majestically and relentlessly forward, [which] showed how you can really get a job done when you have to.'[21] With the completion of this runway, Gatow possessed two parallel runways; the tarmac one for landing and a PSP one for take-off.

Even with new runways at both Tempelhof and Gatow, it was imperative to increase airfield capacity in Berlin if the city was ever to be sustained through the winter. On 5 August 1948, less than two months after the start of the blockade, construction started on a completely new airfield: Tegel, in the French Sector. The requirements here dwarfed everything undertaken at either Tempelhof or Gatow. The new airport required a 5,500ft runway, 6,020ft of taxiways, 4,400ft of access roads, 2,750ft of access railroad, and over 1 million sq. ft of apron.[22] In addition, the airfield needed administrative, operations and support facilities, including a control tower, and GCA radar sites. Since it was also designated to become the main receiving airfield for liquid fuels, huge underground fuel tanks were also planned – and had to be constructed – along with pumps and pipelines.

The future airfield first had to be cleared – of old flak batteries and tree stumps. It had to be levelled and drained. Only then could the construction work itself begin – in the complete absence of building materials and modern construction equipment. In regards to building materials, specifications called for a minimum foundation 2ft thick, which would normally have been composed of concrete, but there was neither cement nor mixers in Berlin. To fly it in would have siphoned off huge numbers of aircraft from the transport of food and coal. However, as one of Tunner's staff put it, the USAF had 'had the foresight' to provide all the material needed three years earlier. 'There's enough brick rubble from bombed out buildings,' he calculated, 'to build a dozen runways.'[23] So the rubble from the bomb-shattered buildings of the city was collected and crushed. The surface asphalt still had to be flown in, though – roughly 10,000 barrels of it.

In regards to equipment, as in any country lacking modern equipment, manpower to a certain extent had to replace machines. Working under the supervision of 15 American officers and roughly 150 enlisted men, who ran the heavy equipment, a total of 19,000 Berliners, 40 per cent of whom were women, contributed their labour to the project. They worked in three shifts, around the clock, seven days a week for a wage of just DM1.20 an hour – and a hot meal. It was, according to one observer, a 'curiously mixed crowd that gathered at Tegel in those summer days: beside the work-accustomed mason stood a narrow-shouldered office-worker, beside former Wehrmacht officers, professors and scientists worked refugees in their tattered clothes and secretaries as often as not wearing silk dresses'.[24] Tunner reports: 'The work began early in September when the weather was still hot, and you could see women in bikinis and men in swimming shorts toiling away.'[25]

Manpower could not replace all heavy equipment and the aircraft of the time were incapable of transporting certain pieces of machinery, notably bulldozers, crushers, graders, etc. Stories vary somewhat, but it seems that somebody remembered a certain welder who had worked for the US Army during the war. This man had developed a means of taking apart heavy construction equipment to make it suitable for air transport in the Pacific theatre where airfields had to be built on obscure islands lacking all such equipment. The FBI tracked down a certain H.P. Lacomb in the Midwest, re-inducted him into the Army and put him on a priority flight to Berlin. Henceforth: 'When heavy machines arrived from the United States, he proceeded to dissect them with his [blow]torch, carefully pack the pieces, and send them off to Berlin. He would then fly to meet them and patiently perform his restorative surgery, putting these priceless steel Humpty Dumpties back together again.'[26]

By this method, a total of eighty-one pieces of essential heavy construction equipment were transported into Berlin, but as one man who drove one of the crushers remembers: 'Maintenance was an ongoing problem because the machines were worked hard and broke down regularly under heavy and constant use. We did a lot of fixing. Working conditions were long and stressful; the Russians were always watching and the French did nothing.'[27]

Initial plans had called for the new airfield at Tegel to open in February 1949. Since this would have meant that it did not open until nearly the end of the winter, when demand was going to be highest, Gen Clay felt this date was too late. There followed talk of opening on 1 January, then on 1 December, but work progressed so rapidly that the first flight onto a runway at Tegel was in fact carried out on 5 November. This did not signify the start of operations, however. Two weeks later, when HQ No. 46 Group sent an aircraft in to test whether the airfield was ready to become operational, conditions were still found to be inadequate. Since no aircraft flew to Berlin without a cargo, an RAF Dakota was sent into Tegel with a mixed cargo of tyres, drums of cooking oil, and crates of condensed milk – a means of testing cargo-handling capacity. The RAF discovered there was none whatsoever. The Dakota had to return to Lübeck fully loaded. Tegel also lacked a control tower, radar, GCA, BABS, and all crew facilities from meals to latrines. Despite these conditions, it was decided to go ahead and start flying the Dakotas into Tegel while the construction of these support facilities continued around them. Despite the bleak weather closing in on Berlin, Tegel ramped up operations rapidly and before long it was carrying its share of the traffic and proved its worth.

Compared to the difficulties and drama of expanding and building airfields in a blockaded city, construction efforts in the Western Zones were pedestrian – but essential nevertheless. While Rhein-Main and Wiesbaden were both more or less ready for operation from the first day of the Airlift, the principle RAF airfield, Wunstorf, was not. There were no hard surfaces except the runway, hangar aprons and a few parking areas. There were no proper facilities for liquid fuels and not enough equipment for loading or fuelling aircraft. At once a huge expansion programme began. Some 5 acres of forest was cleared and roughly 180,000sq. yd of PSP hardstandings and 5 miles of railway sidings were laid down, but despite all this, it was rapidly obvious that, given the number of aircraft involved in the Airlift, a second airfield was necessary. So the RAF began work on turning Fassberg into a second Airlift station.

Fassberg was a former Luftwaffe fighter station. It was converted into a transport airfield in just fourteen days of construction by a joint RAF/ Royal Engineers/German Railway effort. Together they first cleared 5 acres of forest, and then laid down 180,000sq. yd of PSP hardstandings, built a 2,000yd runway and laid 5½ miles of railway track. They provided power lines and approach roads, and built accommodation to house 8,000 Air Force personnel and 4,000 German civilian workers by renovating 12 barrack blocks as well as converting 2 hangars and 2 office buildings. RAF Dakotas started operating from here on 16 July to reduce congestion at Wunstorf, and on 27 July they were joined by three American C-54 squadrons.

Less than a month later, on 22 August, Fassberg was turned over entirely to the Americans, and the RAF transferred their Dakotas to Lübeck. Lübeck too had undergone significant improvement in advance of this move. Although concrete runways existed already, 88,000sq. ft of marshalling hardstandings had to be put in. The railhead capacity was doubled and lighting had to be improved for both the runway and for loading. Initially all Dakotas were concentrated at this field whether RAF, RNZAF, RAAF, SAAF or civilian. It had one severe drawback, however: the eastern boundary of the field lay just 2 miles from the border of the Soviet Zone. Landing from the east meant flying over Soviet territory and in bad weather a blind approach over the Soviet Zone could easily end in double disaster. Tragically, this happened three times during the Airlift, on 17 November 1948, 24 January 1949, and 22 March 1949. All three crashes took place during approaches to the airfield in poor weather, two of them at night, and all three cost the loss of all on board.

By early October 1948, Lübeck had become so congested that on 5 October the civilian Dakotas were moved on to Fuhlsbüttel, the main civilian airport for Hamburg. Here too improvements were made to supplement the existing PSP runway. First, a 5,850ft parallel runway, which opened on 21 December, was built, and in addition lighting and new hardstandings for loading were installed. One innovation Fuhlsbüttel had was soon imitated elsewhere: green lights that ran down the centre of the runway. Fuhlsbüttel, however, lacked GCA throughout the Airlift, which proved a serious drawback.

Late in November yet another departure airfield, Schleswigland airfield, was opened for Airlift operations. This airfield boasted two excellent runways, but it needed an additional hangar, larger aprons and more hardstandings, an extension of the rail spur, and most important an enlargement of aviation fuel storage tanks. Although, once finished, the airfield itself was excellent,

Schleswigland's location on the narrow Jutland peninsula between the North Sea and the Baltic meant that it was often socked in with low cloud and sea fog. It also had consistently lower temperatures in winter, which caused severe icing. It proved to be the Airlift airfield most frequently closed for bad weather. Nevertheless, the need to avoid congestion at the other fields induced the Airlift planners to station some RAF Yorks and civilian companies flying aircraft other than Dakotas at this field.

Last, but not least, Celle was opened as an Airlift field in December 1948. This was built on the site of a Junkers aircraft factory and incorporated all the lessons learned so far in airfield construction for Airlift operations. The runway was 5,400ft long and 150ft wide and constructed of concrete. The hardstandings and taxiways were PSP. There were hundreds of Nissen huts for housing, good access roads and railheads, a fuel complex and the entire layout was oriented towards the 'production line' operations that Gen Tunner preferred and commanded by this time. Celle was built by the British in the British Zone but it was intended from its inception for the USAF and they took over the field exclusively from the start.

BED AND BOARD

So far, the talk has been of the infrastructure needed to keep planes flying, but aircraft do not fly themselves, and the accommodation for their crews was another critical component of the Airlift infrastructure. It is fair to say that accommodation was not adequate anywhere at the start. The build-up simply took place too rapidly. The result was 'living conditions . . . [which] resembled those of a combat-type operation'.[28]

This impression was reinforced by the fact that Airlift personnel generally did not have their families in Germany and aggravated by the fact that the Airlift came on top of an occupation – whose forces, at least in the US Sector, lived very differently from the Airlift crews. The situation is well illustrated by the contrast between the housing provided for the respective commanders of the US Air Forces of Occupation and for the senior commander on the Airlift – both generals. Gen Tunner described the situation in his memoirs as follows:

> I had arrived after office hours, I'd found LeMay at his quarters, a fifty-five-room mansion run by a staff of fifteen servants. It was a beautiful home, exquisitely furnished with fine oriental rugs and the best of European antiques and paintings. It belonged to the Heinkel family, makers of champagne, but had been requisitioned along with eight hundred other houses for the use of

Air Force families. From this palatial residence I went to my quarters, a third-floor walk-up in the Schwartzer Bock Hotel, overlooking a block of burned out buildings. The door to my single room was opened for me, and I found myself looking into the bathroom. That was the only way you could get into the one-room quarters of the commander of the Berlin Airlift – between the tub and the commode.[29]

If those were the conditions for the commander, it is not surprising that ordinary American airmen on the Airlift could expect no luxury. One pilot says his crew, arriving in Frankfurt after flying non-stop from Alabama, was told on arrival that they had a choice between tents and tarpaper shacks. They were further told: 'The tar-paper shacks [were] in a barbed-wire compound at Zeppelinheim, across the autobahn. There [was] a nearby building with showers. [However,] there [would] be a few minutes delay in moving in [because] the shacks were . . . occupied by displaced persons.'[30]

His description of his accommodations continues:

We pulled into a compound through a barbed wire gate to witness a scene that could have been shot from the liberation of a prisoner of war camp. There were already several two-ton trucks in the compound loading non-descript belongings in a variety of bags and battered suitcases. The owners, by their haggard looks and dishevelled mixed dress, had seen happier times. We were adding to their misery. The displaced persons were once more being displaced.

Four walls were all there was there besides a black potbelly stove and metal cots covered with what had once been reasonably good G.I. issue mattresses. There was obviously no washing or toilet facilities inside the buildings.[31]

In addition to the tents and the tarpaper shacks in the Displaced Persons' Camp, Airlift personnel were also housed in the attics of the existing barracks at Rhein-Main and in Nissen huts at Wiesbaden. With respect to the attic housing a veteran remembers: 'The building had suffered war damage, and holes in the roof had been simply covered over with canvas – in late November!'[32] As for the Nissen huts, another American Airlift veteran remembers them as follows:

We slept in old Nissen steel-fabricated huts heated by three pot-bellied stoves that had to be stacked nightly to keep out the blowing snow and cold. . . . A plane was taking off every 3 minutes during our hours of access to the assigned corridor into Berlin. . . . The crew got very little sleep except while waiting our base's turn to access. . . .[33]

There was nothing anyone could do to stop the aircraft noise, without suspending the entire operation, so the best that Tunner could do was to 'pass the word down to housing officers to do their best to put crews working on the same schedules together, so that they could all sleep at the same time'.[34]

Compared to what the Americans had to put up with, RAF accommodation was reasonably good. Despite crowding, the basic substance was of a high standard. Even 'other ranks' remember being housed in 'superb pre-war Luftwaffe quarters'.[35] These had reinforced concrete roofs and triple glazing on the windows against the cold. Crowding meant that initially airmen were housed in the attic in metal bed frames 'so close together that access could only be gained over the foot of each bed' and there were no mattresses. Worse still, as with the US crews, initially there was insufficient care about scheduling and so men working different shifts were constantly waking their sleeping colleagues. The RAF, however (unlike the USAF) did move the Occupation forces out. Thus as the Occupation personnel moved out, RAF Airlift 'other' ranks 'were allotted smaller rooms on the first and second floor' – presumably with better-matched schedules.[36] An AC2 remembers his Airlift accommodation as follows: 'Accommodations for ground crews were sturdy, brick buildings with large, double entrance doors to keep out the cold. Rooms contained only four beds with very efficient central heating. This was the epitome of luxury for RAF ground crews accustomed to Nissen-type huts, containing thirty beds and two coke stoves.'[37]

Aircrew, not surprisingly, describe even better accommodation, although in the early days they were much crowded. Again the basic housing was pre-war Luftwaffe quarters built to give each officer a bedsitter to himself. Airlift requirements meant that at Wunstorf no less than four RAF officers were housed in each bedsitter initially, while others were 'stuffed' into the attic. The attic was particularly unpleasant, as one of the pilots describes it: 'We slept in dormitories in the attic and were called out at all hours of the day and night for duty creating a continual disturbance to others sleeping after their shift of 16 or so hours. One morning I discovered I had flown all night to Berlin and back several times wearing one black shoe and one brown, such was the state of disarray in the attic billet.'

Later, as the additional airfields were built and airlift personnel in the British Sector spread out, it became possible to clear out the attics and reduce room occupancy, and even to provide chambermaid service.

There was also an effort on the part of the British to provide 'off duty' accommodation. As one RAF Airlift participant remembers: 'The powers that be decided that we should have a few days rest every three weeks or so and made Hotel Bad Neindorf [sic] some miles away a convalescence centre. However, it did not last long as it became a hive of high-living and late nights and did not provide the rest for which it was intended.'[38]

If British housing during the Airlift was, thanks to the Luftwaffe and the greater dispersion in the British Sector, on the whole better than the American equivalent, the same cannot be said about the food. According to some accounts, RAF personnel received the same rations as civilians in England – who were also rationed at this time. Other accounts say that they received no better rations than the Germans. At all events, they were fed far less and far less well than the Americans.

Just as during the war itself, American troops were supplied with every luxury America could afford from hot dogs and doughnuts to apple pie and ice-cream. There was no rationing in America and, as Clay catalogued so well, the caloric intake of the average US diet was roughly three times that of the German. At Fassberg, where British staff provided for American air and ground crews, the problems were compounded by taste. One American sergeant put it this way: 'The food was very British – sometimes good and sometimes very bad. We often had mutton for breakfast and warm milk for our cereal.'[39] While some Americans even found the food 'good' the majority 'reacted bitterly to a British diet composed mainly of kippers, fried tomatoes and overcooked Brussel sprouts'.[40]

It is telling that while Americans all but rioted against the British food at Fassberg, RAF personnel remember Airlift kitchens with affection, one airman claiming:

> The amenities at Wunstorf were quite good. The food was better than anything we were given in England. The chefs were the unsung heroes of the Operation. For its duration they provided first class food 24 hours a day. Catering for [Airlift] personnel required work shift patterns around the clock.[41]

The pressure of feeding air and ground crews not just in shifts but continuously seems truly a forgotten achievement of the Airlift. Here too the block system meant that work would come in sudden frantic spurts followed by lulls – yet no one could predict when those spurts would occur since weather and technical difficulties rapidly disrupted schedules. Airfields and their kitchens, therefore, had to be ready to respond flexibly and rapidly to ensure that whenever the crews arrived, tired and hungry, they could get a hot meal. At least some of the men they served remember their services with affection. For one American, the fact that the mess was open 24 hours a day was vitally important to morale and 'the food was great'.[42]

Feeding the multitude was not a job for the military messes alone. Both the USAF and the RAF recognised the need for 'snacks' and 'refreshments' during duty hours for aircrew, and places to unwind for both air and ground crews after duty. The British commandant of Berlin felt that the poorer rations of British troops/airmen in Berlin when compared to both the Americans and French had – or could have – a negative impact on morale. He therefore ordered that the NAAFI be stocked with more 'luxury' goods, at the cost of goods for Berlin. His calculation was that in the total reckoning, morale could be significantly boosted for the price of a single Dakota load per day. In other words, at the price of just 3 tons out of the thousands being flown into Berlin day after day, he could keep his men from feeling neglected and forgotten. Most veterans of the Airlift would probably have agreed with him.

Tunner was a different character. He was concerned not only with providing services but also with improving performance. During his initial assessment of operations, he noticed that pilots wandered off to get themselves coffee and snacks, leaving their aircraft standing around longer than was necessary for unloading. He quickly put an end to this practice by forbidding crews from being more than 10yd away from their aircraft during offloading in Berlin. He then ensured that they received everything they needed – from orders to the latest weather report – at their aircraft, i.e. everything was brought to the aircraft by jeep. Last, but not least, he established mobile snack bars 'liberally stocked with such items as hot coffee, hot dogs and doughnuts, and equipped with a canopy that could be extended in case of rain'.[43]

Not only did the food now come to the airmen, but Tunner ' . . . approached the German Red Cross and asked for their cooperation. . . . They picked out some of the most beautiful girls in Berlin to ride along in the mobile snack bar and dish out the goodies along with enticing smiles. There were no more moans from the crews about staying by the plane. You couldn't chase them away.'[44]

One of those girls remembers it as follows: 'With my mobile snack bar I drove to the waiting aircraft and supplied the three-man crews with hot chocolate and sandwiches. Sometimes I worked straight through for 24 hours. The boys needed a little refreshment. Out of gratefulness one of them gave me a fur coat. I cried from joy. We had nothing back then.'[45]

The British response to this need was characteristically less regimented and more individualistic. Aircrews were not ordered to stay near their aircraft and the services were not organised by senior command but rather 'out-sourced', as would be said today. Namely, there was a Salvation Army canteen, a NAAFI, a YMCA, an American PX and a Malcolm Club at Gatow.

The Malcolm Club was particularly popular, and here too there were girls, but British rather than German. The Malcolm Club at Gatow had been designed to serve the needs of the small Occupation garrison at Gatow, but abruptly it was confronted with hundreds of aircrews passing through the station as part of the Airlift. In response, the Club called in help.

Mrs Bell was tall, dark, light-hearted and a little light-headed hence her nickname [Dizzy]. She was given half a day's notice to get to Gatow, and she threw a few items of personal kit into a hold-all then filled it with tea, sugar and powdered milk, which she was sure would come in handy in Berlin. She decked herself out in her smart air-force-blue uniform and tried to reach Berlin by road. Naturally she couldn't. There was a blockade on, they told her. 'Silly of me,' grinned Dizzy, and hitched a lift to Bückeburg. She was devoted to the Air Force . . . and the Air Force reciprocated by being extremely fond of Mrs Bell. So she had little difficulty persuading the ground staff to look the other way while, quite without authority, she climbed aboard an aircraft that happened to be bound for Gatow.

Quite quickly, a few more of the trim Malcolm Club girls arrived to work under Mrs Bell's direction. They took on a staff of sixty-five Germans to do the manual work and some of the specialised jobs. Three of them were barbers and for the next year they worked from 12 to 14 hours a day.

Meanwhile, in the hut on the edge of the airfield, Mrs Bell and her girls served tea and coffee and doughnuts. The crews ate and drank while their aircraft were being unloaded and sometimes reloaded with manufactured goods or people bound for Western Germany. If the crews were delayed by bad weather or unserviceability, they could go to the main club-house and get a more substantial meal at any hour of the day or night.[46]

And so the men of both air forces were provided for in their own way and on the whole to their satisfaction by the dedication of women and other civilians whose role in the Airlift is far too often overlooked.

Chapter 8

AN ARMY OF WORKER ANTS

One aspect of the Airlift was almost entirely in civilian – indeed German – hands: the on- and offloading of cargoes. It can be argued that cargo handling began when the civic authorities in the besieged city determined the volumes and priorities of goods required for the civilian population of Berlin. The Allies informed the Berlin government of what Airlift capacity was available, and the Berlin government in return 'advised' the commandants of the Western Sectors what they wanted most. In doing so, the city government had to take into account the needs of the city not only for food and fuel, but also for raw materials to keep factories working. They had to meet not only material needs but maintain morale as well. There were many competing demands on the capacity of the Airlift and so despite every effort at 'scientific' methodology, many decisions on what to transport were inevitably political. The Allies were wise to leave these decisions to the German authorities. At the working level, this meant that liaison officers were appointed for the key categories of cargo – food, fuel, medical supplies, clothing, industrial raw materials, etc., and these in turn conveyed the city government's requests to the Air Staff Committee of the Western Allies in Berlin.

The Western Allies then took over the organisational aspects of ordering, purchasing and ensuring the delivery of the required/requested goods to the departure airfields in Western Germany. This was an army, rather than an air force, duty; in the British Zone it was the responsibility of the British Army Air Transport Organisation, and in the American Zone the US Army. It meant procuring and then ensuring transport for the goods needed to the departure airfields. As one historian points out:

The whole business of finding the supplies and getting them flowing at the right rate to the correct base was fiendish. Flour, for example, came from thirteen different mills in the Bizone and two ports. Dried vegetables were supplied by eleven German firms. . . . Butter could not be kept waiting for long because of the absence of cold storage. Dried milk was in terribly short supply on the world market. Every commodity had to be distributed among nine dispatching airfields.[1]

Since many objects were not available in the Western Zones at all, they had to be brought in by ship, predominantly from the US, to Bremen or Hamburg. These goods were then transhipped by rail or truck to the departure airfields. Coal, on the other hand, came primarily from the German mines on the Ruhr, and it was also transported by rail, but not directly to the departure airfields. First, it was sent to dealers in Frankfurt, Hanau, Offenbach and Mannheim for packing in US Army duffel bags, and *then* it was shipped again by rail to the airfields.

Military staff were actively involved in seeking methods of increasing the net delivery of usable supplies and reducing extraneous weight. This entailed such calculations as whether it was more efficient to fly in pre-baked bread, or fly in the flour *and* the coal needed to fire the bread ovens of Berlin. Here it was determined that one-third of the weight of baked bread was water and that it was more economical to fly in flour, yeast and coal. As another example, it was possible to increase calories of diet delivered per ton of cargo by filleting meat rather than sending it on the bone; and no account of the Airlift would be complete without reference to the all-pervasive, much maligned and then again nostalgically remembered 'Pom'. The need to import potatoes in dehydrated form was recognised almost immediately, but the first efforts were disastrous. Six hundred tons of pre-cooked potato flour sent from America proved so unpalatable that the Occupation authorities themselves were ashamed to issue it to the population. After various other sources were tried, it was found that British Pom was the most popular. It was also popularised by the Airlift saying, 'Better "Pom" than "Frau, kom!"' – a reference to the phrase used by the Soviet soldiers demanding unpaid sex from any woman they fancied.

As important as finding ways to reduce the weight of the supplies destined for Berlin was finding appropriate packaging for those goods. This proved a major headache for planners, and not only with respect to coal as described earlier. The need to tranship cargoes onwards to Berlin in relatively small transport aircraft with small doors meant that many traditional means of packing were unsuitable. Newsprint, for example, was usually transported in huge rolls weighing 4 tons a piece – too large to fit through the door of a C-47 or C-54. Milk in canisters was difficult to handle and excessively heavy. Barrels, then a common means of transporting a variety of goods, were dangerous; if the barrels became loose in flight, they could roll about, completely destabilising an aircraft and causing it to crash.

From a planning perspective, packaging had to be found that met a variety of criteria. On the one hand, cargoes had to be packed in the lightest weight packaging practical in order to ensure the highest net delivery of needed goods to Berlin. Packaging also had to be sufficiently robust to prevent damage, spoilage, or loss of cargoes and aircraft. (In one incident, honey in barrels broke while in the air, oozed all over the cargo compartment of the aircraft and then out onto the tarmac when the doors were opened; the trip was a complete waste and the aircraft was unserviceable for an inordinately long time while it was cleaned out again.) Packing things in small containers increased the amount of packaging per net delivered ton of cargo, which was undesirable, but packing things in large containers often made it impossible for one man alone to carry the load from trailer to aircraft and vice versa, thereby slowing down the on- and offloading process. All these factors had to be considered.

Another problem was the behaviour of cargo in the air. Loose cargo could shift, causing a change in the centre of gravity. Issues of hygiene also had to be considered; any aircraft might carry a mixed cargo, and almost all had carried cargoes of coal at one time or another, meaning that coal dust was everywhere and seeped into subsequent cargoes if the packaging was not sufficiently airtight. Yet another consideration was the impact of temperature. In the winter months, cargoes were subjected to freezing temperatures in the cargo compartment, while excessive heat in summer was likely to be even more disastrous. In one case it almost came to a 'diplomatic incident' when the freezing crew of a Hastings turned the heat on in the aircraft – forgetting that they were carrying a cargo of frozen fish.

The airfields each had an operations officer responsible for keeping track of the cargoes. They knew what cargoes were on order for their field and where they were located at any one time. They gave the orders to the German railways (Bundesbahn) to put together a trainload and deliver it at a specific time. Clearly one aspect of this task was ensuring that perishable or urgently needed cargoes did not get delayed, and the Americans and British took totally different approaches to this problem. The Americans liked to have the German railways ship things to the airfields in large quantities and they would then warehouse them at the departure bases. This made it easier to ensure that aircraft capacity could be maximised. While this 'flexibility' optimised aircraft usage, it did not always respond to the needs of Berlin. There were instances where West Berlin factories had to close down for days on end due to a lack of supplies – which were in fact at a warehouse in Wiesbaden or Rhein-Main.

Possibly because their bases were so widely dispersed that it was impossible to have central storage, the British operated a system which would now be called 'just-in-time' delivery. They tried to get an accurate estimate of each daily requirement and to have only those specific goods in the named quantity delivered to the designated airfield, minimising storage. 'Under the British system, goods were put in aircraft for Berlin within hours of their arrival at the base in the British Zone.'[2]

Problems arose even with this system. If an aircraft had to return fully loaded, as did happen if the weather suddenly turned bad in Berlin or when the aircraft developed technical difficulties forcing it to return to base, the cargo – possibly a perishable cargo – was unexpectedly back on the ground at the departure airfield. Thereafter the controllers had to carefully keep in mind just what that cargo was when planning where to put it and when to reschedule it. A cargo of coal could sit outside in pouring rain or hot sun for hours – a cargo of milk could not.

On the whole, deliveries of goods to the departure airfields were the responsibility of the German railways but the Allied military took responsibility of the cargoes at the railhead. In the American Zone the responsible military organisation was the Field Traffic Section and in the British Zone, the RASC especially created the Rear Airfield Supply Organisation. (At Gatow, known as the Forward Airfield Supply Organisation.) These organisations represent yet again neglected, indeed forgotten, heroes of the Airlift. They had the daunting task not only of taking deliveries and storing them as necessary, but actually putting together loads of freight to optimise aircraft utilisation.

The method involved was to pack all cargo destined for one aircraft onto one or more trailer(s), which was then hauled to the aircraft as a single, predetermined and finite unit. The difficulty was not only ensuring that the total weight did not exceed the capacity of the aircraft – bearing in mind that different aircraft types had different capabilities – but also ensuring that each aircraft's space was used to the optimal extent. In other words, both bulk and weight had to be optimised. An aircraft filled to the gills with noodles would in fact be carrying only one-third of its tonnage capacity, but if PSP plates were to be loaded in the hold in the same manner, the aircraft would never get off the ground. The result was an effort to 'marry' cargoes so that both weight and space were used effectively.

The load for a specific aircraft type was loaded onto one or more trailer(s) and directed to a 'holding and consignment' or 'marshalling' area. As aircraft returned from Berlin empty and radioed in to the tower that they were roughly 15 minutes away from landing, this information was passed on to the Army traffic control personnel. These in turn directed specific trailer(s) to the spot where the incoming aircraft would be parked. Ideally, the trailer(s) full of cargo arrived at the parking place at the same time as the aircraft and the loading crews. Then the task of loading could begin at once, while the aircraft was refuelled and the crew, if necessary, changed. Arriving in Berlin, the procedure was essentially the same. Roughly 15 minutes from landing, the pilot radioed in his cargo, and by the time he had cut his engines at his parking place, a team of offloaders would already be alongside with empty lorries and trailers for hauling the cargo away.

Naturally, and particularly in the early days, the wrong configurations of cargo did sometimes get put aboard the wrong aircraft type. At least one Dakota pilot reported astonishing sluggishness at take-off and sweated his way to Berlin suspecting serious technical difficulties in his aircraft (and very likely muttering something rude about what a sluggish old cow they had given him) only to discover on landing that he was carrying the load intended for a larger aircraft. Allegedly, the Dakota had just carried more than twice what it was certified for.[3] The Dakota was a remarkable machine, but three times the load was too much even for it. In another incident, a corporal of the RASC at Wunstorf remembers: ' . . . one evening some bumblers put a York load into a Dakota. That's roughly a 9 ton load stashed into an aircraft that can only lift three. Needless to say, the Dakota didn't get airborne. . . . Fortunately, the terrain was flat and the only mishap was that the farmer out there harvested his turnips a bit earlier than he intended.'[4]

Sometimes the problem of weight was not the fault of the marshalling teams and dispatchers, but rather of the packers. Gen Tunner, after reading repeated reports of 'sluggish' C-54s flying like 'lame ducks', visited the facilities where coal was loaded into sacks for transport by air to Berlin. He found:

> The men were really working away, filling the sacks to the brim and hoisting them onto the big trucks with vim and vigour. They only bothered to weigh about one sack out of a hundred, and when it was overweight, as it invariably was, they simply poured a little coal out and threw it up on the truck. I stepped forward and had fifty of the sacks already on the truck taken down and weighed. Some of those so-called one-hundred-pound sacks ran up to 125 pounds; they averaged out at 115 – a 15 per cent overloading that would mean a ton and a half extra weight on a C-54 full of coal. No wonder the planes seemed sluggish! . . . . It had to be carefully explained to the loading crews that their overzealousness was hurting instead of helping us.[5]

Another serious problem, even if the weight of a consignment was theoretically correct for the aircraft type, was the loading itself. Freight had to be very carefully balanced to ensure that the aircraft's centre of gravity was not altered. Experienced teams placed the light cargo in the front of the trailer so that it was unloaded last and so ended in the tail of the aircraft or spread out over the heavier cargo. In the early stages of the Airlift, it took Air Force personnel to oversee loading, explain about the needs of aircraft in flight and ensure that no aircraft was loaded in a manner to endanger its aerodynamics. Almost as important, even if the aircraft was correctly loaded in the first place, cargoes had to be properly secured to stop them from shifting while in flight. Again, Air Force experts were initially needed to make sure that cargoes were properly tied down.

Some cargoes required special handling. One of these was salt. It was so corrosive to aircraft and particularly their controls, that it could not be carried in normal cargo compartments. To the relief of the USAF, the RAF took exclusive responsibility for supplying the 38 short tons of salt required *each day* in Berlin. At first the Sunderland flying boats were tasked with delivering this cargo, not – as some have suggested – because the hulls were treated to withstand salt water, but because all the controls were in the ceiling and so less subject to corrosion. After the Sunderlands were withdrawn from the Airlift, the British assigned converted Halifax bombers to the salt-run, carrying the salt in panniers slung in the bomb-bay.

Another special cargo was liquid fuel. Initially the cargo tanks of tanker aircraft were filled by the same bowsers as were used to fill their own operating tanks. Loading a tanker by this method took as much as 40 minutes. Furthermore:

> The tricky part of the operation was knowing the right minute to stop the pump. If the operator left it too late, the cargo tanks flooded and covered the aircraft in petrol. One spark after that and the aircraft would explode. . . . [So a soldier sat in the aircraft] watching the gauges and it was his job to shout to another soldier at the door when he wanted the Germans in charge of the pump to switch off. Sometimes the man at the gauges would shout 'off' and the man at the door would shout 'orf' but the German would think they said 'auf' and keep the pump going. When that happened, that particular aircraft lost a sortie.[6]

By using pumps attached directly to underground storage tanks, not only could these misunderstandings be avoided but the time could be cut to just 12–14 minutes. But the problems with the cargo didn't end with loading. Initially, 'the fuel tanks had no baffles installed to prevent sloshing in flight, with the result that the slightest turbulence caused the tankers to career all over the sky'.[7]

Then there were cargoes that were difficult simply for morale reasons. The crew of an American C-54 became outraged when they discovered their consignment consisted of wine destined for the French garrison of Berlin. They promptly refused to fly it, expressing the opinion that wine was not as important as milk and if the French could have wine then the Americans could have coca cola. The equally enraged French promptly dispatched a delegation to the USAF HQ in Wiesbaden with a detailed history to prove that wine was vital to French health. (Modern experts might agree!) The USAF diplomatically agreed and the wine got delivered – probably by a different crew.

On the other hand, there were also cargoes that had a notably positive effect on morale; one RAF Dakota with a load of scotch for the NAAFI was coddled all the way to Berlin by solicitous controllers anxious to ensure its safe arrival. There was also the C-54 crew with a cargo of fresh strawberries. The aroma from the cargo compartment was so tantalising that the crew came to the conclusion that they simply must ensure that they were delivering quality goods to the poor people of Berlin. They allegedly landed the plane 'with every finger sticky, and the throttles, control yokes and seat backs covered with a bright red goo'.[8]

Offloading at Gatow had one distinct disadvantage over offloading at either Tempelhof or, later, Tegel. Gatow lay on the very outskirts of Berlin, beyond most of the verdant neighbourhoods of the rich, and far from the population centres of the city where the consumers of the goods being flown in lived. This meant that even after offloading at Gatow, the cargoes had to be transhipped again onto vehicles to take them fully into the city. To move, for example, 1,000 tons of cargo by lorry from Gatow into the heart of the city required 5 tons of gasoline and roughly 1½ tons of diesel oil. Fortunately, some forty barges had been trapped on the Havel when the blockade began. One tug could haul 3,000 tons of freight on barges at the cost of burning just 1 ton of coal. The forty barges together had a cargo capacity of 15,000 tons, so a large portion of Gatow bulk cargoes were transhipped onto barge and hauled into central Berlin by tug.

While Allied military personnel supervised loading the trailers and the aircraft and both provided and drove the motor transport, the actual work of loading cargoes was done by civilian work gangs. The bulk of those employed to do loading in the Western Zones were Germans (predominantly released POWs) and Displaced Persons (DPs). The latter were former forced labourers, mostly Poles, taken from their homes by the Nazis against their will and forced to work in conditions little better than slavery but now reluctant to return to a home occupied by the Red Army and under Soviet administration.

As many as 16,000 DPs were employed in US Labour Service battalions, earning a hot meal and a roof over their heads more than a 'living'.

In Berlin, the workers were almost exclusively German. Former Wehrmacht soldiers, who had served in technical trades of one kind or another, were preferred. These men tended to be better educated but still possessed a high degree of military discipline, making them particularly easy to control. However, the recruiting was not done directly by the Allies, but rather by the Berlin Employment Office (Arbeitsamt) which sent able-bodied, unemployed men to report to the various airfields. A total of 20,000 Berliners, predominantly workers laid off by the closed factories, eventually found employment at the airfields, primarily as loaders.

The units were organised, where relevant by nationality to minimise conflict and improve ease of communication among workers, into semi-military work crews. Loaders worked 12-hour (later 8-hour) shifts on rations of 2,900 calories per day, and almost every first-hand account stresses that the 'hot meal' at Allied installations was by far the greater incentive than the pay of DM1.20 per hour. 'What could one buy in a ruined, bombed out and now blockaded postwar Berlin? But that good hot meal of meat, vegetables and chocolate for desert was simply priceless at a time when most people were living on the verge of starvation.'[9]

In consequence, the greatest possible punishment was dismissal. Rather than miss a day, men were known to send brothers or sons to take their place. The loading crews also developed strong team spirit. 'Among our group there was a special kind of team spirit and the common need somehow achieved a congruency among people which could never be established in peaceful, normal times.'[10]

German loaders remember that the early days of the Airlift were 'pretty chaotic' and that as many as twenty men would be assigned to offload one C-47 – merely getting in each other's way. One German loader also pointed out that offloading C-47s was particularly difficult because of the tail wheel and the steeply sloping deck of the cargo compartment. This was a problem with all the British aircraft as well. Only the larger USAF planes were at this time designed with tricycle undercarriages and so level cargo compartments.

The lasting image for most observers was simply one of hectic activity. One USAF pilot wrote: 'The place was swarming with people and machines of all descriptions. Semi-trailer trucks loaded, unloaded and in the process were everywhere. Some snuggled up to the silver bellies of the big birds like piglets suckling the sow.'[11]

Things did not look different from the RAF perspective; a squadron leader taking part in the Airlift remembered:

On reaching Berlin we raced for the end of the runway . . . putting our wheels down at maximum undercarriage speed, there was no time to be lost. On arrival the aircraft was besieged by German workers with the unloaders' sacks over their heads as they passed to and from, each with a hundred pounds of supplies on his back like a flow of ants.[12]

Civilians on the Airlift described the offloading as follows:

The large freight doorway at the rear was completely blocked by a lorry which had already received half the load. Eight German labourers were inside the fuselage and in the lorry three Germans were stacking. From the centre section doorway, a chain of four more were feeding a second lorry parked close by the inboard propeller on the port side. We had just taken all this in when two women sweepers appeared and as the last sacks went out through the door, the dust from their brooms met the incoming crew.[13]

German sources reported: 'A landing aircraft had not yet finished its landing run and already the lorries of the offloading teams had attached themselves to its wake. The offloading began at exactly the same minute as the aircraft came to a halt.'

Gen Tunner himself noted:

I'd seen [the] planes being unloaded swiftly and efficiently by sweat-drenched German civilians and I knew that that phase of the turn-around activity was being well taken care of. The Germans were personally involved; they had their own well-being and freedom at stake, and they were working like beavers.[14]

Not only altruism motivated the labourers. The offloading times were carefully and officially recorded. Each month the crew with the best overall record at each airfield was announced and rewarded with cigarettes and chocolate. These items, although highly valued in themselves, had the added value that they also served as currency on the black market. Such rewards were, therefore, far from nominal incentives. Sometimes the Germans had a little unexpected – and unpaid – help too. The son of the chief of transportation in Tempelhof, then a teenager, remembers helping unload planes there in his 'spare time' – just to be part of it all.[15]

Despite Tunner's praise for the German workers, the temptation for pilfering was too great for some. There were strict controls of workers as they came off their shifts, both by MPs and by German civilians hired especially as guards.

One of the German guards tried to explain what it was like: 'Everyone was hungry, and that made a lot of people forget their principles and illegally "accrue" a few items. We had to watch very carefully because there were 3,000 loaders one shift – lasting 8 hours – and all together there were three shifts in this 24-hour airlift operation.'[16]

The methods were ingenious, reminding modern readers of the ingenuity of RAF POWs at German prison camps, made famous by the book and film, *The Great Escape*. 'One favourite trick was to conceal flour and sugar in little bags suspended inside the trousers. When caught, the men would pull a string which emptied the bags and little piles of food would appear all over the tarmac.'[17]

Another highly valued object was fat. This was often smuggled out in the false bottoms of mess tins, in which workers were allowed to take leftovers from the daily meal home to their families. A single control could yield astonishing results. One such control turned up:

34kg of sugar	3 bars of chocolate
400g of tea	20 cigarettes
1.8kg of flour	0.25kg of coffee
28kg of butter	5.5kg of coal
129 tins of canned meat	4.6kg of milk powder

It is striking that the objects stolen were not predominantly the 'currencies' of the black market, i.e. cigarettes and chocolate, but rather the things wanted at home by wives and children: sugar, flour and butter. Furthermore, for a shift composed of 3,000 workers, the quantities are not alarming, speaking rather for the majority that apparently did not even try to take advantage of their position at the source of goods coming into the besieged city. One historian characterised the pilfering as 'pitiable rather than criminal'.[18]

It should not be forgotten that the work these labourers did for a hot-meal and a minimum wage was both strenuous and dangerous. Workers were involved in accidents with both motor vehicles and aircraft. A total of seven German labourers lost their lives in work-related accidents while working on the Airlift. It is fair to say, that given the situation they were in, the Berliners working the Airlift showed far greater honesty than did many of the Occupation troops who never faced the same hardships yet were not above engaging in both minor and even major dealings on the black market.

Before closing this chapter on cargoes it must be remembered that not all cargoes were being transported *into* Berlin. The need to transport cargoes out of Berlin was – at least initially – underestimated and controversial.

The Americans, particularly under Tunner's leadership, were interested in maximising efficiency and clearly it was easier to increase delivery tonnages if aircraft were turned around rapidly in Berlin. Loading return cargoes cost hours and so reduced significantly the number of inbound flights that each aircraft made, reducing daily delivery tonnages. The Americans calculated that for every 100 tons of cargo lifted *out* of Berlin, 40 tons of supplies, that might otherwise have been flown into the city, were sacrificed.

The British, on the other hand, reasoned that failure to fly out products produced by Berlin's factories would result in those factories closing down, putting their workers on the dole, and so would adversely impact civilian morale. Tunner's reduced tonnages were quantifiable, the impact on morale was not; but the British remained committed to flying out cargoes and as the backlog of finished products building up at Tempelhof grew, the Americans simply dumped the problem on the RAF. It was decided that henceforth the RAF would be responsible for flying cargoes out of Berlin – at the expense of its aircraft utility and cargo delivery rates.

Justifiable as the 'back-lift' was in morale terms, it was difficult to organise. Products from Berlin's factories required the same care as cargoes going in – attention had to be paid to the packaging of the individual products, to the mixing of consignments for aircraft by type and to loading the aircraft itself. Again, special problems could arise. Pilots remember the odd feeling associated with flying a load of light-bulbs, which were virtually weightless but very fragile. Others remember their first load of loudspeakers; these had magnets in them which completely confused the aircraft's own compasses. In short, packaging, 'marrying' and loading return cargoes was just as complicated as doing the same for inbound cargoes, while the variety of aircraft employed by the RAF, and the fact that the RAF continued to use Dakotas right to the end, complicated things further. The Dakotas were too small and their capacity too limited for many kinds of heavy or bulky cargoes, but Dakotas could carry passengers and mail – and they did.

While mail was easy to handle since it was not perishable or bulky and was relatively light, passengers could be very difficult. The West Germans trapped in Berlin unexpectedly when the blockade started had been evacuated; those passengers consisted either of military personnel on official orders, civilians on urgent business (and the right connections to Allied or German government officials) or persons deemed a 'burden' to the besieged city. The latter might be sick or elderly persons requiring special medical treatment, which could not be provided adequately in Berlin, or they might be children, who were undernourished and in need of a chance to regain their strength in a healthier environment. People, and in some cases entire families, who feared for their safety and well-being in the Soviet Sector or Zone, also made their way to West Berlin with the sole purpose of being flown out to safety – and they were.[19] Lastly, people whose negative attitude was deemed a morale liability were also flown out. The British commandant believed that anyone despondent about the city's chances of surviving the blockade as a free entity ought to have the 'highest' evacuation priority. He reasoned that one nervous person could infect hundreds of others with the same doubt and pessimism. Civilian passengers paid a flat rate of 16 Marks each; the equivalent of a second-class rail ticket to Hannover. Altogether, the RAF flew out over 50,000 adults and about 17,000 children from the beleaguered city.

Whatever category they belonged to, conditions for passengers were less than ideal. An RAF flight engineer remembers:

> We had an empty plane on the return journeys until batches of mail bags were slung in the back. Then a little later young ladies began to appear in groups of six or ten. They apparently had relatives in West Germany and were being evacuated to relieve the food shortage. Being equipped solely for cargo, these bright cheery things sat on the mail bags for take off and landing. I sometimes wondered what would have happened if we had a bit of a bump.[20]

One passenger described the experience vividly:

> The inside of the machine was filthy from coal dust. The metal seats were fixed on sides of the fuselage and folded down. We sat down and were told to buckle up. . . . With a deafening noise – the freight room of a Dakota was not noise-insulated – the aircraft rolled onto the runway and took off. The flight was due to turbulence at low altitude very rough. . . . My brother, who was looking out of the window, noticed that the engine of the war-weary Dakota was losing oil. After a flight of about 1½ hours we landed at Lübeck. It was not a gentle landing, probably because the runway wasn't in the best condition. . . .[21]

As described, the Dakotas were at best equipped with inward-facing bucket seats down the sides of the fuselage designed for paratroopers, who of course were disciplined. The passengers being flown out of Berlin, particularly the children, often were not. This was one reason why many felt that the most difficult cargoes on the Airlift were children. An RAF pilot remembers: 'When we picked [the children] up at Gatow they would be loaded some twenty-five or thirty at a time by their German escorts, harangued with a briefing in German, and then the doors slammed shut. From then on they were all ours and some were very young. No interpreter to help out should an emergency situation arise.'[22]

Fortunately, there were no accidents involving children, but this is not to say that all flights were smooth or comfortable. Confined to the corridors and their designated height, Airlift aircraft could not avoid turbulence and often conditions were rough; the children were sick. Or, as another pilot remembers: 'Kids wriggle. They wriggle out to play on the icy cold and filthy floor. Then one of them wants to go. And all at once a rush to the tail unbalances the plane. Its nose rises. The captain wonders what the heck is going on, and all this amid the world's number one current crisis with Russian-held territory below.'[23]

Another RAF aircrew recalls:

The real problem arose after landing at Fassberg. A truck was supposed to meet each aeroplane that was carrying children and transport the load to a nearby transit centre. We often had to wait over an hour in the dispersal area at night with aircraft taxiing around until a truck arrived. Safe-guarding the children was rather like shepherding a flock of geese in the dark and not what we had signed on for at all. This led to some pretty hot R/T [Radio/Telephone] exchanges with the tower e.g. 'Where's the bloody truck etc. etc.'[24]

Fortunately, the children appear to have been blissfully unaware of the trouble they were causing. The many stories told of being flown out of Berlin are dominated by the thrill of flying for the first time and memories of kindly pilots inviting small boys into the cockpit or giving away sweets.

Chapter 9

'IS ANYONE IN CHARGE HERE?'

From the start of the blockade, the centralised Soviet Union was facing three Western democracies, each of whom was a sovereign state with their own priorities and agenda. Given the history of friction between the US and France over German policy, Stalin had every reason to believe that the Western Powers would start bickering among themselves and fail to agree on a joint policy at all. Certainly Stalin must have hoped that he could drive a wedge between the Western Powers and exploit their differences. If he had succeeded in dividing them, he might well have also succeeded with the blockade. It is certain that Britain could not have sustained the Airlift on its own, doubtful whether the US would have, and even the loss of the French would have hurt the West as it would have denied them Tegel and the undoubted propaganda value they gained by isolating the Soviet Union.

That the West *did* find a common policy and even a common voice is in large measure due to an initiative by Ernest Bevin and the daily efforts of three diplomats, all but forgotten by history. Just two days after the start of the blockade, Bevin proposed to the United States the establishment of a coordinating committee composed of the US and French Ambassadors to London, and Sir William Strang of the British Foreign Office. These senior diplomats knew each other well, and had been working closely together in the preceding months. Furthermore, they all enjoyed the confidence of their political masters, allowing them a large degree of self-sufficiency in day-to-day matters.

While it made sense to locate this committee in London, in the same time zone as Berlin, it also ensured that the British government had a stronger influence than if the committee had been located in Washington – something which Bevin undoubtedly had in mind when he made the proposal. Washington saw the sense of the proposal, however, and the US Secretary of State, Gen George Marshall, approved the plan the day after Bevin proposed it.

This committee proved an invaluable asset in ensuring that the Western Allies 'spoke with one voice' on the issue of Berlin. The three diplomats managed to retain an overview of the complex situation, openly shared their respective instructions and so prevented suspicions from arising. They managed over the coming months to forge joint recommendations, draft joint diplomatic notes and to keep their respective governments working in tandem and harmony. In the assessment of historians: 'Their professionalism made a great contribution to the smooth running of the political and diplomatic operation, [and] their personal relationship prevented many a misunderstanding.'[1]

Another of Stalin's hopes must have been that the governments in London and Washington would face criticism from their domestic opponents and become weakened. This hope was also disappointed. After all, it had been Winston Churchill, now in the Opposition, who had first publicly sounded the alarm about the 'Iron Curtain', and the Conservatives were staunchly anti-communist. There was no risk of the Opposition undermining the British government's position on Berlin. In the United States, the Republicans were at this time more isolationist than the unpopular Truman, and Truman found himself in the midst of a presidential campaign that he was widely expected to lose. It is both surprising and significant that his Republican challenger did not try to make an issue of the Berlin Airlift in the election. On the contrary, it was one of the few Democratic policies that Thomas Dewey wholeheartedly embraced – an indication of just how popular the Berlin Airlift was with the American people.

While the political consensus in both Western capitals was firm and the diplomatic cooperation between Washington, London and Paris worked well, the same cannot be said about the military coordination of operations. As was mentioned earlier, both the British and Americans launched their own, independent, Airlift operations. Furthermore, they had independent Forces of Occupations, each headed by Military Governors whose activities were theoretically coordinated by the now defunct and inoperative Control Council but who were completely equal to one another. Most importantly, while the British Military Governor, Gen Robertson, and his American colleague, Gen Clay, got along well enough, they each took their orders from their respective governments.

Gen Robertson was in the better position of the two Military Governors. He took his orders from the British Foreign Secretary and the relationship was a good one:

> [Robertson] saw the day-to-day affairs of the zone as his own responsibility
> and did not refer details to London. Higher policy he thought a political matter

and left to Bevin. He gave the Foreign Secretary devoted service and the loyalty which Bevin prized. In return, Bevin gave Robertson total respect and backing; his first response to any German crisis was 'What does the General think?'[2]

Bevin's confidence in Robertson was not misplaced. The general had extensive experience in private industry from the interwar years and was by training an engineer with a strong background in supply and logistics. He is said to have brought 'a flexible mind and a readiness to listen', and clearly possessed 'calm common sense and the analytical clarity and drafting ability of a top-rate civil servant'.[3] He was the right man in the right place at the right time, as far as Airlift operations were concerned.

Gen Clay, who had spent most of the war as chief of military procurement and had a real genius for logistical organisation, was also *eminently* (immanently) qualified for the job he was to assume during the Airlift. He had come to Germany determined to get along with the Russians and convinced that the best way to get trust was to give it. By the time the Airlift was launched, he knew he had given his best efforts to trying to work with the Soviets and they had failed; that made him firmer than many who had not been at the game as long as he had. The Germans viewed him as 'anti-German' and certainly he had no undue sympathy for them, but as a southerner he knew what it was to be defeated and that, perhaps, was the source of his dedication to being 'fair'. For his many good qualities, he was in the unfortunate position of being a servant of two masters. He reported both to the Department of State and to the Department of War. Furthermore, Washington, perhaps because it had no tradition of colonies too far away to micro-manage, had a greater tendency to interfere in the day-to-day affairs of the US Zone of Occupation. In consequence, throughout his tenure as Military Governor, Clay had to spend much of his time arguing his case in Washington either by late night telephone calls or by flying back to the US; and he had to persuade not just the Department of State of his policies, but also the Department of War, the President and Congress.

To complicate the Command and Control situation in Germany further, although the two Military Governors had command authority over their respective armies of Occupation – and the attached air forces of Occupation – they did *not* exercise direct control over the air force units pouring in from around the world and assigned to the Airlift. This meant that, while the army side of operations worked more or less from the start (after the establishment of appropriate subordinate command structures), the air force operations suffered from initial confusion.

In the British Zone, the tensions between RAF Transport Command and the British Air Forces of Occupation (BAFO) were evident right from the start. It resulted, for example, in two group captains with identical instructions (to command all transport operations) being sent to take command of Wunstorf – one was sent from BAFO and the other from Transport Command. Just to add spice to the soup, Wunstorf was still a fighter base at the time and so under RAF Fighter Command orders also.

Under the circumstances, it is not surprising that a squadron leader of Transport Command remembers bringing seven Dakotas to Wunstorf and finding neither marshallers to direct his aircraft to a hardstanding nor anyone at Station HQ who could tell him what to do with them. 'Every corridor and stairway seemed alive with harassed blue-clad pilots vainly seeking instructions.'[4] Another squadron leader recalls the early days as 'a complete shambles' with aircraft taking off as soon as they were ready and crews working until they dropped.[5]

From the point of view of the airmen trying to provide services to the pilots, the situation was hardly better. Norman Hurst, who worked as an operations clerk, remembers the operations room being relocated at frequent intervals, moving about the airfield like a gypsy. It eventually came to rest in a collection of Nissen huts located near the aircraft hardstandings. This hut also housed the Army dispatch unit responsible for loading and unloading aircraft and the aircraft servicing unit responsible for refuelling and maintenance checks. The operations clerk was here confronted by nine separate field telephones on one desk – 'a nightmare when three or more calls came in at the same time'.[6]

In the RAF, the Command confusion at the senior level was initially resolved in favour of Transport Command because it was felt that it possessed the expertise to run a complex transport operation. BAFO, it should be remembered was not at its inception an *operational* headquarters, it was a *policy* headquarters only. It didn't even have an operations room. Sir Kenneth Cross, Group Captain Operations at BAFO starting in January 1947, claims that at the start of the Airlift BAFO 'had been cut to the bone and [we] were not always filled. So we were in the worst possible state to take on an operation of which we knew nothing'.[7] Nevertheless, while Transport Command took over the command of flying operations, BAFO retained responsibility for the airfields, and continued to lobby for control of the Airlift as a whole, a battle they eventually won shortly before the blockade was lifted. Meanwhile, Transport Command ran the show, albeit not without some internal friction because the Yorks flying the Airlift came from 47 Group and the Dakotas from 46 Group. These frictions were resolved when on 22 September 1948 an advanced operational HQ of 46 Group was established at Schloss Bückeburg in Germany with responsibility for 'all airlift operations involving British aircraft'.[8] By 1 December 1948, 46 Group HQ also had administrative responsibility for the airfields supporting the Airlift located in the British Zone and for Gatow. Schloss Bückeburg also housed the headquarters of the British Army Air Transport Organisation tasked with supporting the Airlift on the ground. The establishment of this 46 Group HQ further contributed to close cooperation between the RAF and Army in the British Zone and a smooth-run operation on the whole.

At the airfield level, unified command structures eventually produced the professional operations which later observers associated with the Airlift. Where there had once been one operations clerk there were now four per shift, each man working a regular 8-hour shift. The aircrews also worked on regular schedules, 'reporting to the operations room at a specified time, day or night, and collecting printed flight details'.[9] The latter consisted of crew members, aircraft registration number and parking position, time to start engines, time to taxi, time to take-off and time to each turning point.

In the American Zone the same conflict of interest had emerged between the Air Forces of Occupation and the transport exports of Military Air Transport Service (MATS) in the US. Unfortunately, it was not so happily resolved. Commanding the US Air Forces in Europe (USAFE) at the time the Airlift began was the already legendary first commander of the US 8th Air Force (1942–4), Gen Curtis LeMay. LeMay was credited with developing both pattern bombing and the combat box, as well as the low-level bombing tactics used against Japan in 1945. He was not a man who readily conceded that anyone could do anything better than he could; his successor General Cannon was worse. Impressive as their combat credentials were, neither man had any experience in air transport much less airlift operations. Due to the fact that Gen Clay respected his subordinate air force officers and had no experience of airlift operations himself, he did not see any reason to have them removed. Fortunately for the future freedom of Berlin, senior officers in the Pentagon felt that given the political importance and prominence of the Airlift, it might be sensible to give command of such a massive air transport operation to the best air transport expert they had: Gen William Tunner.

Tunner had been one of the first officers in the entire Air Force to specialise in air transport. He had helped establish the Ferrying Division and nurtured it from a handful of men to an organisation 50,000 strong and delivering 11,000 planes a month to domestic and overseas destinations. In fact, he can be largely credited with creating not only an organisation but an entire ethos and standard for air transport pilots. He passionately believed that transport pilots had a different mission and required different qualities than combat pilots. He was proud to claim that he had 'proved that air transport was a science in itself; to be carried out at its maximum efficiency air transport must be run by men who . . . are dedicated to air transport – professionals'.[10] In August 1944 he had taken command of the highly risky supply operation across the Himalayas – which had already defeated several previous commanders – and turned it into a spectacular success.

Tunner also had a reputation as a hard driver. His nickname was 'Willy the Whip' and he claimed he didn't lose any sleep over it.[11] The official Air Force history of Air Transport Command described him as 'arrogant, brilliant, competent. He was the kind of officer whom a junior officer is well advised to salute when approaching his desk.'[12] He was both the consummate professional air transport commander and the kind of commander who could be expected to get the job done – even if it was a job that the officers appointing him did not believe could be done.

Tunner was duly appointed to command the US airlift operations by the Chief of Staff of the Air Force, Gen Vandenberg, at the express recommendation of Gen Albert Wedemeyer, Director of Plans and Operations of the Army General Staff. He was appointed over the heads of generals Clay and LeMay, but he was made subordinate to both. Unlike the RAF officers of Transport Command, who were outside the BAFO chain of command, Tunner had to report to LeMay and, later, to his successor Cannon. LeMay clearly resented the interference from Washington, which 'robbed' him of control over an air operation which had captured the imagination of the American press and people.

Tunner arrived in theatre, almost exactly a month after the Airlift had started, on 25 July 1948. What he found was then popularly referred to as the 'LeMay Coal and Feed Delivery Service' operating at a frenzy – to the delight of the hoards of journalists who had flocked to Germany to cover the story. It was 'fire-alarm haste coupled with a total lack of long-range planning';[13] and that lack of long-term planning was already starting to have negative effects. Exhaustion was becoming evident among the crews, and 'LeMay was now calling on every grounded flier in the command for part-time duty. Yet most pilots, even so, were lucky to snatch 7 hours sleep in 36'.[14] Meanwhile, the planning and support work those desk officers were supposed to be doing was not getting done, adding to future problems. Tunner rapidly concluded that the Airlift could not last another month the way it was being run. He later wrote:

My first overall impression was that the situation was just what I had anticipated – a real cowboy operation. Few people knew what they would be doing the next day. Neither flight crews nor ground crews knew how long they'd be there, or the schedules they were working. Everything was temporary. . . . Confusion everywhere. . . . I read how desk officers took off whenever they got a chance and ran to the flight line to find planes sitting there waiting for them. This was all very exciting, and loads of fun, but successful operations are not built on such methods. If the Airlift was going to succeed and Berlin to remain free, there must be less festivity and more attention to dull details. . . .[15]

Tunner set to work putting things 'right' immediately. As he reports: 'By the way the crews were lounging around in the Operations room and the snack bar, I wondered how in the world they'd get their planes off in time. Well a look at the records showed they were not getting them off in time. There were frequent delays. The schedule was ragged.'[16] On his third day on the job Tunner put an end to the 'lounging' and instituted the procedures by which the operations officer, weather officer and snack bar all went to the pilot rather than the other way around.

Another immediate change came about when the aircraft in which he was flying to Berlin got stacked up over Tempelhof in bad weather. He resolved immediately that it would never happen again. He eliminated circuits altogether. Henceforth aircraft not only took-off 3 minutes apart, they landed 3 minutes apart. If the weather closed in unexpectedly and landing became impossible, the aircraft were sent home by the central corridor. If an individual aircraft missed the approach for whatever reason it too had to return to its home base fully loaded using the central corridor and got slotted into a new position in the continual flow of flights. The calculation was simple: in the same time it took to land nine aircraft stacked in a circuit, thirty aircraft could land using the straight-in approach, and if an aircraft developed technical difficulties that would complicate the landing, it was told to land elsewhere, not in Berlin, where the air traffic controllers did not have the time and space to deal with a difficult landing. Tunner did not want any 'pranged' machines cluttering Berlin's airfields either. Tunner required the pilots to fly not when and as they wanted, but according to a very rigid plan. They took off at a specific time, flew a specific speed (C-47s flew at 180mph and C-54s at 245mph) to a specific altitude and maintained that speed. They therefore were due over each beacon along the route at an exact, calculable point of time. If they were late they had to speed up and if they were ahead of schedule slow down. Soon planes were less like autos on a highway and more like products moving down an assembly line. Last, but not least, Tunner started requiring all pilots to fly by instrument flight rules regardless of weather, i.e. even in good visibility.

Tunner also instituted changes in the maintenance of aircraft. Typically, aircraft maintenance was done by crews assigned to a particular aircraft doing a variety of jobs. Tunner wanted maintenance to be like an assembly line. Each stage of a particular check was to be done at a different station. The aircraft moved down the maintenance line from one station to another, while the ground crews did the same job on each aircraft that passed through.

Tunner made these changes and others because he was a professional and knew what he wanted from the start, but even for him Berlin during the blockade presented a unique challenge, and Tunner was not the kind of general who thought he knew everything already. The first thing he had done on arriving in the China/India theatre was to fly 'the Hump' himself – with his own hands on the controls and his own feet on the rudder pedals. In Berlin his method was what is now called by expensive management consultants 'managing by walking around' – and listening. He was constantly 'prowling around' because he felt he learned more by seeing things himself than from reading reports. The added benefit was that, because he wore an old flight jacket that was as filthy as everyone else's, ordinary airmen took him for just another Airlift pilot and didn't realise who they were talking to when they complained to him. Another tactic was coming upon men in the dark of night when not only did they not expect or recognise him but they were also tired, less alert, and more candid. 'Aircrews met him as they climbed from their aircraft; maintenance personnel saw him studying repair work at midnight; control tower operators found him looking over their shoulders at three in the morning. . . . Visits, discussions, and casual talk often led to immediate changes.'[17]

Even with regard to his own innovations, Tunner retained an open mind. After instituting the changes itemised above, Tunner invited roughly thirty pilots – not squadron or group commanders – to his hotel meeting room. He provided a keg of German beer and cold cuts and he asked for complaints. It took the pilots a couple of beers to find the courage to talk openly to 'Willy the Whip' but once they started the flood gates opened. The meeting ended up lasting from 10 a.m. until 7 p.m. The pilots had plenty of complaints and Tunner found most of them justified. His staff was tasked with finding solutions. As Tunner reports it:

> Finally a young lieutenant made what many considered the most intelligent suggestion of the day. 'How about getting the Red Cross or somebody to send over a couple of hundred beautiful American girls?'

'We don't have enough housing as it is,' Kenny Swallwell, my engineering officer, said seriously. 'Where would they sleep?'

They all answered at once, and that was the end of the meeting.[18]

By another account, someone at the meeting asked the general if he thought the C-54 could ever replace sex. The answer to that question is also unrecorded. The point remains the same: he could get his pilots talking and he was ready to listen – at least to the serious suggestions.

He had two other important management techniques which he employed well and consciously. First, he institutionalised an outlet for bitching in the form of the *Task Force Times*. This paper was uncensored and Tunner expected and accepted considerable humour at his own expense. He likewise made no effort whatsoever to inhibit the chatter on the air waves that so characterised the Airlift, although this was strictly forbidden in other circumstances and incurred stiff fines in civil aviation. Tunner's entire approach was to set very high standards, but to give his men sufficient outlets for bitching and joking to keep tension and resentment from building up.

His other tactic was to spur competition. He had large chalk 'Howgozit' boards, on which the latest statistics could be noted and placed in prominent places, and he published statistics in the *Task Force Times* by unit, by base etc. The idea was to get participants fired up by the prospect of being the best unit in one regard or another, or at least better than a particular rival, whether it was the other squadrons on the same base, another base, the Brits or the Navy. In short, his tactic was to harness the instinctive competitiveness of healthy, young males for the purposes of the Airlift.

However, it was never at the cost of safety. Tunner was a pioneer in the establishment of accident reporting and investigating. He was also very proud of his safety record, and reducing accidents was always as much of a goal as increasing tonnage. Perhaps the best summary of Gen Tunner comes from Lt Gail Halvorsen, another 'hero' of the Airlift – if for very different reasons. Halvorsen describes Tunner as follows:

> General Tunner . . . came across as a man with a mission, in a hurry to be somewhere. On the surface he was tough as nails, but underneath he had great compassion for those he served. We knew immediately that he was primarily interested in the safety of flight and ground crews.[19]

Tunner himself would have agreed with this assessment. He was certainly a man with a mission: that of getting air transport recognised as a military speciality equal in value to strategic bombing and fighter operations. Tunner was determined to see air transport professionalised, and to this end he devoted considerable time training, leading and reorganising forces that had been neglected and scorned by others. He also evolved and articulated very clear theories about all aspects of air transport. He summarised his philosophy about airlifts in his memoirs eloquently:

> The actual operation of a successful airlift is about as glamorous as drops of water on stone. There's no frenzy, no flap, just the inexorable process of getting the job done. In a successful airlift you don't see planes parked all over the place; they're either in the air, on loading or unloading ramps, or being worked on. You don't see personnel milling around; flying crews are either flying, or resting up so they can fly again tomorrow. Ground crews are either working on their assigned planes, or resting up so they can work on them tomorrow. . . . The real excitement from running a successful airlift comes from seeing a dozen lines climbing steadily on a dozen charts – tonnage delivered, utilization of aircraft, and so on – and the lines representing accidents and injuries going sharply down. That's where the glamour lies in air transport.[20]

The problem was that no matter how much of a professional Tunner was or how hard Tunner drove himself and his crews, he remained a subordinate commander reporting to unsympathetic superiors who retained control over vital aspects of the operation. He was never given control over replacements, promotions, awards or even appointments. He had no command authority over the vitally important supply depot at Erding and the equally crucial maintenance depot at Burtonwood in England. He was dependent on Washington for more aircraft and personnel, and on the theatre for housing, catering, civilian hiring, and other services. Throughout his tenure, Tunner would experience more responsiveness from Washington than from his immediate masters in Europe.

One story is illustrative of both Tunner's problems and his personality. Tunner quickly recognised that the entire US airlift was suffering from an acute shortage of trained aircraft mechanics, and he was sitting in the middle of a country which had produced one of the most technically advanced air forces in history. From his experience in the China/India theatre of war, he had learned to value 'native' labour – despite being warned against 'natives' as unreliable and likely to commit sabotage. To Tunner the most logical solution to his problem was to hire German aircraft mechanics to supplement his USAF mechanics; but Tunner was not free to do so. He was subject to the policies laid down by LeMay and Clay, and these included strict 'anti-fraternisation' restrictions. The Airlift depended, to be sure, upon the unskilled labour of the loaders and unloaders, and on the literally thousands of Berliners who built Tegel airfield and helped keep the other Berlin airfields operational. German women, particularly attractive young women, were also welcome employees at canteens and snack bars, but Occupation policy prohibited the use of *skilled* German labour, especially in close proximity to the aircraft. Only Gen Clay himself could grant an exemption to the policy, and Tunner's orders specifically prohibited him from talking directly to Gen Clay. He was required to go through his superior Gen LeMay in any dealings with Clay.

Fortunately for history, Clay and Tunner met by chance at Tempelhof one day, and Clay politely – and probably rhetorically – asked if there was anything Tunner needed. Tunner replied unexpectedly that, yes, he did have a problem, that he didn't have enough good maintenance personnel, but – before Clay could get the wrong idea – he added that he already had a solution, 'if you will allow me to hire some skilled German mechanics'.[21]

Clay's answer is also very telling with regard to Tunner's awkward situation. Clay not only authorised the use of German mechanics, he specifically told Tunner to tell LeMay that he had personally authorised it. He clearly expected Tunner to have problems with LeMay otherwise.

Meanwhile, after lengthy negotiations, a Combined Airlift Task Force HQ was established in mid-October 1948. This institution was the very sensible, and in fact overdue, joint command for the British and American Airlift operations. Given the predominance of the Americans in terms of aircraft and tonnage, it was inevitable that any joint command with a single commander would be headed by an American, and this may explain British resistance to what was a very logical concept. While the Americans pushed for a single headquarters with a single commander from the start, the British advocated a 'coordinating committee'. The Americans, rightly in this case, did not think an operation with the urgency and importance of the Berlin Airlift could be run by committee. After a series of conferences in which the British made a variety of proposals, the Americans finally got their way – four months into the Airlift. On 14 October 1948 a directive was signed with the stated purpose of establishing a CALTF HQ to 'merge the heretofore coordinated, but independent, USAF–RAF airlift efforts in order that resources of each participating service may be utilised in the most advantageous manner'.[22] Significantly, the mission of the CALTF was not as heretofore with the individual air forces the delivery of an established minimum of tons but rather the delivery of the maximum number of tons possible. At the working level, there were committees each staffed by US and UK personnel for 1. planning, 2. operations, 3. logistics, 4. installations, 5. support and maintenance, 6. communications and 7. coal. There was also a subordinate command tasked with coordinating with the Army in the US Zone, and another coordinating committee tasked with liaising with the commandants of the three Western Sectors of Berlin. Tunner was appointed Combined Airlift Task Force Commander, and Air Commodore J.W.F. Merer was named his deputy. The preponderance of the subordinate officers on the staff were Americans because the RAF simply did not have any surplus personnel; only five RAF officers served on the CALTF in addition to Air Cdre Merer.

Unfortunately, the very next day Gen LeMay was replaced by a new USAFE commander, Gen Cannon. LeMay had resented Tunner's arrival, but had been content to let him 'get on with the job' as long as things appeared to be going well. Cannon, in contrast, felt he had to exercise his command over Tunner. Almost the first thing he did was prevent Tunner from locating the CALTF HQ in the British Zone where it would have been nearer to bases from which, now, the bulk of all Airlift missions were being flown, and closer to Berlin itself. Cannon insisted that CALTF remain in Wiesbaden where he could keep his eye on Tunner. Tunner was also abruptly prohibited from any direct communication with Washington, thereby severely hindering him in many aspects of Airlift administration. Henceforth, when Tunner experienced delays in getting needed personnel, spare parts, or information, Tunner could not, as before, pick up the phone and talk to those responsible at MATS or Air Materiel Command or anyone else. He had to first make a formal request to USAFE and *they* then passed the message on if and when it suited them. Abruptly, just as the weather was closing in, Tunner found himself hampered in his efforts to build up the Airlift by the command structures that had been established for him.

Yet even Tunner's problems pale beside British difficulties in controlling the civilian contractors. The dilemmas of controlling an operation that was ultimately to encompass 27* different civilian companies started with the absurd fact that the Foreign Office signed their contracts. These contracts (not surprisingly given the fact that they were drafted by civil servants with no expertise in managing air operations of any kind) did not establish any minimum standards for aircrew training, qualifications, crew ratios, maintenance scheduling, spare parts depots, etc. The contracts did, however, give the Foreign Office the right to cancel contracts on *one week*'s notice, thereby completely discouraging any would-be contractor from making a significant investment in any of the above. This one seemingly minor feature of a bureaucratic product is perhaps the best indicator of how utterly convinced the Foreign Office was that the 'Berlin Crisis' would be of short duration.

At all events, the Foreign Office gave contracts to more than a score of small charter companies and designated the British European Airways (BEA) as the 'managing agent' for the civil airlift. The idea was that the BEA manager in Germany, Mr E.P. Whitfield, would work together with the RAF and through his staff to coordinate the civil airlift – in addition to his regular duties of managing BEA's Airlift operations and its scheduled passenger services between London and Berlin via Hamburg. The reality 'on the ground' was that when Mr Whitfield and the first civilian companies arrived in Wunstorf they discovered that no instructions had been given to the RAF about what role they were to play or how their operations were to be integrated into Operation Plainfare. There was no accommodation available for the civilians, no hangars and no workshops. In fact, nobody seemed to have the faintest idea of what was going on.

Furthermore, 'no one had thought to tell the civilian companies that [Mr Whitfield] was responsible for running the civilian side of the airlift. They regarded Whitfield as an interfering busybody.'[23] In fact, they ignored him for the most part, and Mr Whitfield discovered that the Foreign Office with its notions of his position was very far away. His control over the civilian companies was theoretical only and the civilian companies more or less did as they pleased.

The civilian companies were on the whole 'sky tramps' – companies formed by 'enthusiastic young men who had survived the war and scraped together every penny to purchase surplus aircraft'[24] usually just as a means to keep flying. Jobs in aviation were few and far between in the postwar years compared to the number of qualified pilots the air forces had produced, and so these charter companies had sprung up. The experiences of Victor Bingham are typical:

> During that period of 1945–1949 many British civil aviation companies were forming and going bankrupt every month, and so one moved from one company to another – and the pay and conditions were awful – but we wanted to stay in aviation – and so we carried on, mainly flying civil versions of the Halifax and Lancaster bombers, with a few flying Dakotas.[25]

These companies survived by flying cargo on a charter basis, but contracts were sporadic and so few had the incentive or the resources to maintain reserves of aircrew, ground crew, equipment or spares. When the Foreign Office offered contracts at £45 per flying hour – or almost £8 above the then commercial rate – there were few companies that did not see the Airlift as an irresistible opportunity. For many it was a desperately needed last chance to avert bankruptcy. Bingham summarised the feeling: 'I was living just outside London, and the company I was flying for went 'broke', but after a couple of weeks I got a job flying from Liverpool to Northern Ireland and back to bring back milk in churns as there was a shortage of milk in northern England. Then the Berlin Airlift started, which meant for both the company and ourselves regular paid work.'[26]

The charter companies were happy to have the Airlift contract, but as the contract did not specify any minimum standards they simply brought along what they had. The type of aircraft varied from the Hythe flying boats of Aquila Airways (manned entirely by former RAF Coastal Command aircrew) to converted Liberators and rundown Dakotas, Yorks, Haltons and the infamous Tudors. These aircraft, depending on the number of hours flown and the maintenance they had received had very different cruising speeds, different optimal altitudes, and different load factors. None had radios which could communicate with the RAF and air traffic control, so these had to be provided by the RAF. Even the Dakotas that should have fitted easily into RAF Dakota operations had a Certificate of Airworthiness issued by the Air Ministry which rated them safe only for *smaller* loads than the RAF was then carrying on its Dakotas. As the army doing the loading could not cope with two different loads for identical aircraft and the objective was to fly in as much cargo as possible, an application to the Ministry had to be filed immediately to enable the civilian Dakotas to carry standard RAF loads. This approval arrived on 15 August 1948.

The problems did not end there. For a start most of these companies did not have sufficient aircrew for 'round-the-clock' operations. In fact, on average the civilian companies had only 1.3 crews per aircraft. That meant that even if they had wanted to, the civil aviation companies could not keep their aircraft flying around the clock. There is a natural inclination for men to want to sleep at night, and so the civilian companies quite reasonably tended to do their flying during daylight, a trend reinforced by the higher demands on pilot competence in darkness and the fact that not all civilian crews were certified for night flying. That left the RAF with the task of filling the night slots.

However, even flying only by daylight in August entailed a good deal of flying, and the civilian companies – whether motivated by altruism, enthusiasm or profit – flew with great keenness when they started on the Airlift, only to soon exhaust themselves. 'A high intensity of operations over a few days was invariably followed by a slump because many of the aircraft were undergoing inspection and maintenance at the same time.'[27] Another problem was crews going on a binge after an intense period of flying and needing to sleep it off.

These scheduling problems were compounded by the fact that many of the smaller charter companies did not have large administrative staffs. They had not needed them before. Even if they had some kind of office manager, they rarely sent him off to Germany as soon as the Airlift contract was signed. The senior captain was generally burdened with all administrative duties 'in theatre' – but he was too busy flying to do anything else.

As for maintenance, none of these companies had maintenance facilities in Germany. When a problem came up that the crew could not handle, the first instinct was to get the RAF to deal with it, and only if that didn't work did they send the aircraft back to the home base in the UK for servicing – and so lose the desperately needed revenue. The same went for spare parts, hangar space, workshop facilities and accommodation; the civilians generally looked to the RAF to solve all their problems more or less without compensation. Friction was largely avoided simply because civil fliers were almost all ex-RAF and often knew the men they were dealing with personally, and the RAF was dependent on the additional aircraft and crews and wanted Plainfare to succeed. But it still amounted to a haphazard, uncoordinated effort without clear Command and Control structures – or at any rate without one that anyone was respecting.

As exhaustion set in among the civilian crews and maintenance problems mounted on their aircraft, the performance of the civilian component of the Airlift started to slip significantly. At the same time, the military component was being made increasingly efficient in consequence of the effective and unified Command and Control structures going into place. When Tunner assumed command of the Combined Airlift Task Force in mid-October, the entire Airlift was on its way to becoming a highly regimented and, to a large extent, an assembly line-like operation. Increasing specialisation of cargoes by aircraft and bases was being put into effect, and the demands on flying discipline were increasing. In this environment, the individualistic civilian flyers, with their tendency to fly when and how they pleased, 'yo-yoing in the corridors to avoid cloud or turbulence and scaring the living daylights out of RAF pilots trying to keep to a steady altitude',[28] increasingly became a problem rather than a solution. Until they were brought more under somebody's control, they remained a wild card in the entire operation.

Chapter 10

POLITICAL PRISONERS

The Soviet blockade of Berlin had from its inception political objectives. As a maximum: a unified, centralised and communist Germany, firmly rooted in the Soviet sphere of influence. As a minimum: the prevention of the establishment of an independent German state anchored in the 'capitalist' camp. In other words, the Soviets sought either a communist or a neutral Germany. To achieve this end, the Soviets attempted to expel the Western Allies from the German capital, discrediting them at the same time, and to force them into negotiating a German 'solution' that was acceptable to Stalin.

Soviet policy, based on the assumption that no airlift could sustain a population of over 2 million people, anticipated that either the Western Allies would concede their defeat and retreat voluntarily from Berlin or that the outraged people of Berlin would force the Allies to withdraw. Various sources estimated that it was only a matter of weeks until unemployment and hunger resulted in widespread riots and a popular uprising against the Western Powers. It was expected that West Berliners would demand, more or less violently, that the Western Allies go home.

One month into the blockade the anticipated riots had not materialised. Instead there was the steady drone of aircraft over the city and morale in the West had sky-rocketed. Moreover, respect for the Western Allies had shot up dramatically. Precisely because the Berliners had expected so little from the West, the mere fact that the West was willing to *try* to sustain the entire city buoyed up hopes and spirits. After all, few Berliners had any idea of just how *little* the Dakotas of the early Airlift could actually carry.

Besides it was summer. It was warm and sunny. People did not need to heat their houses and the power plants of the city did not have to sustain winter demands for electricity with airlifted coal. Berlin was blockaded, but it was not yet a walled city surrounded by barbed wire, watch-towers, minefields and soldiers with orders to shoot to kill. That would come later.

In the summer of 1948, Berlin was an open city only politically cut off from the surrounding countryside and not yet cut in two by a lethal wall. This meant that the initial impact of the blockade was far less than anyone – East or West – had anticipated. To be sure, people resident in West Berlin could not 'legally' purchase goods in East Berlin or, more importantly, the surrounding rural areas of Brandenburg. Commercial traffic in goods from these areas had been shut down, but in reality there were many ways for enterprising citizens to obtain goods from the East. Over 200,000 workers still lived in one half of the city and worked in the other, for example. Families sometimes had one member working for the British or Americans while another worked for the Soviets. Almost everyone had family or friends in the other Sectors of the city. It was only human nature that friends and family shared. In short, by late July it was clear even to the Soviets that spontaneous riots against the West were not going to materialise. New methods were needed to convince the West Berliners that their future lay with the East; and the Allies that it was time to pull out.

POLITICS IN BLOCKADED BERLIN

The Soviets opened their new offensive for winning control of Berlin with the announcement on 24 July 1948 – exactly one month after the start of the blockade – that henceforth West Berliners could avoid the rigours of the blockade merely by registering for rations in the East. In other words, they did not actually have to find housing in the East and then pick up their entire household and move in order to qualify for Soviet rations. All they had to do was 'register'; they were even told where to go. Since Soviet rations were larger and better (because fresh) than the rations available in the blockaded Sectors of the city, the Soviets expected people to 'vote with their stomach' and register in the East. Even the staunchly anti-Soviet SPD, good Marxists that they were, stoically expected that most people would accept the Soviet offer.

Throughout August the Soviets harangued the citizens of the Western Sectors through the media. They advertised the fact that Soviet rations were more generous and of better quality (e.g. no Pom, real potatoes). They bragged that there was so much coal available in the East that they were running out of places to store it. They even offered work to those laid off from their jobs in consequence of the blockade. However, the stampede of hungry West Berliners beating down the doors of the East Berlin authorities, just like the hunger riots, failed to materialise. The Berlin representatives to the Bizone Economic Commission reported the following figures:

	Number of West Berliners who registered for rations in East Berlin	Percentage of the West Berlin population
August 1948	21,000	1.0 %
September 1948	32,000	1.5 %
November 1948	50,000	2.4 %
December 1948	54,835	2.6 %
January 1949	68,959	3.3 %

Although the early numbers appear to be rounded and may only be estimates, the later figures suggest precise information, possibly from an East Berlin source. They clearly show that even in the darkest and coldest part of the year, the West Berliners were not prepared to barter their freedom for a marginally better diet. With a degree of amazement an East German wrote to a friend after visiting a family in West Berlin:

Dear Jack . . . yesterday we visited a family in West Berlin and asked them whether they wouldn't rather register [for rations] in the East, now that winter was here. They rejected the suggestion for the following reasons: In winter there were better rations in the West (noodles, rice, peas) than the East. Recently there has even been fresh meat in the West. But the main reason – and this pleased me – was from principle. They simply hate the Russians. To be sure they don't have any illusions about the Western Allies, but as one put it expressly, 'one has to choose the lesser of two evils'. And they say this although they all work in Russian factories in the Eastern Sector. . . .[1]

The West Berliners were not taking the carrot. That left only the stick.

The Soviets started cracking down on the unofficial movement of goods between the Sectors as soon as the trend became evident. They had stopped all official deliveries of goods with the imposition of the blockade; now they started to control personal vehicles and individuals. This meant the frequency with which passengers on trains returning from the surrounding countryside were stopped and searched increased. Likewise, there were growing controls on the inner-city trams and buses that crossed Sector borders. People travelling on foot or by bicycle across the borders were also stopped and searched ever more frequently. These searches could be brutal and above all humiliating. They ended in, at a minimum, the loss of any goods being transported in violation of the blockade, and often in the loss of other things as well (i.e. anything from watches to jewellery that caught the fancy of the Red Army soldiers performing the inspections). It also became common practice for the conductors on trains and buses to confiscate all Western newspapers; and, of course, the Soviet and East German police increased their measures against the black market.

All these actions led to rapidly escalating tensions, including increasing incidents of Soviet military and East Berlin civil police crossing Sector borders 'in hot pursuit' of smugglers and black marketeers. This inevitably led to confrontations with British and American MPs. Soon the British and Americans started to erect barriers on the Sector borders to prevent these incursions and reduce the risk of direct confrontation. Meanwhile, the elected City Council of Berlin suspended the Chief of Police, Paul Markgraf, a man who had been appointed to his office by the Soviet Military Administration before the Western Allies arrived in Berlin. He was one of the many *fait accompli* which the Western Allies had been forced to swallow when they agreed that all decrees and orders issued by the Soviet Military Administration prior to their arrival would remain in force. Now, with the Control Council and the Berlin Kommandatura moribund, the elected government of Berlin felt they were entitled to act. The Soviets, not surprisingly, did not agree. They continued to view and treat Markgraf as the chief of police, while the Western Allies recognised the authority of a professional police chief appointed by the City Council, Johannes Stumm. (Markgraf, in contrast to the professional Stumm, had very little police experience and all of it dated from long before the war; he had been an army officer under the Nazis, captured at Stalingrad and then prepared for his duties by the Soviets.)

Stumm set up his HQ in West Berlin and invited volunteers to join him in forming a new police force. Many did, at severe personal risk because henceforth policemen of Stumm's force were prime targets for East German kidnappings and beatings. Certainly, any Western policeman who set foot in the East risked arrest, assault and even death.

The Eastern police, however, still ventured into the West, and on 12 August this resulted in a violent confrontation when police from the East met with stones and bricks thrown by angry citizens in the West. Just two days later when the Soviet Sector police again violated the Sector border in an action against black marketeers on Potsdamer Platz and the mob again threw some of the plentiful rubble lying about, the police responded by firing into the crowd. They wounded six people – and set off an even more violent reaction from the crowd. British and American military police rushed to the scene, and so did the Red Army. For the moment a stand-off was achieved, but the incursions by Soviet Sector police continued, as did the kidnapping of and assaults upon Western Sector police.

The Soviets had also turned up the volume in the propaganda wars and the tone had switched from enticing to menacing. Now the Soviets threatened to clamp down harder, implying that they weren't already doing all they could to stop goods from getting into the Western Sectors of Berlin. They hinted that people would soon starve, implying that if a 'real' blockade started the 'pitiful' Western airlift would collapse in chaos. Soviet tanks manoeuvred ostentatiously in the areas surrounding Berlin and paraded through the streets. The message was unambiguous and unremitting: we have the power to make you starve, either join us now or pay the consequences.

The elected government of Berlin, so overwhelmingly anti-communist in its make-up, was clearly an articulate and powerful voice of defiance. It was also vulnerable. Since the Berlin City Council was not an Allied institution but composed entirely of Germans, the Soviets felt that actions against it would not provoke the West. After all, hadn't they meekly accepted a Soviet veto of the freely elected mayor, Ernst Reuter, and so prevented him from taking office? The Western Allies, it was assumed, would not go to any great effort to protect the elected government of Berlin; and to make action against the City Council even easier, the City Hall was located in the Soviet Sector.

On 26 August 1948, the day that the City Council was scheduled to reconvene after a summer recess, the SED called upon shock troops of party loyalists to demonstrate against the City Council. A couple of thousand agitators appeared around the City Hall calling for an end to the 'Government of Division', demanding a common (Eastern) currency for all Berlin, and calling for the reinstatement of Police Chief Markgraf. Appeals by the City Council to the police to clear the mob were ignored. The mob broke (or was let) into the Council chamber and the session was disrupted. All representatives (except those sitting for the SED) left the chamber. The SED members then gave rousing speeches condemning their colleagues to the hand-picked audience that cheered them enthusiastically. A second attempt to open a plenary session of the City Council followed on the next day with the same result. Since no police protection was forthcoming and many councilmen felt seriously threatened, it was decided to postpone the next session until 6 September – and to take some Western Sector policemen in plain clothes with them for protection when they appeared on that date.

The SED, sensing victory, increased the strength of their forces. Bussed in by lorry and coach, the agitators of September were reputedly rowdier than those of the week before. Their force was estimated at 3,000. After the Council session began, the mob stormed the City Hall, smashed the glass doors and again surged into the Council chamber. They overwhelmed the forty-six Western policemen, seizing several and setting upon reporters representing the Western media. Some of the councilmen fled out of back and side doors while others barricaded themselves in their offices. The Soviet Sector police, however, having achieved the objective of disrupting the plenary session then cleared the building. They arrested the Western police but sent the councilmen and women, who were not members of the SED, away. These representatives, following a plan they had worked out beforehand, met that same evening in a locale in the British Sector. They convened a plenary session of the City Council, in which they protested the lack of protection by the Soviet Sector police and agreed that henceforth the City Council would meet in a place where it could conduct its business in peace and safety. The city government had been split in two.

Just how 'representative' was the City Council? It had been elected long before the imposition of the blockade and it was only fair to question whether it still reflected the sentiment of the Berliners. The SED had been able to rally at least 3,000 loyalists to disrupt the sitting of the Council. It was clearly time to test the sentiment of the Berliners by asking them to rally in support of their Council.

The SPD called on supporters to assemble in front of the ruins of the Reichstag, the parliament building of the old Weimar Republic located in the British Sector. Built under Bismarck to house Germany's first unified parliament, it was from here that, after the collapse of the Western Front in 1918, the German Republic had been proclaimed by the SPD leader Friedrich Ebert. It had been gutted in a fire set by a communist agitator in early 1933 – a fire which had given Hitler an excuse to impose dictatorial powers. At this historic venue, the SPD held a rally on 9 September 1948. Without the help of the Occupying Powers, and without bussing in supporters from far and wide, a crowd of over 300,000 gathered.

The principal speaker at the rally was to be the elected (but due to the Soviet veto not acting) mayor of Berlin. Ernst Reuter was an exceptionally important figure at this time because his background gave him credibility that few contemporaries possessed. The salient features which set Ernst Reuter apart from his contemporaries was his freedom from dogma combined with practical experience of government. Reuter had been born bourgeois. As an idealistic young man he had been part of the pacifist and socialist left, but he had fought in the First World War, been taken prisoner in Russia and there become acquainted with Lenin personally. Lenin thought so highly of him, he appointed the German POW 'People's Kommisar' of Saratow in the Volga Republic and Reuter returned to Germany at the end of the war to a leading position in the German Communist Party, the KPD. However, the German Revolution of 1918 so disillusioned him, that he abandoned the communists and returned to the SPD. He was appointed director of Berlin's public transport system in 1925, and elected Mayor of Magdeburg in 1931. When the Nazis seized power he was deemed dangerous enough to warrant immediate removal and confinement in a concentration camp. On release from the concentration camp two years later, he went into exile, first in Holland and London and later in Turkey. Thus Reuter was one of those rare beasts, a bona fide opponent of both the extreme left and the extreme right, with practical government experience.

One might have expected him to be welcome in postwar Germany, but the Americans were not keen to have him return. This may have been deference to their Soviet ally (who detested Reuter for his 'defection') or it might have been scepticism about the sincerity of his conversion; the American intelligence community may have suspected Reuter of being a Soviet 'mole'. Whatever the reason, the American attitude remained ambiguous to Reuter, and it was the British Labour government which arranged for his return to Berlin. Once back in Berlin, Reuter rapidly won the affection, the trust and the votes (82 per cent) of the Berliners, but the Americans let the Soviet veto against him stand without much fuss, disappointing Reuter still further. By the start of the Airlift, Reuter's attitudes reflected those of the people he represented: he was disillusioned with the West and he didn't trust the Western Powers to back the Berliners in their struggle for freedom and democracy, but he hated the Soviets and their system so intensely that he was determined to at least demonstrate that the Germans knew what was being decided in the heart of Europe – and what side they were on.

In this mind frame Reuter stepped up to the many microphones and gave one of the most important speeches ever delivered at this historical site:

> Today is the day on which neither diplomats nor generals speak and act. Today is the day on which the people of Berlin raise up their voices. Today the people of Berlin call out to the entire world. We know what has been going on at the negotiations in the Control Council on Potsdamer Platz . . . and in the palaces of the Kremlin in Moscow. We know that [everywhere] at these negotiations our future is at stake. When these negotiations began, the appetite of the Russian bear was greater than for Berlin alone. He wanted to negotiate about Germany as a whole, and with the deceitful pretence of not wishing to divide Germany, sought to lay hands on that half of Germany which he does not already possess.
>
> Now the negotiations have returned to Berlin. The Generals are again deadlocked. Under the circumstances, we believe it is important that the world hears what it is the people of Berlin really want. . . . We want to make it absolutely clear: we do not want to be bartered!

We cannot be bartered, we cannot be negotiated, we cannot be sold. . . . Whoever would surrender this city, whoever would surrender the people of Berlin, would surrender a world – more, he would surrender himself. . . .

People of the World, People of America, England, France and Italy. Look to this city and realise that you must not and cannot forsake us. There is only one possibility for all: to stand together until this battle has been won, until the enemy has been defeated by a victory over the powers of darkness.

The people of Berlin have spoken. We have done our duty and we will continue to do our duty. People of the World, do your duty too. Help us in the time ahead – not just with the aircraft that fill the air, but with your indestructible commitment to our common ideals – which alone can guarantee all of our futures. People of the World, look to Berlin. And People of Berlin, do not doubt, that this is a struggle we want and this is a struggle we will win.[2]

The thunderous applause of the crowd confirmed his words.

Inspired by Reuter's speech, some of the crowd tried to storm up Unter den Linden – i.e. into the Soviet Sector. The Soviet flag was torn down from the Brandenburg Gate and a Soviet jeep pushed over. The Soviets responded with force, killing a 15-year-old boy and wounding three other demonstrators as well as arresting thirty. The Soviets could not be pushed back or overpowered. They still had the overwhelming preponderance of force on their side, but from that point forward, no one in the West questioned that Reuter spoke for Berlin. Two weeks later, US Secretary of State Marshall promised the United Nations that the United States would not 'trade away' the rights or freedom of any other people. Berlin had not only found a voice, it had been heard and heeded.

Meanwhile, the political unity of the city was being torn apart. Elections for the City Council had been scheduled for 5 December 1948, but the Soviets too had heard Reuter and the cheering crowd before the Reichstag. They were not prepared to suffer a renewed humiliation at the ballot box; and why should they? Other methods had proved so much more successful in Warsaw, Prague and Budapest. Of course, the continued presence of the Western Allies in Berlin complicated things a little.

The Soviet commandant made a show of supporting elections, but only if no 'militaristic' or 'fascist' elements – as defined by the Soviet military government – were allowed to stand for election. This meant, in practice, that only members of the SED or its sympathisers would be allowed to hold office. Since the Western Allies were not about to accept these conditions, the SED called publicly for a boycott of the elections and privately ordered the SED to establish a 'revolutionary' City Council. The SED promptly declared the elected

City Council 'dismissed'. The reasoning was that the elected City Council had, by holding its sessions in the British Sector, 'abandoned their post in an irresponsible manner and in the crudest way violated their duty to the People of Berlin'.[3] The SED then called for a constitutional assembly composed of 'representatives' from Berlin's 'democratic mass organisations' and 'industrial combines' – effectively disenfranchising anyone who was retired, self-employed, a homemaker or otherwise not 'organised'. This assembly duly convened on 30 November, composed entirely of representatives 'unanimously' elected by a show of hands at meetings organised and managed by the SED. This unrepresentative assembly then 'unanimously' elected a new government for Berlin.

To the delight of West Berliners, this sham assembly was held in the Opera, so the City Council it elected was referred to popularly as the 'opera council'. The Western Allies referred to the entire process as sheer 'theatre' and immediately stated that they did not recognise this council as legitimate. Thus from the start, the opera council exercised authority only in the Soviet sector. Here, however, its power was absolute. The day after it assumed power the purges began. Any civil servant or other employee of the city who was not prepared to sign an 'oath of loyalty' to the new council was fired immediately. The stated objective of the council was to 'create the conditions that would enable the reconstruction of Berlin and an improvement in living conditions for the working class'.

Meanwhile, in the West, the long-planned City Council elections, set for Sunday 5 December, went forward. Fears of Soviet intervention – despite their opera council – induced the American commandant in Berlin, Howley, to warn the Soviets via public radio that any use of force to disrupt the elections would be met not by the German police but by the US Army. The Soviets, however, both forbade the elections from being held in their Sector, and also attempted to reduce participation in the West in the hope of discrediting the results and minimising their own humiliation. To do so the Soviets called not only for a boycott of the election by all 'democratic' and 'patriotic' West Berliners, but also made open threats against anyone with ties to the East, particularly those residents of West Berlin who were employed in the East. Workers were warned that those who participated in the elections 'would be noted' and were urged 'not to endanger' their future. Furthermore, 5 December was declared a 'working Sunday' at which special rations and free food were promised. The idea of the latter was to prevent those workers who lived in the West but worked in the East from voting. Workers were required to report for the 'voluntary working Sunday' *before* the polls opened in the West.

Tensions were by now so high that Gen Clay insisted on being flown into Berlin on election day to personally demonstrate the interest of the American military government in the election results and perhaps add more iron to Howley's threats. The USAF was so concerned about Clay's safety, however, that they first made him sign waivers absolving the Air Force of any responsibility and even then the Air Traffic Controllers denied him permission to land until he personally came into the cockpit and ordered them to give the pilot permission to land.

Once again, the Americans had greatly underestimated the determination of the Berliners to exercise their democratic rights. The Soviet scheme to keep West Berliners employed in the East from voting was foiled by a traditional weapon of the 'revolutionary proletariat' – a strike. The transport workers staged a strike from 6 a.m. until 10 a.m. on the day of the election, thereby giving all workers in Eastern factories a legitimate excuse for being late without having to admit that they had used that time to vote in the elections. By the end of the day more than 86 per cent of West Berliners had voted, and they voted overwhelmingly (with 64.5 per cent) in favour of the SPD, the most articulate – and vehement – opponent of the SED at this time.

Two days later, Reuter himself was again elected mayor of Berlin. He immediately formed a 'grand coalition' with the other parties represented on the Council, the CDU and the LDP. There was no longer any question that the Western Allies would recognise him as the legally elected mayor of Berlin, but Berlin was now also irrevocably divided as a political entity.

ECONOMICS OF BLOCKADED BERLIN

The economic fabric of the city, in contrast, had not yet been torn in two. On the contrary, as mentioned earlier, over 200,000 Berliners worked on the 'other side' of the political divide from where they lived. The situation for factories and enterprises of all sorts was even more difficult. Berlin industry and retail establishments depended on power, raw materials, components, products, workers and customers in all Sectors of the city, the surrounding Soviet Zone or even in the Western Zones and abroad. In short, the Berlin economy was hopelessly intertwined with both East and West in 1948.

It was not until the start of the blockade, when factories were cut off from power, raw materials and customers, that the economy started to tear in two. The very complexity of the economic ties between Sectors within Berlin and between Berlin and its surrounding countryside, made it highly vulnerable to the blockade. For factories in West Berlin it wasn't just a question of getting enough coal to fire the ovens or enough food for workers, it was about all the fragile relationships between suppliers and buyers, between salesmen and customers, between producers and markets.

Those relationships were not damaged by the blockade alone; they were almost equally ravaged by the 'counter-blockade'. In July 1948, in retaliation to the Soviet-imposed blockade, Gen Clay forbade factories and retailers located in the Western Zones and in the Western Sectors of Berlin from selling or delivering goods and products to customers in the East. For producers in the Western Zones this generally constituted an inconvenience; it was not always easy to replace good customers at short notice, but on the whole alternatives existed. After all, Marshall Aid was now pouring into all of Western Europe, making customers in France, Holland and Scandinavia far more attractive than Soviet Zone customers paying in the worthless East Mark. However, Berlin factories and retailers could not so readily find new customers in Western Europe. They could hardly get out of the city to make initial contacts. Worse, raw materials and component parts for production were competing with babies' milk and medicines for space on the Airlift transports. Last, but not least, getting their finished products transported out again and to customers on time entailed enlisting the (often reluctant) services of the Allied Air Forces.

The result was that with the introduction of the Deutsche Mark the Economic Miracle started in the Western Zones – despite the blockade of Berlin or the counter-blockade. But that Economic Miracle passed Berlin by, and rather than starting to recover, Berlin's economy went into a sharp decline after the imposition of the blockade, negating all the progress that had been made since the end of the war. It has been estimated that the industrial capacity of Berlin at the end of the war was roughly 38 per cent of 1936 levels; during the blockade it fell to just 20 per cent. Of the roughly 60,000 employers operating in the Western Sector of Berlin at the start of the blockade, nearly one-tenth were forced to close their doors before the blockade ended. In the period of the blockade, June 1948–May 1949, the unemployment rate in Berlin more than tripled to nearly 18 per cent. Although an estimated 56,000 Berliners found Airlift-related employment as unloaders, in airfield maintenance and construction, and as caterers and cleaners for the Allies, these jobs in no way compensated for the jobs lost in Berlin's own economy. The nearly 20,000 Berliners who found employment building Tegel Airport, for example, had employment for just under four months of the ten-month blockade. Furthermore, many of those who were still nominally employed in Berlin's industry were working only a few hours a week – when there was electricity and sufficient raw materials available. No less than 8,738 different employers were reporting working 'short-time', i.e. something less than normal operating hours.[4]

Rising unemployment resulted in reduced tax revenues for the city and increased city expenditures in the form of unemployment benefits. The situation was so dramatic that it is fair to say the blockade bankrupted the city of Berlin. The Allies started pumping aid into the city and the emerging governing bodies in the Western Zones voted to divert some of their own revenues to Berlin while also approving a special tax for the support of Berlin. A short-term crisis was avoided, but henceforth the city of Berlin became dependent upon subsidies; a lasting and often forgotten negative legacy of the blockade.

While Western Germany experienced a dramatic increase in economic activity and in its wake prosperity, and East Germany became increasingly isolated from the West and ever more dependent upon and integrated economically in the Soviet block, Berlin became a centre for smuggling and racketeering. No business in Berlin at this time was bigger or more lucrative than the black market.

Berlin's Sector borders had been drawn by foreign soldiers with the objective of controlling a soon-to-be-captured enemy capital by joint military Occupation forces. The Sector boundaries had no economic logic, and nor were the Sectors designed to be self-sufficient or defensible. Entire housing complexes straddled the Sector borders throughout the city, providing marvellous opportunities to move goods across the borders illicitly. All over the city, there were places where one could enter a house through the front door in one Sector, and then by crossing the multiple courtyards or moving through the interconnected cellars emerge from the front door of a different house in a different Sector. There were never enough police or soldiers to control these rabbit warrens of routes across the Sector borders. It was only decades later, with the construction of the Berlin Wall in 1961, that courtyard by courtyard and cellar by cellar the passages would be bricked up, cemented, and turned into barricades. Throughout the blockade, these hidden – but not really secret – passageways served those 'enterprising' Berliners willing to take the risk of dealing on the black market.

There were many such 'enterprising' Berliners. After all, with so little legitimate employment available and with wages so poor, the black market was practically the only avenue to tangible economic success. There are, in deed, many parallels between the situation of Berliners in 1948 and black youths living in America's inner cities, for whom drug trafficking appears to offer the best opportunity to break free of poverty and hopelessness. So the black market boomed, fuelled not – as earlier – by the worthlessness of the currency *per se* but rather by the endless opportunities for arbitrage and trade offered by two currencies with radically different fixed exchange rates and huge differentials in the availability of products across a very short distance.

Illicit markets existed in practically everything as long as it was coveted, in short supply, durable and could be transported and concealed by people on foot. Cigarettes, of course, were the most common and familiar black market product because they acted as a secondary currency (less important now that a hard currency was also in circulation). Other common black market commodities were coffee, rice, silk stockings, soap and chocolate. Indeed, the breaking of the 'Cadbury Chocolate Ring' was one of the infant West Berlin police force's greatest successes. After a hot tip and days of observation, raids led to the arrest of twenty-six people on one day and a further sixteen suspects two days later. Huge stores of Cadbury chocolate were confiscated. The chocolate ring was as much a feature of Berlin in the blockade as the chocolate bomber, whose tale will be told later.

DAILY LIFE IN BLOCKADED BERLIN

What was life like for the average Berliner during the blockade?

Impressions and experiences varied as much as the population itself. Much depended on where one lived – in which Sector, whether housing was largely intact or badly damaged, whether it was centrally heated or not. It depended on whether one had work or not. It depended on whether one had a garden plot for growing one's own vegetables or not. It depended on family circumstances such as the number of household members under one roof and whether the principal breadwinner was at home or still in a POW camp far away. It depended too on political inclinations, and the temperament and emotional stability of the observer.

One dominant fact remembered by almost all observers, however, was the darkness. One resident of Berlin at the time felt: 'It was as though Berlin was dead. The electricity was turned off most of the time, and there was no glimmer of light. . . . There were no street lights, and the merest flicker of ghostly candles glowed through the windows of the houses that had escaped destruction.'[5]

Other residents describe how the prevailing darkness evoked primeval fears. The darkness was dangerous. In it lurked not only the usual dangers of thieves and murderers, but kidnappers and Russians. Women, it is said, walked only in the middle of the wide empty streets, frightened of every building and side-street where Russians might still be lurking. Even the Americans stationed in Berlin remember that a flashlight was essential for movement, and one mechanic stationed at Tempelhof claims that if he strayed too far after dark, 'I had to thread my way through streets of rubble back to Tempelhof by following the C-54 landing lights on their final approach.'[6]

Another Berliner described life in blockaded Berlin to a friend outside the city in a letter:

> We sit and wait. We grope about the apartment like the blind. We yawn and talk about the blockade. Whether the Airlift will work and whether Berlin will be able to hold out. . . . Then 'Ah!' we call out simultaneously, 'Light!' We run about, we laugh and shout, as if we had been drinking wine. The stove! The radio! We cook, we wash, we iron, we listen to the news. Above all, we listen to the news. RIAS broadcasts every hour, all through the night. We listen to the East Radio and the West Radio. Overhead the droning of the aircraft. Every 3 minutes. . . . It is a matter of nerves. Between midnight and 2 a.m. [when we have light] we feel we have not lost our nerve. We aren't doormats, but heroes.[7]

As temperatures dropped, the lack of heat became as characteristic of the blockade period as the darkness. Houses with 'central heating' – i.e. heated with oil or gas from a central heating plant – were basically unheated. The best people could do was wear layers of winter clothes, including their outdoor coats, in their houses. Many people, particularly the elderly and small children, spent almost the entire winter in bed wearing as many clothes as they could under the bedclothes. If they had an electric stove, this could be turned on full during the few hours during the day when there was electricity. Some people would boil water on the stove to distribute steam heat throughout the apartment, but this generally froze on the ceiling creating a thin layer of ice, so the benefits were doubtful.

Older houses which had individual coal-ovens in each apartment could still be heated to a certain extent with coal, but this had to be flown in and so was tightly rationed. Given the demand for coal for the power plants producing the essential electricity for the city, the hospitals, bakeries, and factories, the authorities had determined that that only 22,000 tons of coal per month could be allocated to private households. Furthermore, these coal supplies were not distributed evenly. Households with children, elderly or ill members received higher rations, leaving an 'ordinary' household (i.e. without any of the above special categories) with as little as 12.5kg of coal per month. This induced many otherwise honest citizens to turn to dishonest means of obtaining a bit more fuel. One favourite means of supplementing coal rations, for example, was for agile boys to climb onto the back of coal lorries and shake or scoop off what they could to an accomplice on the ground. Another young Berliner remembers that his aunt and uncle tore down an old wooden fence in the dark of night for the firewood it would provide. His aunt 'kept a watch for the police, and if they approached, [his aunt and uncle] embraced and pretended to be lovers'.[8]

The Western Allies, after calculating how much heat 22,000 tons of coal would produce for a population of over 2 million, came to the conclusion that they were heading for a disaster. They decided on 7 October that it would be necessary to supplement the coal supplies with wood. It was already possible for people to burn the roots of trees already cut down if they were willing to do the work of digging them up, but city-dwellers, often women with no man in the house, found the task of digging and sawing very daunting. Furthermore, ovens designed for coal did not always burn wood well. People still tell horror stories of apartments filled with filthy black smoke for the sake of a pitiable amount of heat.

Nevertheless, the Allies, faced with a severe shortfall in coal and remembering the bitter winter of 1945/6 in which hundreds of people had frozen to death in Berlin, decided that Berlin's remaining forests would have to be sacrificed. An estimated 350,000cu. m of wood was thought needed. To the utter surprise of the Allied military authorities, a public outcry ensued. The Berliners made it clear that they preferred freezing to deforestation. The City Council, responding to the public outcry, proposed cutting down 'only' 120,000cu. m, or roughly one-third of the Allied figure. The Allies agreed to start with this figure, fully expecting that the Berliners would become less 'ecological' when the weather got colder. They did not, and Berlin's forests, although mutilated, were not destroyed.

Another shortage that characterised the blockade was petrol. There was no petrol for private vehicles, and petrol for official vehicles – even of the Allies – was strictly rationed. Buses of the public transport network and ambulances had priority. Throughout the blockade, there was not one petrol-powered taxi operating in Berlin. People were dependent on public transport, bicycles, or their own two feet. The trams and underground only operated from 6 a.m. until 6 p.m. The last trams of the day were therefore always overcrowded, with people clinging to the outside as the overloaded, ancient tramcars swayed and strained through the streets, hardly able to carry their excessive load. Those bicycles which had not been 'confiscated' by the Russians were often in poor condition or completely lacking tyres, thus one RAF airman remembers vividly the 'most unforgettable noise of the steel rims on the cobbled streets'.[9] The sheer distances in Berlin, a city encompassing 889sq. km, however, made walking completely impractical in many instances.

One resident, who had been a teenager at the time, summarised all these features together simply and nostalgically: 'Cold showers and early meals, and walking home at night in the dark as there was no street lighting, nor was the U-bahn working.'[10]

Shortages of soap and deodorant were another feature of the blockade period that left memories. The German ration was just one-quarter of that for Occupation forces, or roughly one bar of soap per month per person. Clothing was effectively unavailable (except silk stockings), and even sewing and mending was difficult since thread, needles and cloth came into the city only in very limited quantities.

Clothing, however, could on the whole be made to last a little longer. Food was needed daily. Rations were meagre, as noted earlier, as little as one-third of the average daily caloric intake of Americans at this time. One child growing up in Berlin at this time remembers: 'My family, which consisted of my widowed mother, my grandmother, three boys and a girl, was allotted one stick of margarine a week. My grandmother sliced it so thin, you couldn't see it when spread on a slice of dark bread.'[11]

But the Allies were, in fact, with admirable efficiency, ensuring that everyone in Berlin got enough calories per day to survive. The *form* in which those calories were delivered, however, left much to be desired. Quality and variety was sacrificed to sheer quantity and even the Allied garrisons suffered from the decline in palatability, if to a lesser degree. The quality of food at official American functions was so bad that the Soviets felt justified in complaining about it. The American commandant, Col Howley, was not fazed, however. When his counterpart, Soviet General Kotikov, complained that the chicken served at an official luncheon was 'tough', he fired back: 'It ought to be. It had to fly all the way from Frankfurt.'[12] For everyone living on food brought in by air transport, the greatest problem was simply that virtually everything flown into Berlin was dehydrated.

The dried food spawned many jokes. The Berliners noted that probably even their humour was flown in by the Airlift – i.e. very dry. Others said that all that was missing was for the Allies to fly in the water in dehydrated form. Mothers were delighted with the powdered milk 'because you didn't have to wash the diapers any more; it was enough just to shake them out'. As Christmas approached, the rumours flew that the Allies would fly in 'powdered Christmas Trees' – just add water. Nevertheless, for all the hardships, the Berliners reminded each other that 'things could be worse: the Americans could be blockading the city and the Soviets attempting to supply us'. Or they complained that, 'From morning to night we're heroes. Wouldn't it be nice to relax once in a while?'

The dried food spawned creative cooking as well as jokes. The elder generations particularly had experience in the art of stretching inadequate rations going back to the First World War. People turned balconies and window-sills into tiny kitchen gardens. Likewise, the land between the boulevards, unused railways and parks were dug up for vegetable gardens by those who did not already have one of the many garden plots which had become a feature of the Berlin landscape long before the war. Stinging nettles, dandelions and other objects generally viewed as inedible found their way into the Berliner diet. That said, it is notably not a feature of blockade stories that pet owners had to fear for the lives of their beloved four-legged companions. Hay was – over the protest of some Americans – even flown in during the blockade for the horses of Berlin, most of which were in British ownership.

For as long as possible, the Berliners also sought to supplement the dried rations provided by the Airlift with fresh fruits, vegetables and dairy products from the surrounding countryside. Berlin was traditionally fed from Brandenburg, the rural province surrounding it. Berliners had long travelled to Brandenburg for fresh things. During the war, the tradition of the 'hamster' trips to purchase foodstuffs from farmers to supplement official rations had started. There were two kinds of 'hamster' trippers: those who went with empty sacks to scavenge for leftovers in already harvested or abandoned fields or look for wild mushrooms, nuts and fruits, and those who travelled with silver, porcelain, linens and other objects of value in order to trade with farmers. During the blockade these 'hamster' trips continued. According to the East German police, in the period between 27 September and 3 October 1948 alone, an estimated 400,000 'hamster' trips took place, bringing in no less than 7,000 tons of foodstuffs to the beleaguered city.

Clearly, the Soviets could not allow this to continue if their blockade was to be a success. A crack-down was inevitable. In early September, as the political tensions and divisions in the city were sharpening, the overcrowded trains arriving in Berlin were with increasing frequency met by a cordon of Eastern Sector police blocking all exits from the station. Everyone would then be forced to surrender all their treasures. 'Crying, helpless and full of hatred', the returning 'hamster' trippers had to obey – and go home empty-handed to their hungry parents and children. And that was true whether the returning 'hamster' was resident in East or West Berlin.

On the positive side, no account of Berlin during the blockade would be complete without mention of the CARE packages, more than 200,000 of which reached Berlin during the blockade. This was a private initiative, founded in November 1945 by twenty-two different charitable organisations and dubbed Cooperative for American Remittances to Europe – CARE. Millions of Americans donated $10 apiece and this purchased the contents of one package full of basic necessities. The contents of each package varied slightly; they were not identical but the value of each was the same. Common contents were: canned meat, canned milk, sugar, coffee, chocolate, cigarettes, soap, matches and toilet paper. Berliners, particularly children, report that often they saw many things for the first time in their lives in a CARE package – dried cake mix, canned maize, crackers, peanuts and peanut butter. What one did not wish to consume personally, one could sell or trade for objects one did want. Yet the most valued object in the CARE package was often the little note from the donor with his/her name and return address. This personalisation of the giving gave it an incalculable dimension far beyond the caloric value of the contents. From thank-you notes grew correspondence, which sometimes led to visits across the Atlantic in both directions. When the author first went to Berlin in 1992, she was thanked on more than one occasion – merely because she was an American – not for the Airlift as a whole but for the CARE packages.

However, man does not live by bread alone. Significantly, the introduction of the blockade resulted in the founding of a new university in Berlin, the Free University. Leading professors and thousands of students refused to continue teaching or learning in a university guided not by science and intellectual curiosity but rather by dogmatic ideology. Although dissatisfaction with the rigid and blunt imposition of Marxism–Leninism into all faculties, and the purging of professors with independent thought pre-dated the blockade, the Airlift became a catalyst to action. The professors and students left the famed Humboldt University, located in the Eastern Sector of the city, and started holding classes in whatever buildings they could rent scattered about in the Western Sectors. The symbolic importance of such a move should not be underestimated. To move away from the Sector in which supply of all basic necessities was unrestricted and demonstratively locate in a city under siege merely for the sake of intellectual freedom gave the name of the new university, the Free University, real meaning.

But the founding of a new university had little impact on the daily lives of most of West Berlin's inhabitants. For them, after food, heat and light, nothing was more important in this period than news. Berlin had a long tradition of competing newspapers going back more than a century. After the censorship of the Nazi era, the press had flourished in Occupied Berlin – fostered by the fragmentation of the city into competing political systems. The various political parties eagerly sought to influence the population for their own cause. All three Western Allies had a strong commitment to the freedom of press and had quickly recognised the potentially insidious effects of the Soviet-controlled press, which received massive financial and bureaucratic support from the Soviet Military Administration. In consequence, although the West was reluctant to support one paper or another, the Western Powers were generous with imports of newsprint and licences for a variety of papers.

1. A woman searches for fuel in blockaded Berlin. *(Landesarchiv Berlin – LAB)*

2. A meal in blockaded Berlin. (*US National Archives and Records Administration – NARA*)

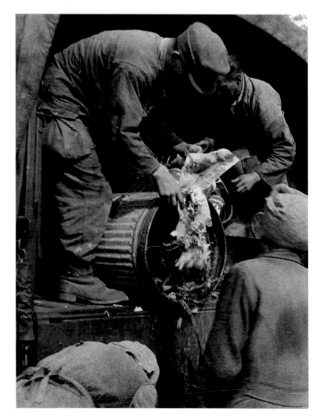

3. Life in blockaded Berlin could be very hard. Here, someone is going through the rubbish. (*NARA*)

4. Berlin from the air, 1948. (*Lt Gail Halvorsen*)

5. A day-care centre for children in blockaded Berlin, one of the few places with heating. (*LAB*)

6. A child buys bread made in the blockaded city. Note it is wrapped in the East German newspaper *Neues Deutschland*. (*NARA*)

7. Throughout the blockade a variety of newspapers were available to West Berliners. (*LAB*)

8. Radio in the American Sector (RIAS) provides news broadcasts via loudspeaker during the power cuts in West Berlin. (*LAB*)

9. C-54 approaches Tempelhof airfield over the ruins of West Berlin. (*NARA*)

10. Construction work at Tegel airfield. (*NARA*)

11. On final approach, a Dakota C-47 lands at Tempelhof airfield. (*LAB*)

12. RAF Dakotas on the apron at Fassberg. (*Rusty Waughman*)

13. *Left*: A Berlin child is delighted to receive a gift of chocolate in blockaded Berlin. (*LAB*)

14. *Below*: Berlin schoolchildren run through the street playing 'Airlift'. (*LAB*)

15. Berlin toddlers play 'Airlift'. (*LAB*)

16. A crowd estimated at about 300,000 gathers at a rally to protest against Soviet policy, 9 September 1948. (*LAB*)

17. *Above*: Dakotas being loaded at an airfield in Bizonia. (*NARA*)

18. *Left*: An RAF Sunderland flying boat prepares to land on the Havel. (*LAB*)

19. The trans-shipment of coal from freight train to loaders. (*NARA*)

20. Loading an RAF York. (*Norman Hurst*)

21. C-54s wait for take-off. (*NARA*)

22. Loading aircraft at Rhein-Main. (*NARA*)

23. A cargo of flour for Berlin. (*NARA*)

24. A C-54 lands at Tempelhof. (*NARA*)

25. RAF Dakotas ready for take-off at Fassberg. (*Rusty Waughman*)

26. The line-up of C-47s offloading at Tempelhof. At the time, Tempelhof was the busiest airport in the world, with more traffic than either New York or London. (*NARA*)

27. A C-47 offloading at Tempelhof. (*NARA*)

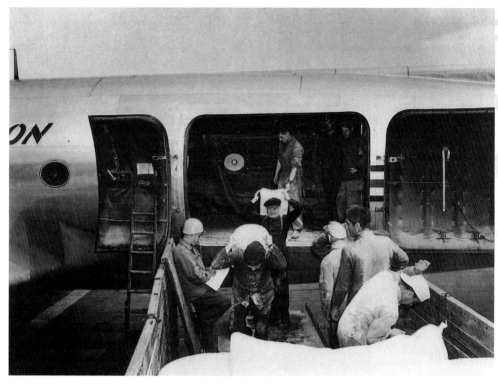

28. A team of German labourers offloading in Berlin. (*NARA*)

29. German passengers aboard an RAF transport aircraft. (*LAB*)

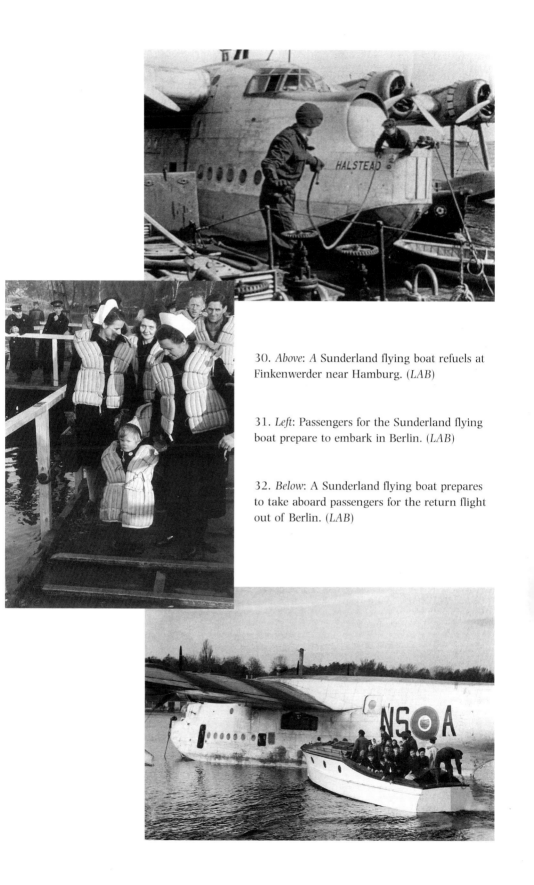

30. *Above*: A Sunderland flying boat refuels at Finkenwerder near Hamburg. (*LAB*)

31. *Left*: Passengers for the Sunderland flying boat prepare to embark in Berlin. (*LAB*)

32. *Below*: A Sunderland flying boat prepares to take aboard passengers for the return flight out of Berlin. (*LAB*)

33. An Airlift airfield by night. (*NARA*)

34. A night landing. (*NARA*)

35. 200-hour checks are made at Oberpfaffenhafen. (*NARA*)

36. Airfield checkpoint at RAF Wunstorf. (*Norman Hurst*)

37. Maintenance in the snow. (*NARA*)

38. Tempelhof airfield by night. (*NARA*)

39. Maintenance by night. (*NARA*)

40. Pilots are instructed on flight patterns during a pre-flight briefing. (*NARA*)

41. Weary pilots get the 'gen' at a pre-flight briefing. (*NARA*)

42. *Above*: RAF Honington.
(*Ministry of Defence – MOD*)

43. *Right*: RAF air traffic
control ops room. (*MOD*)

44. *Below*: USAF air traffic
control at Wiesbaden.
(*NARA*)

45. RAF dance band in action at the NAAFI club. (*Bob George*)

46. USAF operations briefing. (*NARA*)

47. Leading Aircraftman George. (*Bob George*)

48. Rhein-Main squadron room. (*NARA*)

49. Wreckage of a Halton. This Halton broke in two on landing, possibly overloaded. (*Brian Hansley*)

50. Wreckage of a USAF C-54 at Tempelhof. (*LAB*)

51. Wreckage of a USAF C-54 – miraculously no one was seriously injured in this crash. (*LAB*)

52. Wreckage of a USAF C-47 in the Handjerystrasse in West Berlin. Although all crew members were killed, there were amazingly no civilian casualties. (*LAB*)

53. Lt Halvorsen, Sgt Elkins and Capt John Pickering. (*Lt Gail Halvorsen*)

54. Lt Gail Halvorsen stands before his C-54. (*Lt Gail Halvorsen*)

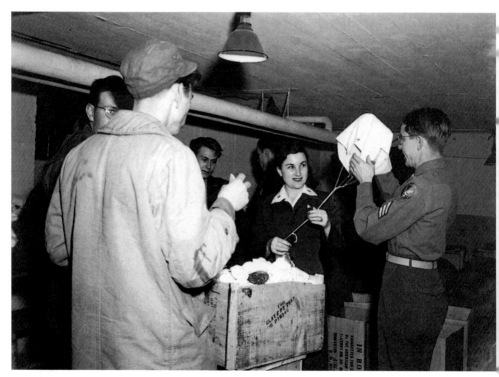

55. Parachutes for Operation Little Vittles – the distribution of chocolate and candies to the children of Berlin by aircrew flying in the Airlift. (*Lt Gail Halvorsen*)

56. Lt Gail Halvorsen surrounded by parachutes for Little Vittles. For the candy drops to the children of Berlin, aircrew initially used their own handkerchiefs. When word about the American pilots' generosity got publicised, contributions poured in from all across the US. (*Lt Gail Halvorsen*)

57. *Above*: A Berlin child collects a Little Vittles parachute out of the snow. (*NARA*)

58. *Below:* Lt Gail Halvorsen and his fans. (*NARA*)

59. One of Gen Tunner's mobile snack bars. (*NARA*)

60. USAF canteen at Rhein-Main. (*NARA*)

61. An RAF York delivers the one-millionth ton of supplies to blockaded Berlin. (*NARA*)

62. A symbol of Berlin's morale: products produced in blockaded Berlin carry this picture of the Berlin Bear breaking his chains. (*LAB*)

63. Berlin from the air, 1948. (*Lt Gail Halvorsen*)

At the start of the blockade, the Western Allies had been dismayed to discover that the usual reels of newsprint could not fit through the doors of their transport aircraft. Rather than let the newspapers close, however, paper factories were commissioned to produce a particularly lightweight paper that could be transported by air in a different format – and this cargo was given a high priority. Consequently, five daily newspapers were kept alive in Berlin – put to press each evening literally by candlelight – throughout the blockade. Not one of West Berlin's newspapers missed a single edition after the initial few weeks of the blockade – and sales were high. Furthermore, papers were also imported from West Germany and so Berliners always had a range of opinion and viewpoints from the Social Democratic *Vorwärts* and *Der Sozialdemokrat* to the more conservative *Kurier*, *Der Tagesspiegel*, and *Abend*.

The importance of newspapers at the time can be measured by the fact that Soviets viewed these Western papers as a threat to their control over the Eastern Sector and Zone. The description of events was so at variance, that it was obvious to readers that one – if not both – sides were lying. By 24 August 1948 the situation was considered so serious that the Soviet Military Administration felt compelled to forbid the sale of newspapers published anywhere outside the Soviet-controlled areas. The East Berlin post-office workers forthwith voted 'spontaneously and unanimously' to discontinue deliveries of papers from the West because of 'anti-Soviet agitation'. The West Berlin news-stands responded with a boycott of the Soviet-controlled publications. In retaliation, the transport police, i.e. those police responsible for order on Berlin's commuter trains (S-Bahn) – all of whom were employees of the Soviet-controlled Berlin Transport Authority – started confiscating Western print media sold in the news-stands located in the S-Bahn stations. They ripped the advertisements for the 'anti-Soviet' press off the walls and they forcibly expropriated any Western papers in the possession of passengers as well. Right up until German reunification in 1990, there were many Berliners who, remembering these events, boycotted the S-Bahn, preferring other means of transportation to control by – and payments to – the East. Strangely, the Soviets never seemed to grasp the simple fact that their actions to make Western newspapers inaccessible only made them more desirable.

Yet perhaps even more important than print media at this time in history was radio. To counter the near constant outpouring of Soviet propaganda on the airwaves of the Berliner Rundfunk, a new radio sender had been established in February 1946 in the American Sector. Named exactly that, Radio in the American Sector or RIAS, the station grew rapidly in popularity until by July 1948 it had an estimated market share of 33 per cent. After the start of the blockade, RIAS suddenly became *the* most popular radio station in and around Berlin. RIAS broadcast 24 hours a day, and since much of the city was without electricity much of the day, they sent out trucks with loudspeakers to read the news out on the streets. A fleet of twelve vehicles manned by newscasters started cruising the city's streets. They were 'hailed, like the airliners themselves, as public idols'.[13] Reporters of RIAS remember vividly going out into the pouring rain wondering if it was worth the trouble only to find crowds of Berliners already standing at every corner, soaking wet but patient in their hunger for news.

RIAS, powered by a 100,000-watt transmitter, could reach not only the Soviet Zone around Berlin but into Poland and Czechoslovakia as well. There were those living under Soviet Occupation that went to great efforts to ensure reception of those broadcasts, and in return the Soviets felt compelled to try to jam them. (A favourite Berlin cabaret wrote an entire song inspired by the Soviet jamming sounds. Each verse is ended by a chorus of jamming noises and the next verse shifts to a different key to intimate the shift of frequencies.) The Soviet-controlled Berliner Rundfunk employed three times the number of people that RIAS could afford, but it had only one-tenth the number of listeners.

RIAS was a success primarily because 'the free voice of the free world' offered listeners news in a format that did not insult their intelligence. The Soviet-controlled media's refusal to admit there was a blockade, and its efforts to portray the Airlift as 'a second bomber offensive', discredited it almost beyond repair. So did claims broadcast by Soviet radio that Berlin was the site of violent protests against the Western Allies, who had shot into the crowd killing 'hundreds' who lay unburied on the streets. That might convince the citizens of Moscow and Leningrad that they were on the side of History and Truth; it did not play well even on Alexanderplatz, seat of the Eastern Police, let alone on Wittenbergplatz in the West.

RIAS furthermore brought news in a timely fashion – as it was breaking – not after it had been reported to the Politburo, a response had been meticulously formulated by the Soviet authorities and then translated, distributed and released to the Eastern news media hours and days after the event. Last, but not least, RIAS news was also popular because it dared to, and got away with, critique of the Western Powers in its commentary. Clay's policy of not exercising his right to censorship was one of his wisest and most successful Occupation policies.

Yet it would be wrong to think that RIAS was popular because of its news programmes alone. It also broadcast a variety of entertainment programmes, including radio drama and jazz – then still considered a little racy and daring.

(It had been forbidden under the Nazis and was alien to the Soviets.) RIAS offered Berliners cultural features and theatre reviews, sports and local news as well.

That there was so much to report upon may surprise many. Certainly visitors to Berlin seemed to miss much of what was going on. The Malcolm Club's 'Dizzy' Bell found Berlin a barren place. She complained:

> The city was grimly depressing, for people were living in holes all over the place and there were only a few spots open. . . . There was nothing much you could do in Berlin, except sail on the lovely lakes. You couldn't window-shop, for example, because there was nothing in the windows except cardboard hams and other such unappetizing articles. There was nothing in the cafes either.[14]

But Mrs Bell contradicts herself somewhat by telling about visiting nightclubs – a rather adventurous undertaking because one had to 'avoid the police' who closed down nightclubs operating when lighting was switched off, which, of course, was most of the time. 'The party . . . would take candles, dodge the patrols, and put the candles on their tables so that they could see something of what was going on.'[15]

In fact, there was a great deal of other, more traditional entertainment offered in Berlin during the blockade as well. There were live performances of everything from serious drama and opera to cabaret and musicals – although performances were often scheduled at unusual times in order to ensure electricity. In some ways the cultural offerings were greater than they had been for decades because world-famous performers from the Marlowe Players of Cambridge to the American comedian Bob Hope made their way to Berlin in order to demonstrate solidarity with the Berliners and the Airlift. But Berlin's own artists were also active, producing contemporary plays like Carl Zuckmayer's *The Devil's General* and classics like the *Troubadour*, the *Fledermaus* and *Figaro*. As long as the weather was warm, the Berlin Philharmonic and the RIAS Symphony Orchestra performed in open-air theatres. There was rarely a theatre, opera or concert performance that was not sold out in advance.

During the blockade, sporting events also continued to take place, from football matches to tennis tournaments and even horse-racing. Maybe these events did not attract the leading athletes of the world, but they still offered the Berliners relaxation and diversion from the grim realities of life in the blockaded city. In the many sport clubs, Berliners also kept fit and socialised.

A Berliner argues: 'It would be completely wrong to imagine that the Berliners [during the blockade] were depressed and disinterested, or sat helplessly upon the piles of rubble gazing up at the aircraft flying overhead. Not at all! It wasn't like that at all! That would have been completely incompatible with Berlin mentality.'[16]

Nothing characterises Berlin's mentality and spirit better than a political cabaret, conceived as a single broadcast in December 1948 that so perfectly fit the mood of the times that it instantly became a sensational success. Instead of a single broadcast, it was turned into a series, a monthly programme, and would ultimately have 130 episodes. It was broadcast for over fifteen years, from 1948 until 1964. It was the 'Club of the Island Dwellers' (*Club der Insulbewohner*).

In the opening broadcast, the 'Islanders' rather unexpectedly discover that they are living on an island in the middle of a 'red sea'. They declare that, in consequence, 'the roar of the four-engine aircraft is music to our ears. Who can speak of noise?' However, the programme was not really about the Airlift. Like good cabaret anywhere it poked fun at society, politicians and, above all, the audience in little skits and dialogues and chansons. The West Germans, referred to by the Berliners as 'Wessis' and considered a distinctly different animal from the Berliners themselves, were often the butt of jokes – and the earnestness of Eastern news media and party 'functionaries' offered a wealth of material as well.

One skit, for example, describes the visit by an admiring reporter to a factory in the East. The factory is a completely unique and innovative industrial complex because it works in three shifts around the clock to 'construct culture'. The foreman from the poetry division explains: As it had become evident in the postwar years that 'many so-called artists were unable to resist the temptations of the monopoly-capitalist political dividers' of Germany, and to prevent such an 'important consumer of culture', as the citizens of the 'monopoly-capitalist-free' Soviet Zone from being deprived of culture, the 'politically responsible cultural-renewing civil servants' had decided to establish this factory.

Another skit recorded the 'secret' meeting of the East Zone 'Carnival' club, called together to receive their 'confidential guidelines' on how to behave during the 'spontaneous celebrations'. First of all it is explained that Carnival is not – as the liars in the West suggested – a Christian tradition but was invented by the 'Brothers' in the East, just like the fast that preceded it also came from the Brothers. Jokes, the members are instructed, are supposed to be directed at all figures of authority, except all those in the East, of course. Then a variety of songs are selected for singing during Carnival – one being eliminated because it is 'too obvious' that 'one is always happy at a People's Own Factory'. The final song, which the participants find 'just lovely', is sung by a young lady who proudly tells how her 'Darling is with the Peoples' Police . . .'. And she only, only, only hopes that he won't go over to the other side. . . . In another skit, one of the West Berlin gossips complains that there is less of everything – except the Peoples' Police, who are now defecting by the sixes and sevens.

The essence of the Islanders' viewpoint is captured in their theme song, which some claim became the unofficial 'anthem' of West Berlin. This song was adapted from month to month to take into account current events, but it always started and ended with the same lines: 'The Islander doesn't get rattled, the Islander doesn't like fuss. . . . The islander hopes absolutely, that his island will become mainland again.'[17]

Chapter 11

THE AIRLIFT FALTERS

By late autumn 1948 it was beginning to look as if the Islanders might indeed get their wish sooner – but in a manner other than expected. Namely, they might cease to be 'Island inhabitants' not because their island had been reattached to the 'mainland' in the West, but rather because their island was swallowed by the 'red sea' around them. Despite all the efficiency introduced by Tunner and the undiminished political commitment in Washington and London, the fact of the matter was that the Airlift was slowly failing.

Although significant increases in tonnage delivered could be recorded compared to the early months, by September the Airlift was still supplying barely 40 per cent of what had once been brought into Berlin by land and water. The West Berliners were being asked to live on official rations of just 1,600 calories per day, less than Germans in the Western Zones or in the East. Furthermore, these rations were only bearable because they could be supplemented by kitchen gardens and 'hamster' trips to the surrounding countryside. More ominous still, the stocks in the city, particularly of coal, were being drawn down week for week. In short, the Airlift was not keeping up with even summer needs, and the weather was about to turn bad.

By the end of October, the deliveries of coal were running at roughly three-quarters of requirements, while Clay – on the basis of the more accurate and comprehensive information now available to him – actually increased the estimated daily requirement of total airlifted tons from the initial 4,000 short tons per day to 5,620 tons. The statisticians kept adding up the requirements, comparing them to capacity and coming to the same conclusion: the Airlift would not be able to sustain West Berlin through the winter – unless something changed dramatically.

The key factors leading to this conclusion were: that short days and poor weather would reduce the number of flights into the city, and that the absence of dietary supplements from fresh-grown vegetables and produce of the surrounding countryside plus cold temperatures would increase demand for both airlifted food and coal. Official British projections of maximum delivery rates based on historical records of weather conditions and the available Airlift fleet concluded that poor weather would reduce the average daily tonnage delivered to the city by roughly 33 per cent. This in turn would result in all remaining stocks being completely depleted by the third week in January. At that point, people would start to starve and freeze and the Airlift would be seen to be a failure. The Allies would have no choice but to capitulate.

In one area the shortfalls were already acute. This was with regard to liquid fuels. Initial estimates had called for the delivery of 220 tons of liquid fuel daily, calling for a tanker fleet of thirty-one aircraft. Delays in converting aircraft into tankers, and delays in fitting what tankers there were with the necessary navigational equipment to enable flying in poor visibility, meant that in fact only eleven tankers were operating on the Airlift by the end of 1948. They were flying in an average of only 148 tons of liquid fuel per day – a shortfall of over 70 tons daily. In fact, the Western Allies would already have run out of liquid fuel in November if they had not 'simply purloined Soviet stocks which happened to be stored in the Western Zone'.[1] By the end of the year those stocks too were gone. Berlin had to live on what the civilian air fleet could fly in each day, and this fleet was still patently inadequate.

It is fair to say that the entire Airlift fleet was inadequate. This was not because something unexpected had come up, but simply because the Western Allies had failed to do what they knew they must. For example, as early as 13 August, the British government had been warned that the civilian aircraft used on the Airlift had to be fitted with the Rebecca-Eureka navigational equipment if they were to fly in bad – read winter – weather. But that cost money, and so, although nobody actually objected or even questioned the logic or necessity of refits, 'somehow' nothing actually happened. Then the fog closed in, the civil aircraft were stuck on the ground, and Berlin's liquid fuel reserves drained away.

Things were no better on the American side of the Sector border. Clay had been convinced very early on that the Airlift could succeed only if they had enough aircraft. His staff had worked out the exact numbers for him. He needed no more and no less than 225 of the large C-54s with their 10-ton cargo capacity. This meant an increase in the C-54 fleet then flying by 116 aircraft. He requested this increase on 10 September and again on 23 September, but the planes did not materialise, or rather, only about fifty of them did – provided by both the Navy and the Air Force. Clay complained about the shortfall on 4 October and again on 14 October. When he received no adequate response, he flew to Washington to present his case in person.

This seemed to work. The National Security Council approved the assignment of a further sixty-four C-54s to the Airlift on 18 October 1948, and President Truman himself signed off on it on 22 October despite the objections of the Joint Chiefs of Staff, which felt their ability to conduct other missions was being seriously impaired. The ordered redeployment of aircraft brought the entire fleet of C-54s assigned to the Airlift up to 224. The problem was that the Air Force and Gen Clay had different notions of what '224' meant.

When Clay said he needed 224 C-54s for the Airlift he meant 224 aircraft carrying freight to Berlin every day. The USAF viewed '224' as the number of aircraft *assigned to* Operation Vittles. This included not only all the aircraft that were hauling freight but also those undergoing repairs and servicing. It included the aircraft being flown to the US for 1,000-hour checks, and the aircraft being flown back to Germany after those checks. Last, but not least, it included the C-54s used for training pilots in Great Falls, Montana, for future Airlift duties. In short, when the USAF gave Clay his 224 aircraft for the Airlift, what he actually got was 169 C-54s hauling freight on any one day.

The Airlift was not failing only because of insufficient aircraft. It was also failing because the aircraft on the Airlift were not being used optimally. For example, the block system, the idea of flying 'blocks' of aircraft from different bases within specific 4-hour time slots, had been a great improvement over the initial chaos of everyone just taking off when they felt like it and improvising from there. Safety and efficiency had increased significantly as a result, but the block system had its drawbacks as well. The 4-hour cycle was ideal for the C-54s with their large cargo capacity which entailed longer loading and unloading times, but was highly inefficient for smaller aircraft such as the Dakota, Lancastrian or Tudor. These took less time to on- and offload so they often ended up sitting around, fully loaded and fuelled, just waiting for their 'slot' in the flow of traffic. Neither did the 4-hour cycle suit tankers or aircraft with return cargoes that had to load at both ends of the flight. They often took just marginally longer than 4 hours to load, but if they missed their slot they had to wait nearly 4 hours for the next block. The result was that the British aircraft, both the RAF's Dakotas and the civilian Lancastrians, Tudors, Haltons and Hastings, were being kept on the ground longer than necessary and not making the contribution they *could* have made. Aircraft capacity was being wasted.

Another problem was that the hastily repaired and newly built runways with their rubble base had developed serious weaknesses. To be sure, they were not disintegrating like the PSP did, but the runway at Tegel, most notably, had developed undulations in the surface that affected tailwheel aircraft (all British) more severely than US (tricycle) aircraft. Tailwheel aircraft tended to bounce their way down the uneven surface of the runway like kangaroos (usually to a chorus of 'one, two, three . . .' from the crews of all aircraft within sight of the landing craft). If there was a crosswind, these bounces could be dangerous. No less than six Haltons were completely written off and five damaged as a consequence of accidents resulting from the rollercoaster runway surface. They too constituted a reduction in total Airlift capacity.

More difficult to quantify but no less devastating for the Airlift's inadequate results was a deterioration of morale – particularly among USAF crews. The initial enthusiasm had long since worn off, and the thrill of being part of a great historical event and the greatest humanitarian operation in living memory had been ground down by sheer exhaustion. Tunner was the first to admit that morale was lagging by the end of 1948. He pointed to three major problems.

First and foremost was the sheer uncertainty associated with the assignment to Berlin which made planning impossible for the men and their families. Tunner pointed out: 'Even for military personnel and their dependants, used to uncertainty, this situation was extreme, and it got worse. In the cases of practically every man, the TDY [temporary duty] was extended another 30 days and another and another.'[2]

The second problem, as Tunner saw it, was that Soviet agents intentionally undermined morale with a clever campaign:

Of all the Communist hostile acts, perhaps the most damaging was their poison-pen campaign. Mysterious letters would come to our pilots, letters mailed both in Germany and in the United States, reporting the infidelity of wives and sweethearts. Some degree of bitterness already existed between many couples over the extended periods of temporary duty, and even to those husbands who normally shared a firm mutual trust with their wives the letters could cause nagging doubts and a resulting drop in morale.[3]

Last, but not least, Tunner cited the negative contrast between working and living conditions for Airlift personnel compared to the Occupation forces:

The Berlin Airlift was particularly frustrating in the regard that the Airlift personnel lived and worked side-by-side with occupation forces. [While the Airlift personnel worked literally 24/7] the occupation people had as soft a job as you could find in the military establishment, working a couple of hours a day and scrounging the rest.[4]

In addition:

The housing provided my personnel in Wiesbaden and Rhein-Main was grossly inadequate. Airlift men were crowded together in poor quarters. The occupation forces, who were permanent duty and assigned permanent establishments, lived like kings in contrast and this made the quarters of the Airlift personnel seem even more miserable.[5]

Morale was particularly bad at the bases in the British Zone which were run by the RAF. This was mainly because, as mentioned earlier, American and British tastes and standards in food differed substantially. However, there were other irritants: seating in and prices for the station cinema, traditions of courtesy (or lack thereof from the British point of view), and the dimensions (which were impractically generous from the American point of view). But goodwill on both sides managed to brook most of the differences and ultimately it was the stress of the Airlift itself that caused the greatest deterioration in morale.

By November 1948, American pilots on the Airlift were admitting to journalists that they intentionally tried to dodge work if they could. One pilot was reported saying: 'What I try to do is to fly one flight a day instead of two.'[6] Another pilot said candidly: 'I've had enough. I want to go home. I've got enough problems of my own without worrying about the ones the Germans have. They asked for it, didn't they?'[7] At Rhein-Main some pilots started to refuse point-blank to fly any more and were sent home without disciplinary action.

Even those who kept doing their duty were developing serious signs of fatigue. An enlisted man reported that: 'Some of the crypto boys would go around talking to themselves in Morse code.'[8] There were instances of men jumping out of low windows in order to break their legs and get sent home. It was also reported that when one C-54 overshot the runway at Tempelhof, the crew got out of the wreck and just went AWOL before the rescuers reached them.

The most common indication of fatigue-induced morale problems was excessive drinking. Excessive drinking and its associated brawling was so bad that the MPs are said to have 'prayed' for bad weather. No one had a worse reputation for drinking than the British pilots on the civilian airlift, particularly the aircrews of Flight Refuelling. Allegedly the company had to keep 150 aircrew on the payroll to ensure thirty-two were sober enough to fly all serviceable aircraft on any one day. The most famous incident resulting from excessive drinking by civil airlift crews was the night in Hamburg when civilian aircrews returning from a night on the town noticed that a German street-car repair crew had left all their equipment on the site of the repairs. Unable to resist temptation, the aircrews welded the tracks together resulting in total chaos in the Hamburg's commuter traffic on the following day. Another group of drunk aircrew allegedly hijacked the Lübeck–Stockholm express and forced it to deliver them to their airfield. Although it is unclear if it was the objective of these crews to get repatriated, that was the result. And because that was what happened, their escapade begged imitation from those who were fed up with the whole thing and wanted to go home.

On the whole, however, British morale was better – if only because RAF and civilian crews could get home on a regular basis. The civilian firms even started to set up married quarters, and let men's families follow them to Germany. If the trips home were too short to be completely satisfying, British airmen were on the whole glad to be in a job – and pilots particularly glad to be in a *flying* job – at a time when the economy in Britain was very precarious.

The RAF found in internal surveys that only 8 per cent of aircrew complained about the number of hours they had to fly. What they didn't like (85 per cent of those questioned) was the irregularity of their schedules which meant irregular meals and sleep. RAF medical officers furthermore noted that too many pilots were living off Malcolm Club snacks and not getting proper meals. Even if the RAF never equalled the civilian pilots with their inebriated escapades, it is safe to say that RAF aircrew have never been accused of being shy of drinking.

Yet by far the most dangerous negative influence on the performance of the Airlift came from the top not the bottom. Just after the equinox, when the days were becoming shorter than the nights, Gen Tunner got a new boss. Gen LeMay had never been welcoming, but he had let Tunner do his job to the best of his ability. From the day, 15 October 1948, that Gen Cannon became the Commander-in-Chief of USAFE, Tunner found himself increasingly inhibited in his ability to run the Airlift.

The problems started with his new orders which expressly prohibited him from speaking with the various commands in the US which supported the Airlift from afar by providing it with aircraft, supplies, maintenance, training and replacement pilots. One immediate consequence was that Tunner lost the ability to control intermediate maintenance on Airlift aircraft. The vital 200-hour checks were conducted not at the squadron level but at the central maintenance depot in Burtonwood, England. Tunner himself had been behind the move from Oberpfaffenhofen to Burtonwood because he thought that winter conditions in Bavaria would impact negatively on maintenance results, while Burtonwood not only enjoyed a milder climate but was large enough to accommodate the assembly-line type of maintenance procedures that Tunner favoured. All Tunner's planning had been based on the assumption that at Burtonwood eight 200-hour inspections would be carried out every day. In anticipation of Burtonwood taking over the burden of 200-hour checks, Tunner had transferred maintenance personnel away from the squadrons in Germany and from Oberpfaffenhofen to Burtonwood.

In November, however, it rapidly became evident that Burtonwood was not completing 200-hour inspections on eight aircraft per day; it was barely managing two per day. Since aircraft due for maintenance were grounded until the inspections could be completed, this amounted to aircraft coming off flying but not being replaced by those whose inspections were completed. The poor performance of Burtonwood translated into a shortfall of 35 aircraft every week or 150 in a month. Clearly the entire Airlift would grind to a halt very rapidly unless something could be done to improve efficiency at Burtonwood. Tunner flew to Burtonwood and identified a long list of problems – and fixes. But Burtonwood was not under his command. He could not implement a single change. All he could do was beg Gen Cannon to take action.

Meanwhile, Tunner was too devoted to his mission to let these shortages even develop. If Burtonwood could not deliver, then the only choice Tunner had was to transfer the responsibility for 200-hour checks back to the squadrons. Since many mechanics had already been dispatched to Burtonwood, this meant that those few mechanics still in Germany had to do more than ever. Tunner himself says: 'The men remaining had to carry a double load and they were justified in resenting it bitterly. It meant 12-hour days for my maintenance men.'[9]

Neither was overworking the only problem Tunner's mechanics faced. Even something as simple as spares and tools became a problem. The reason was not that these were absent in theatre, but rather that Gen Cannon – not Gen Tunner – controlled the supply depot at Erding, and he had other priorities. 'Cannon proceeded as if Operation Vittels amounted to only a subsidiary concern for USAFE; under his regime, spare parts and tools craved by [Airlift] mechanics . . . would remain on the shelves at Erding Air Force Depot in Bavaria in case they should be needed by any USAFE unit in Germany.'[10] Tunner more generously suggests that Cannon's staff simply did not know what they had because the stuff had been dumped there after the war and never properly inventoried. To allow Tunner to request supplies from the US might have prompted the Pentagon into pointing out that the requested supplies were already at Erding, and this in turn would have exposed the chaos and lack of inventory at the depot. That, however, would have reflected poorly on Cannon, so the best bureaucratic solution to the problem (from Cannon's point of view) was to ignore it. Whatever the reason, Tunner's mechanics were reduced to buying tools on the local economy.

Tunner's problems did not end there. Aircraft returning to the US for their 1,000-hour checks were also being lost to the Airlift for far longer than anticipated and planned. Instead of being absent from theatre for twenty-two days, they were gone fifty-seven days. The reasons for the delays were legion: first and foremost, to the commanders at the scattered maintenance facilities in the US, the Airlift was far away and its urgency completely alien. No one in Texas or Idaho was working around the clock, seven days a week.

Then there was the problem of finding pilots to fly the aircraft across the Atlantic. With the bulk of the USAF's multi-engine transport pilots flying the daily runs to Berlin, there was a shortage of pilots to take over the task of transatlantic ferrying. There were a substantial number of trained women transport pilots who had been qualified on four-engine aircraft during the war. The majority of these pilots had even been part of Ferrying Division, then under Gen Tunner, but the USAF had discharged the women in haste before the end of the war, did not acknowledge them as veterans, and was in fact doing its best to pretend they had never existed. Certainly, no one in the USAF dreamed of reactivating them, so the Airlift just had to live with the slower return of aircraft, and President Truman had to order even more planes to be assigned to the Airlift to ensure that Clay had the aircraft he needed actually 'hauling freight'.

The final problem created by Tunner's unsatisfactory command position was that he had no control over assignments and leave for his personnel. Tunner argued then and later that no commander of a major operation should be denied these tools. What it meant was, quite simply, that he could not give the men what they wanted most: certainty about their tours of duty. As he did not know how many or when replacements would arrive, he could not tell the men under his command how long they would have to serve. This was worse even than the war, when aircrews flew a set number of missions and then returned home. Every wartime airman could count his missions and look forward to the day when the last one was complete. Not so during the Airlift. There was no prospect of relief and return home. This, as has been mentioned several times already, created severe morale problems and spawned much dark humour as well. A fictional 'diary' started circulating which described the Airlift in the year 2000 with the pilots then in their 70s and 80s pottering about still hoping for relief. . . .

Tunner was equally powerless when it came to improving housing and food for his troops – an utterly frustrating situation for a commander. As he puts it: '. . . all that my officers or I could do was point out wherein the trouble lay to the responsible persons . . . and hope that something would be done. But instead of action we got excuses and empty promises.'[11]

These various factors combined had contributed to a decrease in Airlift efficiency at the very time when it needed to increase. As predicted and expected, the weather turned nasty in November. The first problem was fog. Visibility was so bad on so many days in November that Tunner reduced the minimums for flying from 400ft visibility to 200ft. But this wasn't enough to overcome the problems. The meteorologists were predicting that the fog might persist for weeks, and on Sunday 28 November it got substantially worse. A fog blanket spread across Europe from Finland to Italy that was so dense that it closed down practically every airport in all of northern Europe for the next 100 hours. On 29 November, the Airlift came to a complete halt.

With Berlin's coal reserves down to just two weeks, Tunner gave the order to fly 'zero-zero' – i.e. zero ceiling and zero visibility. Never a man to order others to do what he would not do himself, on the evening of 29 November in the dark and the dense fog Tunner took the controls of a heavily laden C-54 and flew it to Berlin.

> . . . the Follow Me jeep guiding Tunner's C-54 along the taxiway and out to the active runway had to be guided itself by two men walking ahead and carrying flashlights . . . Tunner's flight was quickly cleared for departure. After all, the commanding general of the Combined Airlift Task Force was at the controls of a coal-laden aircraft, and if he wanted to fly in weather that had even the birds walking, no one was going to deny him.[12]

Despite Tunner's example, only ten aircraft reached Berlin on 30 November. Of those ten aircraft, seven had been British, guided by their superior on-board navigation equipment and their professional navigators. On 1 December, with only marginally better conditions, fifty-four Airlift sorties were flown – a dramatic improvement over the day before – but in fact bringing in a pittance; less than 500 tons of supplies. Again these flights came predominantly from Wunstorf and flew to Gatow, where the better GCA was located, but at least the precedent had been set and henceforth much flying was done in such hair-raising conditions. This meant in practice that:

At Rhein-Main, C-54s took off on nights when the fog was so bad that even buses in nearby Frankfurt had stopped running. . . . Truck convoys from the railheads to the airfields were guided by men walking ahead with flashlights and drivers stayed on the road by following the red taillights of the truck ahead of them.[13]

[At take-off, the pilot] had first to position the nose above a white line, then taxi blindly into nothingness. Once the airspeed indicator showed 100mph, the plane fought into the solid overcast to fly on instruments all the way to Berlin.[14]

[On landing] the fog was so thick that pilots were unable to pick out the beams of the flashlights of the ground crew guiding them to their hardstands. . . .[15]

Gen Clay experienced the dismal conditions personally, describing them as follows:

When we arrived over Berlin, both Tempelhof and Gatow airports reported equally unfavourable conditions so our pilot decided to make a pass at Tempelhof. Thanks to the effectiveness of GCA and its well-trained operators, we landed without accident but with our brakes hot. When the tower directed us to the taxiway we found the visibility so poor that we did not dare move farther down the runway. We were unable to follow the jeep that was sent to guide us and finally reached the unloading ramp guided by an airman under each wing signalling with flashlights.[16]

At Wunstorf, exclusively RAF, the minimums were officially fixed at 200ft ceiling and 400yd visibility. The professional pride of the RAF is demonstrated by the following incident. Sqn Ldr Bevan-John of No. 51 Squadron was acting as tower control officer one night, intent on bringing all his planes safely in.

No runway lights were visible, yet to his astonishment every man joining the circuit reported as if by rote: 'Two hundred feet – four hundred yards.' As the last man touched down, Bevan-John summoned them to the bar for a drink, then challenged them. 'You lied to me, didn't you? How much could you see of the true conditions?' It was New Zealander Les Gow, replying for all, who embodied the spirit that would see the airlift through: 'We couldn't even see the bleeding runway.'[17]

And this was all before the temperatures dropped below zero.

In the damp, any drop in temperature resulted in icing, and ice on flights to Berlin started to become common. There were many, many close calls involving ice. At Celle ice sometimes formed so rapidly that between leaving the hardstanding and reaching the start of the runway, ice had formed so thickly that the aircraft could not take off. Ice caused a C-54 on approach to Tempelhof to lose all four engines at once. The pilot landed short, in the stone-hard graveyard before the airfield, bounced over the perimeter fence, and landed on the runway without harm to man or machine.[18] At least nine of the fatal crashes during the Airlift occurred in poor weather in winter, suggesting that ice may have been a contributing factor. Cockpit recording devices had not yet reached the level of sophistication we know today and nor had crash investigations, which were furthermore hampered by the fact that several aircraft went down in the Soviet Zone and the Allies were never given access to them for investigative purposes.

Tunner's example of flying in fog might be inspiring, but even he did not want men to fly to their deaths. That meant that a combination of fog and ice shut the Airlift down. In mid-December and again at Christmas these conditions caused flying to be suspended altogether.

Several patterns emerged in all this. First, that there was often – though not always – different weather conditions in the north than in the south. This justified the decision to keep Rhein-Main and Wiesbaden fully operational, despite the greater distance to Berlin, because it proved possible to fly into Berlin from these airports on some days when the airfields in the British Sector were closed. Second, Gatow was closed less frequently than Tempelhof or Tegel. This was both because of better GCA and because there was less risk to the civilian population. A mistake at Tempelhof might take hundreds of West Berlin civilians to their deaths; at Gatow an accident was more likely to take only Soviets or livestock as collateral casualties. Third, the Yorks were usually the last of the aircraft to stop flying due to weather, but even they had to reduce cargoes in favour of extra fuel in case they had to divert to the South of France. (One rather suspects the crews hoped for this!) More likely, however, was simply getting socked in at Gatow and spending the night in Berlin, unable to return until the next day.

All these conditions combined to create a 23 per cent drop in delivered tons and a 16 per cent drop in flights in November compared to October – an already inadequate month. Just 3,786 tons were delivered on average per day in November, or more than 1,800 tons too little each day, making a total of 113,600 tons. This amounted to a shortfall of 54,000 tons of desperately needed goods. December saw a slight improvement to 141,500 tons, but this was still below the deliveries of October and more than 32,000 tons short of monthly requirements.

Although by 1 January the situation seemed to have stabilised with regard to food (i.e. people were getting enough to live on and one month's reserves could be maintained), coal stocks were still dwindling at an alarming rate. There was hardly more than a week of reserves left, and even more severe fuel rations were put into effect, reducing above all the hours of electricity available to retail consumers. Efforts to fly out 'extra mouths' were increased, but there seemed little hope of sustaining the city through the remaining three months of dark and cold. The Airlift appeared to have done its best – and fallen short. Disaster appeared to lie just around the corner.

Chapter 12

GENERAL WINTER *VERSUS* FATHER CHRISTMAS

The turning of the year 1948/9 was a deciding moment for the Airlift. The Russians were fond of saying at the time that 'General Winter' was their ally. 'He' had certainly stood by Russia in 1812 and by the Soviet Union in 1941–3. The obdurate refusal of the Soviets to negotiate or even seriously discuss a lifting of the blockade reflected their unshakeable faith in the 'General's' partisanship. Even if surprised by the willingness and ability of the West to supply Berlin by air during the long warm days of summer, the assumption in Moscow and the Soviet Military Administration in Germany was that General Winter would defeat the Airlift.

However, instead of being particularly harsh, causing airfields to close under the burden of snow, or aircraft to ice up and fall from the sky like ripe fruit, or Berliners to flood to the East to register for coal rations, the winter of 1948/9 proved astonishingly mild. There were fewer deaths from cold in Berlin, despite the blockade, than there had been in the first postwar winter. From the Soviet perspective, General Winter became a defector.

But his defection alone does not explain the success of the Airlift. As the days got darker and colder and the reserves were run down, there was a very real chance – objectively speaking – that the morale of the city would break. Just as dangerous: the resolve of the Western Allies could have evaporated. In Washington, and particularly in London, bureaucrats and politicians alike would have been perfectly justified in reassessing the situation, calculating the still-escalating costs of the operation and the chances of success – and concluding that a 'policy change' was appropriate.

Such decisions have been made before in far less difficult situations. Examples from history are legion. Napoleon's defeat at Waterloo was militarily less devastating or costly than his defeat at Leipzig two years earlier, but after Waterloo the French political class was no longer willing to follow the dictator/emperor. The German Luftwaffe's offensive against Fighter Command's airfields in late summer 1940 was systematically beating down the RAF's ability to defend Great Britain, but the political preference for 'punishing' England by bombing London turned an imminent victory into a significant defeat. More recently, the United States soundly defeated the North Vietnamese during the 'Tet' offensive of 1968 – but the will of the American public to continue the war in Vietnam was broken and a military victory led to a political defeat.

A different constellation of public perceptions and political responses could have produced completely different results for the Blockade of Berlin in 1949. The stumbling of the Airlift in November and December 1948 might have become the catalyst for cancelling the entire operation if the will to continue had not been manifest in both the Allies and the Berliners. It was not the concrete measures instituted to ramp up the Airlift further that were critical at this point in history, but rather the psychological impact of Father Christmas. Not objective facts, but perceptions were what saved the Airlift – perceptions and a fundamental change of attitude on the part of both occupiers and occupied.

The change was so profound that it has become a cliché to say that the Berlin Airlift turned enemies into allies. This assessment of the situation may have found its earliest expression in testimony by Gen Clay before a joint session of Congress on 27 May 1949, only days after the lifting of the blockade. While the Airlift itself was still in progress, the senior American military commander reported to the highest representatives of the American people: 'I saw in Berlin the spirit and soul of a people reborn. Two and a half million Germans had a second opportunity to choose freedom. They had foregone their first opportunity, they did not forego their second opportunity.'[1]

In Berlin the transformation was more subtle and gradual, but with time the term for describing the Western Allies changed from 'Occupiers' to 'Protective Powers'. British commentators stressed that: 'The . . . defeated enemy rapidly became our allies in the operation against the Soviet blockaders.'[2]

It has been suggested by the more cynically inclined historians that since people cannot afford to have two enemies at once, it was the change of attitude towards the Soviet Union that fathered the change in attitude between Western Allies and Germans. There is certainly some truth to this. Politically it is difficult to maintain focus and allocate resources if there are too many enemies, and militarily it is always undesirable to be fighting on several fronts at once. Even on a personal level, it is easier to have only one enemy. One RASC corporal making his first trip to Berlin during the Airlift reported:

> I don't remember all that much – we saw the bombed city of Berlin but that was the same as everywhere we had seen before, Hannover especially. But then when we went down this narrow cutting with high banks on either side and were told that we were being watched by Russians above us it became frightening again, especially when told that just a couple of weeks earlier there had been shots fired.[3]

Yet this 'one enemy at a time' theory is too simplistic to accurately describe the changes in perception and attitude that took place in what is historically a very short space of time.

In the summer of 1945, Germany was still the devil incarnate to the Western world, and Berlin especially was the 'heart of darkness' – the HQ of the National Socialist State and the site of the Wansee Conference, at which the 'final solution' for the systematic extermination of European Jews had been adopted.

The hostility towards Germany during the war itself, based largely on a fear of military competence and the hypothesised inherent aggressiveness of 'Prussian militarism', was intensified – and materially altered – by the liberation of the concentration camps in the closing days of the war. Whereas in previous wars, war-weariness had a tendency to spawn pacifism more than hatred, the unprecedented scale and the nature of Nazi atrocities filled people with revulsion towards the Germans that went far beyond the usual bitterness towards a foe. The crimes against humanity committed in the name of the German people caused, not only ordinary men and women, but scholars and intellectuals to hypothesise that there was something fundamentally – even genetically – *wrong* with the Germans. The enemy was no longer just 'Prussian militarism' and the 'German General Staff' but rather the entire German people, who were collectively blamed for the atrocities and defamed as inherently, albeit intelligently and industriously, depraved.

These attitudes manifested themselves in many ways and were nowhere stronger than in France. The French Military Governor, General Koenig, did not believe it was possible to establish democracy in Germany; he considered the Germans incapable of practising an essentially French system of government. His deputy, General Noiret, was equally negative about the German capability to learn peaceful coexistence and so preferred long-term, indefinite Occupation of Germany. The French Foreign Minister wanted the entire industrial heartland of Germany, the Ruhr, to be kept under 'international' control in perpetuity, and wanted Allied troops stationed permanently on the west bank of the Rhine in addition to the complete annexation of the Saar. The French as a whole believed the Americans (and to a lesser extent the British) were naive to think the Germans could be reformed.

Although the Americans proclaimed their conviction that any people in the world could learn pluralistic democracy, Germany was viewed as a particularly 'hard case'. President Roosevelt retained a deep-seated dislike of the Germans going back to his youth, when he had briefly attended school in Germany; he viewed the Germans as arrogant and provincial. Gen Clay went to Germany convinced that his job was to solve 'the German problem'; i.e. providing Germany with security while ensuring that that it did not ever again become a threat to its neighbours. Among American policy makers it was accepted as fact, without further reflection or analysis, that Germany was responsible for starting both world wars; the logical conclusion being that there was something inherent in the German character that made them irresponsible partners in the international community. The role of the Allied Occupation was therefore to 'reform' Germany and transform it into a nation capable of decent behaviour. This was boiled down into the official policy summarised as the 'four d's' – de-Nazification, demilitarisation, de-industrialisation and democratisation.

Nor were the attitudes towards Germany confined to the American political and military leadership. The contempt for Germans was manifest in many ways by ordinary Americans. The very flour sent to Germany to keep the population from starving was sent in sacks from the Abilene Flour Mills of Kansas with the stamp: 'We come as conquerors, not liberators.'[4] American officers arriving in Berlin in 1945 reported without embarrassment: 'The German prisoners, though laconic, scowled at my motion picture camera. I felt a sense of poetic justice watching these blond-haired Blitzkriegers painstakingly dismantling the outer rim of Fortress Europe.'[5] There was a widespread feeling among the ordinary people in the United States that if the Germans were hungry and homeless then they had only themselves to blame. An American correspondent summarised the feelings: 'When you see absolute devastation you do not grieve. . . . Our soldiers say, "They asked for it."'[6]

Gen Clay, perhaps because he came from the South and remembered post-Civil War 'reconstruction', rapidly recognised that reform and progress were not possible if policy was vindictive. A new democratic nation could not develop if virtually the entire population was excluded from any meaningful kind of participation in politics or society because of their 'Nazi' past. The American concept of 'collective guilt' meant that the American policy of de-Nazification conflicted head-on with the American policy of democratisation. Likewise, since the American goal was an independent (if pacified) Germany rather than perpetual Occupation on the French model, de-industrialisation interfered with the re-establishment of economic self-sufficiency. Therefore, in a relatively short period this component of official policy also had to be jettisoned.

What remained were the two pillars of Clay's administration: democratisation and demilitarisation. Furthermore, because 'collective guilt' was unviable when trying to establish a functioning economy and government, 'collective amnesty' became the effective practice if not the official policy. As the images of the concentration camps faded and troops were rotated out, it became impossible to sustain non-fraternisation rules and hatred. As Clay himself admitted, it simply went too much against the grain of the average American soldier to ask him to stop being friendly – added to which it has never been possible to stop large numbers of healthy young men from interacting with young women.

At both official and personal levels, British policy was more subtle and the attitudes more differentiated than America's. Even during the war, the British recognised to a greater extent than the Americans that there were many shades of grey among 'Nazis'. They were likewise more sceptical of the Soviet Union and so more sensitive to the need to maintain allies on the continent of Europe. Britain did not ever embrace the concept of 'collective guilt' to the same degree as America and so from the beginning was always willing to utilise capable German specialists in efforts to re-establish a working German administration. As a result:

> The British occupiers in Germany behaved less as conquerors, more like conscientious colonial civil servants. They were dedicated to sound administration, the creation of democracy in industry and government, the inculcation of liberal values, a mission to instruct and improve. . . . The Zone was treated as a colony for which the administrators felt responsible, but for whose inhabitants they had no affection and little understanding. The British remained aloof in their clubs and requisitioned houses, viewing the Germans as natives. . . . British intentions were basically decent and benevolent, but tended to be concealed by reticence.[7]

These official attitudes were reflected in the personal remembrances of British airlift veterans. At the Royal Air Force Historical Society Proceedings in September 1989, Sir Kenneth Cross, who was with BAFO during the Airlift, reminded participants: 'We didn't have a great deal of affection for the German nation and it would be wrong for anyone to have any views to the contrary. When it came to doing the Airlift, it was a professional job and whether it had been Hindus or Germans, the Air Force would have done it.'[8]

Many ordinary pilots and airmen felt the same. A civilian flight engineer, Victor Bingham, remembers that the Airlift had nothing to do with humanitarian efforts: 'If it had been flying to Timbuctoo we would have been just as interested.' Bingham goes so far as to flatly deny that the Germans ever turned into Allies: 'Not to us they weren't, more like a Cold War encumbrance.'[9] Captain Roy Day, another civilian airman, felt simply that his attitude towards the Germans did not change during the Airlift adding: 'I do not think we had strong political views; we were just doing a flying job.'[10] Norman Hurst, RAF ground crew, claims that: 'I can truthfully say that on no occasion did we ever discuss Germany or the German population. It was not due to indifference but the fact that it was not a particularly interesting subject . . . we had our national problems . . . Britain was just about played out. Six years of wartime effort and stringency just about exhausted the population.'[11]

In short, British crews, no less than British policy, were on the whole more aloof than American crews.

Yet they were human too and many – even or particularly former Bomber Command personnel – remember being shocked and appalled by the scale of destruction found in Germany. The first troops who marched into Germany in 1945 might still have felt that Germany 'deserved' what it had received. They had fought their way across North Africa and up through Italy, or landed on the beaches of Normandy and clawed their way forward in hard-fought battles. They were battle-hardened, and many had seen close friends die beside them. But by 1948, the troops and particularly aircrews coming to Germany for the first time, had been at peace for over three years. Many RAF ground personnel were postwar conscripts who had never known war first hand, and even for the veterans the scars of war had started to heal and were not so raw. Virtually every observer admits that in Germany they were confronted with destruction far worse than they had known at home or had expected to find.

One RAF conscript described what he found in Germany as follows:

The troop train . . . wound its way through a neat, clean and tidy Holland into a truly devastated Germany. Like most of my friends I was absolutely horrified at the scenes which met my eyes – every town it seemed, consisted only of piles of rubble with just an odd fireplace or wall still standing. Where, and how, the occupants lived I never knew, but conditions must have been terrible for them, war or no war. The war still loomed large in our minds but to see such ruin 3 years after it had ended was shocking. My friend lived in Stepney, London and I'd seen a lot of bomb damage there, but nothing on this scale. Even today it makes me shudder.[12]

For Americans, who had nothing with which to compare the destruction, the impact was often greater still:

Nothing I had read, heard, or seen, prepared me for the desolate, ravaged sight below. The gaunt, broken outlines of once majestic buildings, struggling toward the sky, supported by piles of rubble at their base, irregularly stretched from one end of the city to the other – mottled mass of total destruction.[13]

Even returning aircrew often admitted that they had not truly pictured the effects of their raids until confronted with the results. Few men felt guilty for what they had done – they still believed in the cause they had fought for and they had too many friends whose deaths they did not want to consider wasted – but there seems little doubt that the scale of destruction produced the first hint of sympathy for the Germans.

However, friendships are not built on pity, and many observers reported with alienation the way in which the Germans huddled in their ruins, listless and, in the eyes of many, sullen. The sight of appalling devastation may have paved the way to a change in attitude, but the change itself was sparked by the unexpected defiance of the Berliners to the blockade. As has been recorded earlier, the Allies seriously expected the Berliners to give in to the Soviet pressure. The assumption was that the Germans, who had wantonly trampled on their own freedom just fifteen years earlier, would not value it now. When they unexpectedly chose freedom, they surprised the world and ignited a new interest in Germany and especially Berlin.

Suddenly the images of Germany presented to people in Britain and the United States weren't the Nuremburg Trials, but rather the speech of Ernst Reuter defiantly demanding support in the cause of freedom. Berlin rubble women were no longer portrayed as the piteous defeated enemy or an economic burden, but rather as heroic foot-soldiers in the struggle against communism. The degree to which the Berliners were willing to suffer hardships – and even joke about them – made them seem human in a positive sense. Lingering wartime distrust and dislike and postwar pity and contempt gave way to outright enthusiasm. The very unexpectedness of Berlin's resistance is what captured the imagination of Germany's former enemies. News commentators expressed their amazement and then their admiration. Clay summarised these feelings saying: '. . . [T]he courage of the people of Berlin . . . had regained for them the respect of the free people of the world.'[14] Some Americans went even further in their admiration, reflecting: 'I wondered . . . why it was that these Berliners seemed to know what freedom really was and what it was worth, even more than I.'[15]

Notably, these changed attitudes focused on Berliners. In Allied circles it was noted with disapproval that the rest of Germany's attitude towards Berlin was lukewarm rather than enthusiastic. While other German states did make some tepid gestures of support and the Economic Council eventually levelled a special tax for Berlin making a degree of financial support available, the feeling of Western observers was that this support was reluctant and half-hearted. British observers particularly felt that if there were a siege of London, for example, they would be far more supportive of their capital than the Germans were being about theirs. On the whole, only the German political class seemed to care what was happening in Berlin, while the average German was more concerned with finally having enough to eat and starting to rebuild his economic existence.

For those directly involved in the Airlift – as opposed to those listening to the news on the radio from their living rooms – it was the tangible gratitude of the Berliners to the foot-soldiers of the Airlift that changed attitudes most. Every day thousands of Berliners gathered on the street outside Gatow airfield 'clapping and cheering as the four-engined Yorks taxied in'.[16] Tempelhof, more centrally located, attracted even greater crowds, estimated at up to 10,000 on any one day. People climbed on the rubble, perched in the trees, stood upon parked cars and trucks, and waved from balconies and the rooftops.

A *Picture Post* article about the Airlift published 18 September 1948 claims that: 'For all these people [air and ground crews] the apparently genuine gratitude of the Germans for what is being done is the main incentive. At Gatow, the Station Commander has received many gifts for presentation to the flight captains.'[17] Many of these gifts were touching in their simplicity. Captain Edward Hensch remembers receiving a package sent anonymously to a 'blockade flier' which contained a porcelain snail, a few flowers and a toy walrus made with rat fur. Another pilot tells how two small boys collected broken pieces of marble from the ruins and set them in metal bases to make book-ends dedicated in thanks to the Airlift crews. The humbleness of the gifts brought home to the aircrews just how little the Berliners had left to give. In consequence crews were touched by the gift of a watch that had survived Soviet plundering, or by a piece of china that had survived the air raids, by a handmade carving or a beat-up teddy bear. . . .

Even more important than these brief encounters was the impact of more lasting human contact. As Clay had been forced to recognise early on, it was beyond the power of any higher authority to keep young men away from young women, and if you didn't let young men meet young women in an open and ordinary way than they would inevitably find each other in the dark with all the accompanying disadvantages of disease, violence and crime. With remarkable agility, the 17- and 18-year-old recruits of the US Army and Air Force, the products of the almost unimaginable provinciality on a continent not yet connected to the world by television or internet, soon found their way around the *Kneipe* of Berlin and *Biergarten* of West Germany. Some remember with pleasure the restaurants of Celle. Cpl Jack Fellman soon learned to frequent those 'neat little' Berlin *Kneipe* with a back door 'for a hasty exit in case the MPs came.'[18] Sgt John Zazzera, stationed at Rhein-Main, remembers:

> Off-duty time was great. It was a great time for checking out the area, including wine, women and song. My friends and I frequented the Palmgarden, a favourite spot, but we soon 'graduated' to local German establishments in Offenbach. I met a German girl in one of them and almost married her.[19]

Despite the pressures they were under, an amazing number of men assigned to the Airlift did marry German women.

Another kind of interaction with Germans was job related. For the civilian crews, there was the staff at the hotels where they stayed and relations often became very cordial here. One of the civilian pilots recalls the following story:

> I landed at Buckeburg in very bad weather. We went to the transit Mess which was in the local Schloss. We were the only ones there except for the little German girl who was the receptionist, cook and general factotum. We told her to go home and that we would look after ourselves. Very soon afterwards a very large German appeared who said, 'Did you send my daughter home?' We said, 'yes.' His reply was: 'you come.' He took us back to his farm where they were celebrating their Harvest Festival. We spent the rest of the night there among some very friendly, happy folk.[20]

Airlift personnel also met the Germans loading and offloading their planes. An American Airlift pilot wrote of his first encounter with the Germans face to face as follows:

It was my first close up, eyeball-to-eyeball meeting with Germans. . . . As I looked from one to another to find the monster, the hardened stare, the 'superior' eye or defiant look, it wasn't there. I suddenly realised that the closest man to me had his hand extended to me for a handshake and the one behind him was raising his for the same purpose. Then I noticed the look in their eyes as they gazed at the flour bags, then back to us, as though we were angels from heaven delivering the news of the resurrection.[21]

An RASC lieutenant writes:

I thought I knew about Germans – that they were obedient to authority, with little sense of humour, hard-working and dull. . . . These fellows were half-starved, yet cheerful, and cracking with repartee. I never understood the quick Berliner Deutsch, or the reasons for the gusts of laughter that erupted from the stevedores as they toiled over the salt bags . . . [but it was always there].[22]

The British engineer in charge of building a bridge across the Havel remembers that he could not speak a word of German and the German engineer working under him could not speak English but 'both of [us] could read plans and got on very well'.[23] Likewise, the ground crews discovered that the German mechanics hired to help service aircraft shared a common language despite their lack of English: a devotion to aircraft and flying. Although earning far less than their British and American counterparts, by all accounts, they worked with the same dedication. Tunner had found a former Luftwaffe maintenance officer, Major-General Hans Detlev von Rohden, who had actually served in the air transport division of the Luftwaffe and was familiar with the problems facing the Airlift as well as being fluent in English. He naturally selected the best of his former colleagues and subordinates and translated the US aircraft manuals into German. The German crews were then trained on the aircraft engines in German and supervised by German-speaking Americans. With time, however, their proficiency was so great that the Germans themselves took over key positions. Tunner concluded: 'The German mechanics proved to be so capable that eventually eighty-five of them were assigned to each squadron. We had more German mechanics than American!'[24]

Clearly this kind of experience built up trust and respect between the men working together on the same aircraft day after day; and the experience was not confined to the USAF. The British charter companies likewise turned to German mechanics for DIs and emergency maintenance conducted in Germany. One of the civilian charter employees remembers: '[The Germans] were extremely keen to do even the most menial tasks around the aircraft. Flying was in their blood.'[25]

Speaking of encounters with Germans generally, however, many RAF personnel retained an ambivalent attitude towards them, well summarised by a sergeant of the Signals Regiment, who put it this way:

> Most of the communications network stations were manned by Germans and supervised by Royal Signals personnel. Many had worked for the German post office, were very knowledgeable and could speak good English. None of them were ever Nazis, to hear them tell it, and although I could not forgive them for the hurt they had caused this world, individually they could be nice people. But collectively, Nazis or not, they had been a bunch of real bastards.[26]

An RAF mechanic noted: 'Although I liked the vast majority of those [Germans] I did meet and we got along well as I recall, all my RAF colleagues noted with some amusement that all the Germans we met had fought against the Russians, none against the Western powers.'[27] But this was not always the case. Indeed, occasionally it was the reverse – the shared experiences of war – that formed the bond. Master Signaller Robert A. Hide had been shot down over north-east Germany following a raid on Berlin in March 1944. He was badly burned on his hands and face, but treated with 'unbelievable compassion, sympathy and first aid' by the Germans who first found him. Throughout the Airlift he felt that he had 'to reciprocate the compassion and sympathy that had been afforded [him] in the hour of [his] need'.[28] Another former RAF Bomber Command pilot, DFC, AFC, reports:

> I became friendly with a German wood-carver who had a nephew working with him who had been a Fw190 night fighter pilot. We got on very well. We used to exchange reminiscences and found we had both been involved in the same operations on the same nights as each other.[29]

From the German side of the divide the transformation process was not quite as difficult. By the time the war ended, the Germans had long since lost their arrogance or sense of superiority and the fear and hatred of the Soviets had made them look to the West. As mentioned earlier, many Germans seriously believed that the Western Allies ought to join forces with them to fight the Soviet threat. They had then undergone a greater or lesser amount of disillusionment with the Western Allies, but at no time did they see them in the same negative light that was the case in reverse. The issue for the

Germans was therefore less one of transforming an enemy into a friend than of regaining faith and trust after a perceived 'betrayal'.

The sense of 'betrayal' intensified at the very start of the blockade. From the Berlin perspective, the Soviets had behaved badly from the moment they entered the city, but the use of a blockade to starve them into submission after all the other humiliations was the absolute 'last straw'. At the very moment in time when the West was offering an unprecedented gesture of friendship and material support to all of Europe – including the defeated Germans in the form of the Marshall Plan and a sound currency – Soviet policy used the threat of starvation to force an entire city into submission. Even devoted and lifelong socialists and communists felt that the Soviets had gone too far and in so doing revealed their true nature. Residents of the Eastern Zone wrote to relatives in the West begging them to tell the Americans that 'the inhabitants of the Russian Zone are happy about each plane . . . which in spite of all SED propaganda brings food for a besieged city, which is not a fortress but a helpless heap of stones'.[30] The more the Russians tried to vilify the Airlift, the more they made themselves look ridiculous, and Berliners, East and West, didn't like being 'treated like idiots'. As Reuter's speech makes very clear, the Berliners were determined to resist the Soviets not *because* of the Western Allies, but rather despite them. As one Berliner put it:

> Of course we noticed the increased number of flights by the DC-3s going into Tempelhof, but we thought the Allies were just flying in the necessary food and supplies for themselves and their families. No West Berliner ever dreamed that the Airlift was meant to support all the people in the Western Sectors.[31]

The Berliners expected to be left in the lurch, but they chose not to cave in to Soviet pressure despite that expectation because they wanted to show the world that they were not being 'sold' willingly.

Neither did the Berliners see themselves as being 'in the same boat' as the Allies. The Allies, after all, could always 'go home'. The Americans particularly belonged to a nation untouched by war and producing unimaginable surpluses of everything. That made them different from the Berliners – quite apart from the better clothes, food, accommodation, heating, pay, etc. of the Occupation forces. The Berliners noted cynically that the Allied HQ was not subject to the electricity blackouts that affected the rest of the city, and that the NAAFI and PX still sold luxury goods – which found their way on to the black market just as before. The issue was not one of being in the same boat, but rather of temporarily sharing the same goal: breaking the Soviet blockade and defying the Soviets.

Just as Berlin's defiance surprised the Allies, the Allies' willingness to try an Airlift for the civilian population surprised the Berliners. A Berlin taxi driver was quoted in *Stars and Stripes* saying:

> Sure we lost our faith at first. . . . We thought the West would pull out. Now we have [our faith] back again. . . . You hear? There is another plane. And there another. Our faith, Mister, doesn't come from our hearts or our brains anymore. It comes through our ears.[32]

Put another way, one Berliner admitted, 'he was at first dubious over the possibility of the Airlift's success, then hopeful, and finally, he noted with jubilation, he reached the stage of "earplugs on the bedside table"'.[33] Another Berlin resident remembers it like this:

> They turned and came in over Neuköln and it was terrible because they had to go between houses to land. And, you know, if an airplane or two didn't come you actually woke up because something was missing. You knew something was wrong. The noise of the planes didn't bother us at all. As a matter of fact, we felt secure. As long as we heard those planes flying, we felt like everything was all right. But I remember waking up sometimes and thinking something was wrong. There was no plane.[34]

Another Berliner reports: 'As the number of aircraft increased from day to day, we started to hope. Daily I went to the edge of the airfield and I counted the incoming planes . . . I was very impressed. And then the C-54s arrived.' He adds: 'General Tunner and General Clay often drove through West Berlin in their military vehicles. Wherever they stopped, they were recognised by the Berliners and enthusiastically greeted. It made a great impression on us that these two, notoriously not very German-friendly generals, now offered us their hand in friendship.'[35]

It was not just the generals they admired and thanked. Cliff Wenzel had flown Halifaxes in the Second World War with Bomber Command. He was on one of the first crews to be deployed on the Airlift by the RAF. He was then flying with his own brother as his navigator, and on the first night after their arrival, the Wenzel brothers went around to the 'local' for a beer. The Germans seeing the RAF uniform walked out. 'Just three weeks later,' he claims, 'with the Airlift in full swing, we couldn't *buy* a drink – the Germans insisted on buying every round.'[36] Another Berliner reports: 'Everyone, even people like me, who had previously viewed the Victors with suspicion, abandoned this attitude and sought every sort of possible contact with the fliers and soldiers. If you ran into soldiers or airmen on the street, you would stop, shake their hand, and say simply "thanks".'[37]

But a British report noted that although the Airlift had done 'considerably more than pronouncements by Anglo-American leaders' to persuade the people of Berlin that the Western Allies intended to stay in Berlin, the Berliners still felt that the Western Powers ought to 'bare their teeth still further' if they were to obtain any concessions from the Russians. American opinion polls revealed that although 87 per cent of Berliners thought the blockade would succeed and 95 per cent of Berliners preferred the blockade to being absorbed into the Soviet Zone, 24 per cent of the population still wanted all occupying powers to leave.

Thus it was not the Airlift as such – or rather the Airlift alone – that transformed 'enemies' and 'occupiers' into 'allies' and 'protecting powers' but rather, again, personal contact with the people involved in the effort. Some of this was the result of official efforts: there were open houses at the departure bases where the Germans were invited in to see what was going on; in Berlin there were concerts, dances, parties, award ceremonies and the like to bring Germans and Allies together in benevolent settings for friendly interaction; German youth organisations volunteered to help out with loading and offloading on Sundays to enable regular workers a day off. Most important, there were a large number of German workers, whether working as loaders, offloaders, mechanics, cleaning women or canteen help, who came in daily contact with the Allies. One of those workers remembers:

> As you know, things weren't exactly booming in Germany at the time and one was happy to get hold of any sort of job. It was particularly advantageous to get a job with the 'Amis' because of the one 'square meal' a day. And even the work clothes were provided by the Army in the form of black-coloured, practical and completely indestructible canvas fatigues. I still wear my overalls to this day whenever I work in the garden. I owe the not exactly popular Soviets for some of the most pleasant months of my life.[38]

Another worker remembers with approval:

> The working environment was collegial and relaxed. Sometimes one didn't even notice that one was talking to a high-ranking officer. We couldn't read American rank insignia. There was always one in the group who could speak a little English so soon small deals developed between the Germans and Americans. . . . The Americans also took us along to Friedrichstrasse [in the Soviet Sector of Berlin] where there were two great restaurants, the 'Alt Bayern'

and the 'Rheinterrasse'. We'd exchange 5 West Marks for 30 East Marks in advance and then we'd sit there at the same table with the American and Russian soldiers acting as the interpreters.[39]

For others the encounter was brief but the impact lasted a lifetime. Ingeborg Lee wrote decades after the event the following story:

> I was born and raised in Celle and was almost 3 years old in early 1949. My mother had taken me in my stroller to look at the first dolls available in Celle after the War. We were admiring the beautiful dolls displayed in the window of the small toy store, when an American flyer . . . approached us. He said something that my mother couldn't understand and lifted me from my stroller. He then walked into the toy store with me and said something to the sales lady. I remember vividly his turning to me and telling me to pick out a doll. I pointed to a large one and it was handed to me. This wonderful American then placed me and my beautiful doll back in my stroller, mumbled something to my mother (who, I guess, was still in shock) and left.[40]

Children often seem to be the best ambassadors. A Royal Canadian Air Force (RCAF) navigator, coming to Berlin to visit the grave of his elder brother shot down over Berlin flying a Halifax on the night of 20/21 January 1944, remembered how he came with hatred in his heart, but found he could not keep it burning when confronted by the children playing in the rubble of the shattered city.[41] Three years later an RAF operations room clerk, who had confessed to his superior that he didn't understand what Operation Plainfare was all about and was therefore taken aboard a flight to Berlin, remembered vividly a little blonde girl aged about 10 or 11. The child he noted 'was a great favourite of the aircrews' who gave her sweets and biscuits 'which she carefully stowed away in her haversack'.[42] It was that stowing rather than eating that brought home to the observer the seriousness of the situation in Berlin: even children had learned to save and hoard anything of value.

As Christmas approached, Allied personnel demonstrated their vulnerability to the appeal of children in need. The personnel of Gatow, for example, organised a party for German children and fed about 500 in two days. One participant remembers: 'They hadn't seen so much food in years. They looked very thin and pale. We also gave up our chocolate rations. And at the end of each party they had a present and best of all an orange. Yes, an orange. Our food was pretty lousy. But we did our best for those kids.'[43]

American airmen asked their relatives to send gifts to the children of Berlin rather than to themselves. The appeal was answered and thousands of gift packages arrived in the departure fields intended for the children of Berlin. They called it Operation Santa Claus, and it was the strongest weapon the West had against General Winter because it was these gestures that truly turned enemies into not just allies but friends – often lifelong friends.

Arguably, no children have made a greater impact on international relations in the twentieth century than the thirty or so children who happened to be standing at the perimeter fence of Tempelhof airfield the day Lt Gail Halvorsen, USAF, decided to make a quick sightseeing tour of Berlin. Nothing can do the story justice except to quote Halvorsen's own words as he describes the fateful encounter:

> The first thing that caught my eye was about thirty kids in the middle of that grassy strip watching the planes swoop over the roof tops to a landing just behind where I was standing. Now the children were watching me, an American pilot in uniform. . . .
>
> It was a mixed group. Most of them were between the ages of 8 and 14 and evenly split between boys and girls. They were not especially well dressed but their clothes had been kept in good repair. Some were patched. All were clean.
>
> After a few giggles and animated discussion between themselves, they appointed two or three as spokespersons for the group. Children were taught English in the schools and several of the kids spoke it quite well.
>
> The group was there because they had a tremendous investment in the outcome. . . . Some children were timing aircraft arrivals and could tell of the weekly increases in the number of landings.
>
> One of the first questions was, 'How many sacks of flour does each aircraft carry?' There had been some discussion about how many equivalent loaves of bread came across the fence with each aircraft. Were we really flying in fresh milk for the younger children? What about the other cargoes? How many tons? One question came right behind the other.
>
> Then I received a lesson about priorities. They were interested in freedom more than flour. They fully recognised that between the two there was a real relationship but they had already decided which was pre-eminent. I was astonished with the maturity and clarity that they exhibited in advising me of what their values were and what was of greatest importance to them in the circumstances.
>
> In the months between when the aircraft over Berlin changed their cargo from bombs to flour the children had witnessed an accelerated change in international relations. These young kids began giving me the most meaningful lesson in freedom I ever had. . . .
>
> One of the principal spokespersons was a little girl about 12 years with wistful blue eyes. She wore a pair of trousers that looked as though they belonged to

an older brother and a pair of shoes that had seen better days on someone half again her size.

'Almost every one of us here experienced the final battle for Berlin. After your bombers had killed some of our parents, brothers and sisters, we thought nothing could be worse. But that was before the final battle. From that time until the Americans, British and French came into the city we saw first hand the communist system. We've learned much more since that time. We don't need lectures on freedom. We can walk on both sides of the border. What you see speaks more strongly than words you hear or read.' Her sentences came out with difficulty and not just as quoted but with the same points and emphasis.

A boy, not much older and standing nearer continued, 'We have aunts, uncles and cousins who live in East Berlin and in East Germany and they tell us how things are going for them. When they are here they use our library to read what is really going on in the world. They can say what they think when they are over here among family with known friends. . . .'

None had asked if I had been in one of those bombers in former times. I certainly wore the uniform they had been taught to hate; a symbol of death from the skies. Yet in neither their conversation nor in their tone of voice was there a sign of resentment or hostility. It was freedom, not flour, that they were concerned with that warm July afternoon in 1948.

Those who had parents, or a single parent, or only brothers or sisters, all believed that someday there would be enough to eat, but if they lost their freedom they feared they would never get it back.

What they referred to as freedom was the idea that they could be what they wanted to be, to choose their course in life without being told what they would be, that they could really have open access to a free press, and speak freely their thoughts on a subject without fear. Very high on their priority was to be able to travel if and when they had the means.

The wistful blue-eyed girl made the point that they could get by with very little for quite a while if they knew they could depend on us to stick by them and do the best we could.

The conversation, laboured as it had to be given the language barrier . . . had consumed more time than I had allowed. . . . 'Sorry kids, I must go,' I waved over my shoulder. My overriding thoughts were to get that jeep and make up for precious lost time. It would be nice to get back to Rhein/Main in time to have 1 or 2 hours sleep before our flight shifts start again. In that frame of mind it was unlikely that a totally different outside thought could get inside my head and affect my course of action, but it did. . . . By now I was 50yd away, headed for my jeep, but my mind was still back at the fence.

What really makes those kids so different? . . . I stopped in my tracks. . . . Not one of almost thirty kids, most of whom hadn't had any gum or candy in 2 or 3 years, was willing to become a beggar and ask, verbally or by body language, if they could have some chocolate or gum. . . . Thousands of American GIs filled the special craving of countless little ones and did so willingly, even by design. It became a conditioned response: a group of kids, their immediate, strong request, hand in the pocket for pre-placed goodies for such an encounter, and the pleasure of dispensing some. Here had been no request. . . .

Instinctively I reached in my pocket. There had been no preparations for such a moment. All there were was two sticks of Wrigley's Doublemint gum.

Thirty kids and two sticks, there will be a fight, I rationalised, making a last ditch attempt to resume my course to the jeep. . . .

I glanced over my shoulder. The children were there, even pressed against the barbed wire fence, still waving as is the European custom, until the departed guest disappears down the road. . . .

I turned abruptly and headed for the fence.

Within the first three return steps the children stopped waving. They expectantly awaited my arrival at the fence. Then they saw my hand come out of my pocket and something, unmistakably, was in it!

Their interest and intensity of expression changed in a flash. There were some who jockeyed for a better position to discover what I had. . . . In the last few steps I broke the two sticks of gum in half and headed for the children who had been the translators.

Their hands were now through the barbed wire. . . . The four pieces were quickly placed. . . . In all my experience, including Christmases past, I have never witnessed such an expression of surprise, joy, and sheer pleasure that I beheld in the eyes and faces of those four young people. Nor do I remember such disappointment as was evident in the eyes of those who came so close. . . .

There was no fighting or attempts to grab away the prize given to the four who were carefully removing the wrapper. . . .

The quiet was broken with a rising babble from the rest. They were requesting a share in the tin foil or the outer wrapper. Strips were torn off and passed around. The recipient's eyes grew large as they smelled the bits of wrapper and recalled better times. . . . What I could do with thirty full sticks of gum! . . . Immediate thoughts of when I could come back to the fence were answered by: It will be a long time. . . .

Just then another C-54 swooped over our heads, across the fence and landed. Two little plumes of white smoke came off the main tyres as they touched down on the pierced steel planked runway. . . . That plane gave me a sudden flash of inspiration.

Why not drop some gum and even chocolate to these kids out of our airplane the next daylight trip to Berlin?

You will get in a heap of trouble if you are caught, came a quick and rational response.

This whole blockade is a violation of human rights. Compared to mass starvation this couldn't get me more than a minor court martial, I answered myself.

Why not get permission? You know how long that will take? The airlift will be over by then and it is just a one-time thing, besides, we'll only be about 90ft in the air, answered my desire.

To my own astonishment and dismay I found myself in the next moment announcing the plan for all to hear.

At first their response was cautiously reserved for fear they had misunderstood. I took the opportunity to add, 'I will do this thing only if the persons who catch the packets will share equally with everyone in the group.'

By now, those most proficient in the language had confirmed this crazy, unbelievable proposition to the others and the noisy celebration had already begun. Added to the celebration were shouts of 'Jawohl! Jawohl! Jawohl!' from everyone in answer to the requirement to share. Then it became very quiet.

The little girl with the wistful blue eyes was prodded to be the spokesperson. 'They want to know which aircraft you will be flying. Such a small package would be too easily lost, especially if you come late and we have tired by watching all day in vain,' she excitedly stammered out while gazing intently into my face.

. . . There was no way to know what specific plane I would be assigned on any flight. . . . 'You kids watch the aircraft approaching Tempelhof, especially when they pass over the field. When I get overhead I will waggle the wings of that big airplane back and forth several times. That is the signal. . . .'[44]

By Halvorsen's own account his gesture was entirely spontaneous – and it was intended to be a one-time operation. He expected to get in trouble for it and agonised about the fact that his rations were so small that it wouldn't be enough for thirty kids. He had to win over his crew-mates as accomplices. Although they shared Halvorsen's conviction that he was going to get them all into 'one big mess of trouble', they readily agreed and pooled their rations to make the first – and they thought last – 'candy drop'. To ensure no one got hurt, they tied handkerchiefs to the candy to make tiny parachutes that would slow the fall and make the tiny parcels more visible.

The very next day they put the plan into action. The kids recognised the signal and went wild with enthusiasm, but in the cockpit there were increasing doubts both about the risk of harm to the kids and the risk of getting in trouble with the USAF. Halvorsen took them in like he was on a bombing run, ignoring the threat of flak and fighters. They hit the target dead on. By the time they were taxiing to the offloading ramps the kids were waving the captured parachutes through the fence at every passing C-54 and cheering them all indiscriminately. Once the aircraft was on the ground, the kids could not tell which of the many identical planes had delivered the goods.

The next day there were more kids, waving furiously again. And the next day and the next. By now it was clear to Halvorsen and his crew that they had got away with their unauthorised act of generosity, but the kids were still there, hopefully waving to each incoming flight. That was too much for these typical and ordinary airmen to take. They saved up the next week's sweets rations and made the next drop to the patiently waiting and still cheering children. A week later it was the same thing all over again; but then the weather closed in. Halvorsen had to check in with Base Operations while in Berlin, and he received the shock of his life. One of the tables in the ops room was stacked high with mail – and it was all addressed to 'the Chocolate Flier', 'Uncle Wiggle-Wings' and variations on the theme. The sight filled Halvorsen with terror – the certainty of his impending discovery. As soon as he told his crew, they agreed they had to quit immediately!

The resolve lasted only a few weeks, then they all broke down again. They had each secretly saved up their rations and had more than ever, so they agreed to do 'just one more big drop'.

It was fateful. The next day when they landed at Rhein-Main after a routine flight they were met by a staff officer and Halvorsen was ordered to report to his commanding officer. As Halvorsen tells the story the confrontation went as follows:

'Halvorsen, what in the world have you been doing?' came what seemed to me a very stiff query from the good Colonel Haun.

'Flying like mad, Sir,' came my best reply.

'I'm not stupid. What else have you been doing?' came a better question.

Then it was I knew that he knew. . . . 'Oh well,' I thought, 'there must be something else besides flying.'

This fine commander who had accepted my transfer from the C-74 squadron in Mobile in order that I could join the airlift was now in a position to correct the error. He was much firmer than I had ever seen him before.

'Didn't they teach you in ROTC at Utah State to keep your boss informed?' came a burst that cast questions even on my earliest military training, let alone a great University. More seriously, it also indicated he had been going over my file. How else would he know where I had those two quarters of college work. Things looked grim.

Then in one motion he reached under the desk, as though he was searching for a whip, but came up with the *Frankfurter Zeitung*, a newspaper, and put it where I couldn't miss it.

'Look at this,' he invited. 'You almost hit a reporter in the head with a candy bar in Berlin yesterday. He's spread the story all over Europe. The General called me with congratulations and I didn't know anything about it. Why didn't you tell me?'

My reply was rather weak, 'I didn't think you would approve it before the airlift was over, Sir.'

'You mean to tell me that after we had dropped thousands of sticks of bombs on that city and the Russians are now trying to starve the rest of them to death, that you didn't think I would approve dropping a few sticks of gum?' he ended incredulously with volume to spare.

'Guess I wasn't too smart, Sir.' I admitted.

'General Tunner wants to see you and there is an International Press Conference set up for you in Frankfurt. Fit them into your schedule. And Lieutenant, keep flying, keep dropping, and keep me informed.' He smiled for the first time as he finished and shook my hand.[45]

The significance of this encounter is not just that Halvorsen's superiors gave him the go-ahead, but that Gen Tunner had the political savvy to instantly seize upon the propaganda and psychological value of the unauthorised action. In a way, that combination of individual initiative and then, as it turned out, massive and professional marketing, almost epitomises America. English participants have complained that they were 'too poor' to engage in the kind of 'extravagant' enterprise such as Halvorsen's and thereby miss the point that Halvorsen himself couldn't afford it any more than they could. Furthermore, many individual English airmen *did* share their candy rations with Berlin's children. The British were not less generous than the Americans. What made Halvorsen's actions unique and spectacular was the willingness of the Commander-in-Chief of the Combined Airlift Task Force to turn a spontaneous gesture of generosity by an individual into a media event; which should not in any way detract from it. Once Halvorsen's candy drops were approved and publicised they developed a life of their own. Other men started leaving their candy rations on Halvorsen's bed. Men contributed their handkerchiefs for parachutes. When these ran out, old shirts had to be cut up. Finally some old silk parachutes were contributed and cut up into smaller 'chutes'. Since these were so precious, they were deployed with notes asking for their return. Although eventually all but one was lost, they were used and reused many times before being taken out of service by someone who could not resist the fine silk. Many children started returning the other parachutes too. Meanwhile, two German secretaries were detailed to read and answer the fan mail.

That mail brought not only expressions of gratitude, but also requests from children who had not been fortunate enough to receive any of the bounty falling from the skies. At the polio hospital, for example, there were many children who longed for something to cheer them up, but could not get out of their beds, much less clamber over rumble, chasing tiny parachutes. They begged Lt Halvorsen to ignore the signs for quiet and to go right ahead and fly low so he could drop the goodies in the courtyard of the hospital. Halvorsen wisely chose to deliver the goodies in person instead.

Children in the Soviet Sector of the city wanted their share too.

The kids in East Berlin wrote great letters explaining how they would come over to West Berlin and catch some of these wonderful surprises. They hoped I wouldn't take offence that someone from the Russian Sector was collecting bounty intended for the Free Berliners. They hastened to assure me that it wasn't their doing that they lived in East Berlin or even, in some cases, East Germany. They didn't have anything to do with setting up the blockade nor the East–West boundaries. They had to live over there because that is where their parents lived. An admiration was often expressed for the Americans.

The bottom line in the letters from East Berlin always came down to, 'Is there any chance you could drop these packages to us in East Berlin when you make your approach to Tempelhof? You have to fly right over us before you turn to land.'[46]

Halvorsen didn't see why he shouldn't drop over East Berlin either and so he did so. The Soviets responded with a démarche and the State Department told the War Department that Halvorsen had to desist. The fear at the State Department was that Halvorsen's actions might upset the delicate balance that prevented the Airlift from sliding into war. The Airlift had up to then been scrupulously confined to the letter of agreements between East and West. No matter how ridiculous it seemed, Halvorsen's drops over East Berlin infringed on Four Power status by crossing the invisible line of interfering in the other power's Zone/Sector and so threatened to unravel the entire tapestry of hostile – but peaceful – coexistence. Halvorsen conceded defeat and thereafter confined his drops to the West. Even these were not always successful.

A certain 9-year-old, Peter Zimmerman, was most unfortunate. He sent Lt Halvorsen a map in his first letter with very precise instructions: 'As you see, after take-off fly along the big canal to the second highway bridge, turn right one block. I live in the bombed-out house on the corner. I'll be in the back yard every day at 2 p.m., drop it there.' But despite Halvorsen's efforts this operation failed.

> We carefully followed the map to Peter Zimmerman's house. Kids in the back yard. Bon Bons away! Next week a letter from Peter: 'Didn't get any gum or candy, a bigger kid beat me to it.' The next try was futile. His letters had always contained pencil sketches of animals or landscape scenes. One picture depicted an aircraft with little parachutes coming out of it. The words, 'No chocolate yet', were written on the tail section and suggested his continuing plight. The last letter didn't have any works of art only: 'You are a Pilot? I gave you a map. How did you guys win the war anyway?'[47]

Meanwhile, Halvorsen's idea was still growing. By now the interviews had been broadcast and the news had reached the states. People all across the country, mostly women, started sending handkerchiefs. Halvorsen reports: 'Many handkerchiefs had the donor's name and address written on them. The wire services also made mention that I was a bachelor, which explained the black-laced and perfumed contributions. We dropped them all.'[48]

And it wasn't just handkerchiefs which started to pour in. Many contributions came from servicemen throughout West Germany, while in Chicopee, Massachusetts, an old fire station was converted into an 'assembly station' for what was now being called Operation Little Vittles. No less than twenty-two schools organised themselves to assemble thousands of custom-made cartons, ribbons and handkerchiefs into parachutes and containers for 18 tons of candy and chewing gum contributed from various sources.

The drops also became more organised. Various drop zones were identified and designated on maps. Crews departing from Wiesbaden and Rhein-Main would stop by to pick up their box of sweets and be given a drop zone. Staff organised outings for children at which a candy drop was the highlight. Operation Little Vittles was by the end very much an 'official' operation which even included Halvorsen turning over his job as 'Commander' to another pilot when he got rotated out of Berlin in January 1949.

Symbolic of the entire operation was the role of one key contributor, a representative of the Amercian Confectioners Association. Halvorsen describes his meeting with Mr Swersey as follows:

I arrived at the Manhattan Hotel on time and was greeted by the maitre d'. He ushered me to a beautiful table decorated with a bouquet of fresh flowers and linen napkins. A large, well-proportioned man arose and warmly greeted me. 'I'm Mr Swersey,' he announced without any airs or reservation. 'Have a seat.'

After the last fork was used he got serious. 'I represent the confectioners of the United States and you have already received quite a few supplies. We are really excited about what is going on over there and want to do more. What can we do?'

If I had ever heard of a blank check this was it. . . . I honestly don't remember what that number was. It must have been ridiculous. He didn't even bat an eye.[49]

And he delivered. Just before Christmas a boxcar full of candy, gum and chocolate arrived at Rhein-Main for delivery to Berlin.

What makes the story particularly significant is that Mr Swersey was a Jew, but as he told Halvorsen: 'Kids are the hope of the future and whatever has gone on before is now in the past.' That was the importance of not only Little Vittles but the entire Airlift. The war against Germany was over; the Cold War had begun.

Chapter 13

WINNING THE FIRST CONFRONTATION IN THE COLD WAR

The struggle for control over West Berlin had become the first confrontation of the Cold War. There had been other skirmishes including the loss of Western influence all across Eastern Europe, behind what Winston Churchill dubbed the 'Iron Curtain'. But these battles had largely been lost before the West was even aware of what was at stake. Furthermore, throughout the Cold War, many 'battles' were fought by proxies and fought on the fringes of the superpower's spheres of influence – Korea, Vietnam, Angola. But in Berlin in 1948 the Soviets had provoked an immediate and direct response from the United States right in the heart of Europe.

It was clear to both superpowers that far more was at stake than the right of the Western Allies to remain in Berlin: the battle for Berlin was about the balance of power in Europe. The Soviets had underestimated the willingness of the West Berliners to suffer for their freedom and underestimated the resolve and logistical capabilities of the Western Powers to keep Berlin alive without land access. By December 1948 the Soviets were nevertheless on the brink of victory, and just as no amount of technical capability would have been of use without the political will to continue the Airlift, willpower alone could not win this battle. The Airlift had to be made to meet the minimum needs of the civilian population.

As the New Year started, even without a particularly harsh winter and with Berliners' demands remaining impressively humble, the Airlift was falling short by about 1,000 tons a day. The principal reason for this was that not all the aircraft required, requested and promised were actually flying the Airlift and those that were flying were spending far too much of their time in maintenance and too little of their time 'hauling coal' – or liquid fuel as the case might be.

The problem with the civilian tanker fleet was by this time acute. The conversion of the aircraft to fuel carriers, and the outfitting of those aircraft with the navigational equipment required for Airlift operations, had taken far longer than intended. As a result, instead of the planned fleet of thirty-one tankers on 1 January 1949 only eleven tanker aircraft were available to carry liquid fuel into Berlin. Two weeks later, however, the fleet had grown to twenty and by the end of the month to twenty-seven. In addition to increasing the fleet, a variety of improvements were made in early 1949 to both the departure and receiving airfields to increase the rate at which liquid fuel could be loaded and offloaded. These measures included electric pumps which cut loading times almost in half from 20–25 minutes to 12–14 minutes. Likewise, at the other end, five large tanks fed from eighteen offloading bays around a circular island were installed at Gatow along with floodlights to enable night operations. At Tegel four underground tanks with 160cu. m of storage capacity and the facilities to offload ten aircraft simultaneously were built within fifteen days. Two pipelines fed from the underground tanks at the airfield to a central storage tank 2½km away at Plötzensee. Together, these measures led to a significant increase in aircraft utilisation rates and so to deliveries. The last week in February 1949 marked the turning point for liquid fuel. On that day the daily average of liquid fuel delivered to Berlin exceeded plan, allowing for the building up of reserves to commence. Thereafter, liquid fuel was not a problem.

Meanwhile, Gen Tunner had finally received the support he needed to overcome the obstacles put in his way since command of USAFE had been turned over to Gen Cannon. In addition to Gen Clay, whose nagging finally resulted in the last nineteen of the promised aircraft finally joining the Airlift fleet in January 1949, Tunner obtained the support of the civilian Secretary of the Air Force, Stuart Symington. The latter was travelling through Germany with the US Vice President and the Secretary of the Army. Secretary Symington indicated an interest in seeing the Airlift and Tunner took him at his word. Being a man who never stopped working himself, Tunner took the Cabinet member on a tour of Rhein-Main airbase on Christmas Day. Tunner describes how thoroughly the Secretary carried out his inspection, introducing himself to the men and asking intelligent questions. He quickly saw for himself many of the problems that Tunner had been complaining about. But the climax came when, in Tunner's own words:

we stopped behind a grimy mechanic working on an engine. He looked around to see this obviously important civilian standing over him, flanked by a lieutenant-general [Cannon] and a major-general [Tunner], and tried to come to attention.

'Relax,' Symington said, for the hundredth time that day. 'I'm Stu Symington. Just wanted to see how you're getting along with that engine.'

'Oh, I'm going to get it fixed all right, sir,' the mechanic said, 'but I could do it better if I had better tools.'

'What's the matter with your tools?' Symington asked.

The mechanic held up a screw driver, a wrench, and a pair of pliers. 'See these?' he asked. 'Well, I bought 'em myself right here in Germany, and they're all I got, and I can't get any more, and they ain't worth a good god-damn.'

There was a long silence. Symington looked at me. 'This is what you've been telling me all along,' he said. Cannon turned red. I said nothing; I knew I was ahead. Other men backed up that first mechanic. At the completion of our tour, Symington was all business. He wanted facts and figures furnished him immediately, in black and white. . . . On the morning of the 27th I personally placed in Symington's hands a thorough and meaty memorandum . . . 'Supply and Maintenance Problem – First Airlift Task Force'. It specifically cited the difficulties in 200- and 1,000-hour inspections, level of supplies, shortage of shop equipment, and training of mechanics, as well as the situation in housing facilities and allied matters. Each problem was followed by our recommendation for its solution.[1]

Almost more amazing, the Secretary did not forget what he had learned after returning to Washington. Almost immediately orders started to come down the chain of command giving Tunner virtually everything he wanted from the increase in 200-hour inspections to the arrival of long-needed supplies in a steady flow. 'Frankly I was amazed at both the amount and the immediacy,' Tunner summarises. 'From then on our problems in the areas of housing, inspections and shortages of supplies were of far lesser significance.'

Almost with a single blow, Tunner had at last managed to solve long-standing and festering problems with regard to both maintenance and morale. The delays in getting aircraft back from 200-hour and 1,000-hour checks closed the gap between Clay's idea of how many aircraft the Airlift needed and the number of aircraft the Air Force had allocated.

As the C-54s started returning to their duties much more rapidly, the tonnages started climbing again. Already in January, the Airlift delivered greater tonnage than in any month previous – despite the dark and the cold – just short of 172,000 tons, or more than 5,500 tons per day. Due to a serious deterioration in the weather, February saw a slight drop, but the tonnage delivered was still above any previous month except January, i.e. was still better than October 1948, the best month of the previous year before the winter weather had set in. By March the Airlift was delivering 196,150 tons (an average of 6,327 per day) and in April 1949, the Airlift broke 200,000 tons by a margin of more 35,000 tons. The daily average was now 7,845 tons. More than 26,000 sorties had been flown in the month of April alone. The crisis was over and the Airlift had clearly succeeded.

These improved figures were primarily due to aircraft utilisation rates, but a number of other adjustments also made significant contributions to the overall capacity of the Airlift. One of these was the decision on the part of the British government that the Airlift was a long-term commitment after all. In fact, about this time, the British government came to the conclusion that the Airlift was likely to go on for at least another two years. Once this fact was accepted, the responsible staffs moved away from 'improvisation' and 'muddling through' to careful and thorough long-term planning that took into account the need for training and supplies and maintenance on a continuing basis.

Key to improving British performance was improving the quality and efficiency of the civilian component because the RAF was pretty much performing at peak efficiency already given its resources; the civilian fleet was not. As a BAFO memo put it: '[Civilian] serviceability varies from day to day, the number of sorties which they are ready and able to undertake also varies, and their total daily is unpredictable for planning purposes.'[2]

The RAF viewed the situation as so critical that there was consideration given to requisitioning the civilian aircraft and putting service crews into them – or reactivating the crews and putting them under military discipline. In the end a far better solution was found. The various government departments involved in the civil airlift finally got a committee together that hammered out a new policy including placing all civilian companies under a unified command and, above all, putting the civilian lift on the same long-term basis as the RAF lift.

This entailed a number of adjustments. First, it was decided to restrict the types of aircraft flying the Airlift to make it easier for blocks to maintain timing and spacing. Secondly, the civil air fleet, already concentrated at two departure airfields, Fuhlsbüttel and Schleswigland, was now sent to Tegel (rather than Gatow) reducing the need to thread them through USAF air traffic bound for Tempelhof and RAF air traffic heading for Gatow. To improve morale, housing was provided in hotels in Hamburg while construction began on accommodation blocks at the airfields that would give pilots single rooms and ground crews double rooms. New contracts stipulated a minimum standard of two crews per aircraft and also set measurable minimum servicing standards. Last, but not least, BA's senior representative, who had long been nominally in charge, was now not only freed of all other duties so he could devote himself to running the civil airlift, he was also given the means to control his wayward sheep: the power to conclude or take away contracts.

The need to weed out companies that couldn't or wouldn't pull their weight was critical to the success of the civil airlift. Now, at last, poorly performing companies were sacked and a number of smaller operators disappeared from the Airlift. Other companies were given the ultimatum to convert their operations to tankers or lose their contracts. Meanwhile, the superior companies got proper contracts with three-month notice periods and bonuses for more efficient performance, thereby encouraging both investment and better administration and management.

The results were felt almost at once. Companies like Flight Refuelling and Lancashire Aircraft Corporation restructured their operations and ramped up their maintenance organisation. Flight Refuelling, for example, hired a new executive for Germany, Wg Cdr Johnson, who set about throwing out the bad crews and the drunks, establishing strict rules – and enforcing them. He also engaged eight wireless fitters and ensured that ground staff worked 12-hour shifts with one day off per week and one week off every month. Trips home to the UK were paid at company expense. The ground crews, like the aircrews, were almost all ex-RAF, and they responded well to the new routine. Lancashire Aircraft Corporation was also able to do all the maintenance, installation of navigational equipment and conversion to tankers at its own workshops in England. Now that the contract allowed for long-term planning, the company could engage 16 fully trained aircrews and roughly 100 ground engineers, all based in Germany, to keep its fleet of 13 tankers operating. And it did.

Already in March the number of sorties flown by civilian aircraft on the Airlift increased from 54 to 70 per day, and the number of flights continued to increase until June 1949 when, after the lifting of the blockade, the Airlift peaked and started to wind down. In the period between January and June 1949 the civil airlift was extremely well run and efficient. Leonard Vincent Knowles, a wireless fitter, who worked on the Airlift with the RAF until December 1948 and thereafter with Flight Refuelling, claims that by April 1949 there were clear schedules in 4-hour cycles that enabled every aircraft to make 6 flights to Berlin in every 24-hour period. There were workshops 'purpose-built' for the lift, accommodations in hotels in Hamburg were first rate and, due to the discipline introduced by Wg Cdr Johnson, anyone responsible for a flight getting cancelled – whether it was a pilot due to drunkenness or a fitter who overlooked something in a daily inspection that resulted in unserviceability – was subject to instant dismissal. Knowles noted that although he didn't hear of anyone actually getting the sack, a new pride in accomplishment – even competition for punctuality and the best serviceability records – ensued. Clearly the civil airlift had been turned around.

Meanwhile, other changes were made to improve efficiency of the Airlift as a whole. The USAF converted a squadron of Flying Fortresses into weather observation aircraft based at Burtonwood, which flew over the Atlantic reporting to Wiesbaden on weather conditions; as a result long-range weather forecasting improved. Pilots were also issued handbooks with the instrument approach charts for twenty-six different airfields in Europe in case they had to divert due to weather. The RAF made a very unique contribution to the problem of birds flying in the corridors; they deployed a team of trained RAF falcons to Gatow that preyed in a natural way upon the local bird population – and kept them out of aircraft engines.

The capabilities of GCA had also increased. There were two sets of GCA at each airfield and each GCA controller handled aircraft at 2-minute intervals, which meant each controller was directing three aircraft in the traffic pattern at one time. One USAF GCA controller stationed at Wiesbaden remembers: 'On an 8-hour shift I would talk down three blocks of twenty-eight C-54s, roughly one a minute. The weather was zero/zero and after landing a cleat track would have to tow the aircraft to the loading zone because the pilot couldn't see the lights on the taxi strips.'[3]

Pilots on GCA approach were instructed *not* to reply to the instructions as was standard procedure in civil aviation. Instead pilots were told to simply obey instructions instantly. If they received no instruction for longer than 5 seconds, they were to climb to 800ft and return to the last navigation beacon. In theory, enough time was allowed between aircraft to permit adequate separation in the event of a missed approach. Aircraft missing their approach might be diverted to one of the other two airfields in Berlin if there was a break in the traffic – or they might be sent back to their home base.

Modern readers should note that although Airlift pilots almost uniformly report feeling very safe, in fact by today's standards the equipment was very primitive. Another problem was the sheer dependency on voice communications; these were limited by the channels available and were subject to interference due to intentional jamming and weather conditions. Still, at the time of operation, these were the most sophisticated means of air traffic control in operation anywhere in the world – and they worked.

Another important improvement was an end to the system of 4-hour blocks. This system, introduced early in the Airlift, had often resulted in Dakotas and Yorks sitting around waiting for hours until the next available 'slot' came up. It had been replaced over time first with 2-hour and then later with 1-hour blocks. This meant that by early 1949 almost all aircraft, regardless of their capacity or whether they were taking on return cargoes or not, rarely had to wait long to get back into the stream of traffic. For the notoriously undisciplined civilians, the previous practice of just 'popping in and making a mess of an RAF block' was halted; if the civilians missed their time slot they too had to sit on the ground just like everyone else – and that meant losing money. Very soon the companies themselves started to sharpen discipline as noted earlier.

Flying in the corridors was also much more strictly regulated. To the outsider it looked as if 'the machines came so close behind one another it was like a train with wings'.[4] But it was really much more complicated than that. Sqn Ldr Robinson, a veteran of over 200 Airlift sorties remembers:

> A typical stream would consist of a block of twelve RAF Yorks from Wunstorf in line, 2 minutes apart. At the first turning point we would slot in behind a block of say, twelve USAF Skymasters, who slotted in behind twelve RAF Dakotas, and later possibly twelve RAF Hastings aircraft like a continuous, often unbroken conveyor belt all the way to the Northern corridor and on into Berlin via Frohau Beacon, where we split and diverted to our particular airfields of Gatow, Tempelhof or Tegel.[5]

To keep such a system functioning, aircraft now not only reported with their call sign as they passed key beacons, they also reported the number of seconds early or late, their air speed and whether this was increasing or decreasing. Altogether the Airlift was becoming very routine.

A York pilot remembered these latter days of the lift as follows:

> You reported to the Ops Room and you were given an aircraft, rather like booking a boat on a lake, and you went out and found it and you clambered in and you had a sheet of paper that told you what time to start up and what time to taxi, and how long the slot was for the airfield; Wunstorf characteristically might be twenty aircraft, so had a half-hour sortie 'gate' as it were, a slot, and there was no question of flexibility on this.[6]

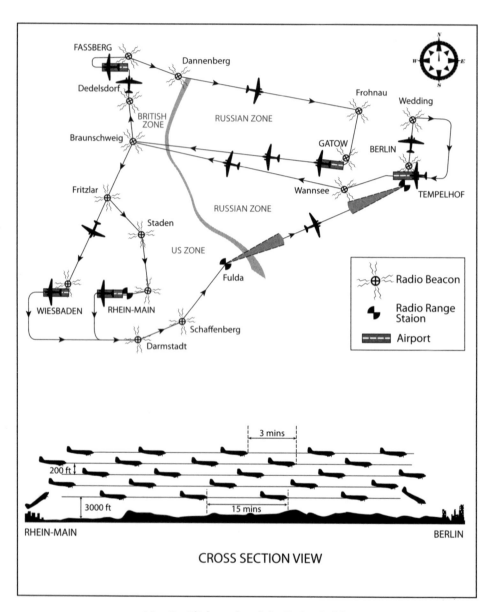

FASSBERG
Dannenberg
Dedelsdorf
BRITISH ZONE
RUSSIAN ZONE
Braunschweig
Frohnau
Wedding
GATOW
BERLIN
Fritzlar
Wannsee
TEMPELHOF
Staden
RUSSIAN ZONE
US ZONE
Fulda
WIESBADEN
RHEIN-MAIN
Schaffenberg
Darmstadt

Radio Beacon

Radio Range Staion

Airport

3 mins

200 ft

3000 ft

15 mins

RHEIN-MAIN

BERLIN

CROSS SECTION VIEW

Map 3: Flight paths of the Berlin Airlift.

The American routine was slightly different but essentially the same:

> Usually each pilot was informed the day before of the time he was required to report to the flight line. . . . Upon arriving at the ready room, pilots were briefed on expected weather and winds, and given a flight plan detailing relevant on route information such as headings, times over points on route and so on. They were also informed of any unusual conditions or activity going on in the corridor. When the C-54 assigned to a particular crew was brought on line, a taxi and take-off time was assigned to it by Operations. This time had to be adhered to very closely, so the aircraft from different bases could slot into their assigned places in the flow of traffic in the corridor. . . .
>
> Crews reported to their aircraft 20 to 30 minutes prior to taxi time. A pre-flight check was completed, and the load checked with the loading crew. The engine run-up was carried out after the aircraft had taxied to the end of the runway; after informing the tower that he was ready for take-off the pilot then awaited instructions, including the en route altitude through the corridor.[7]

When returning, the routine was as follows:

> On initial contact with GCA the pilot reported the condition of his aircraft and whether or not he was loaded. Aircraft which required no maintenance before making another trip were reported 'positive', those that required maintenance as 'negative'. Similarly, loaded aircraft were reported as 'positive' and unloaded aircraft were as 'negative' – so a loaded aircraft requiring no maintenance would be reported as 'positive, positive'. If the aircraft was serviceable on landing it was immediately assigned another taxi and take-off time. The pilot reported to Operations, where he was given another flight plan – then 30 minutes before the scheduled taxi time it was back to the aircraft. . . .[8]

On average this worked out to each crew flying between two and three round trips to Berlin a day.

All this routine and precision naturally tended to make flying the Airlift monotonous and a bit boring. To counter this, the pilots kept up a great deal of repartee over the airwaves that helped keep everyone awake. Not everyone approved. One American Airlift veteran remembers one night when his crew was joking around and suddenly a British voice interrupted the 'merry making' by saying: 'This is Wing Commander (name forgotten). You Yanks are to maintain strict radio silence!' As he reports: 'Everything went dead until out of the void came a soft voice saying, 'I wonder if the * * * really is a wing commander.'[9]

Gen Tunner, however, otherwise a terrible stickler for flying 'by the book' and following rules to the letter, recognised the importance of this 'wisecracking' and joking. Professional that he was, he realised that bored pilots are more likely to get careless and so more likely to make mistakes – particularly in an environment like the Airlift where precision counts. The fact that he tolerated the flippancy and non-regulation communication that filled the airwaves during the Airlift is testimony to its importance; and everyone who flew the Airlift remembers it with affection.

Unfortunately, very little of this chatter survives (and some would have been unprintable in any case), and almost none of the humour inherent in it can be conveyed to the uninitiated reader. In its mildest form it involved some kind of play on the call-sign of an aircraft: 333, for example, was turned into 'State Express' because this was a well-known brand of cigarette at the time, the Lancastrian with the call-sign 'TB' only announced his presence by coughing, and the Tudor with the call sign 'CD', usually converted to 'D- for Dog', responded to communications in the positive by saying 'woof'. The Americans, it is said, corrupted the designation for the key beacon north of Berlin, Frohnau, into 'fraulein' and dutifully reported their position as 'on top of the fraulein'.

Other remarks were nothing more than quick wit made hilarious by unexpectedness and the fact that it usually came 'out of the blue', such as the American pilot who overheard a hot exchange between AVM Bennett and a controller and defused the situation anonymously by remarking in a heavy American accent, 'Hey, if you guys are gonna start shooting down there, I just ain't gonna land this ship.'[10] Or, in another instance, a pilot reported he had 'lost' his No. 3 engine, only to promptly receive the helpful advice from a colleague over the airwaves that he should 'try looking on the starboard wing'.

A pilot who bounced on landing invariably had an audience counting the number in a loud chorus of 'One, Two, Three, Four . . .'. Commentary on flying techniques was standard operating procedure, and the controllers were not above asking pilots to 'please take better care of our runway next time' and the like.

Much of the humour depended on 'being there', 'being an insider', knowing the rules, the personalities, the popular songs, radio shows and film personalities of the time – and the individuals involved. As one RAF pilot stressed, since the RAF flew in squadrons and knew each other well, they recognised voices over the R/T and knew more about one another than merely the professional side. They often used christian names rather than call-signs.

Last, but not least, much of Airlift humour depended on accent. Both British and Americans took pleasure in teasing each other about their respective means of 'mutilating' a common tongue. Accents could also lead to confusion. Controllers at Gatow expecting an RAF Dakota were astonished to hear a broad Great Plains accent coming over the airwaves. Instantly assuming that a USAF C-54 had somehow slipped into the pattern by mistake, they enquired of the aircraft: '123, are you a Skymaster?' To which the pilot (a Canadian as it turned out) replied in his drawl, 'Ah don't think so. Ah'll take a look. Ah was a Dakota when Ah took off, but maybe Ah've growed some.'[11]

From the perspective of the ground crews working at the departure airfields, the routine was equally well organised and looked like this:

There was usually a 'wave' of RAF aircraft and then a 'wave' of civilian machines of all sorts. After a 'wave' had taken off a 'wave' of machines returning empty would promptly land, taxi in to the appropriate parking area and would be set upon by refuellers, servicing personnel, and loaders all feverishly preparing for the next trip. . . . While we refuelled the aircraft, it was being loaded with supplies.[12]

There was a downside to all this efficiency; a USAF pilot said he never knew the ground crews, or even what squadron he was flying with. Furthermore, the very precision and comprehensiveness of the GCA tended to deglamorise the entire operation. According to Jack O. Bennett, pilots wisecracked that 'a smart monkey could be trained to bring the airplane in on instruments with this backup'.[13] Flt Lt 'Ted' Edwards remembers that 'the crew was fond of turning on George [the autopilot] . . . and retreating to the main cabin for a round of cards, much to the anxiety of the already nervous German passengers'.[14] An RAF radio operator provides another example of how routine it had all become. On one flight into Berlin his skipper dozed off and was asleep as they made their first radio contact with air traffic control in Berlin. The Master Signaller decided he didn't need to awaken the pilot and turned the aircraft himself onto the course and altitude prescribed:

With undercarriage lowered, flaps extended, and the runway dead ahead, I suddenly decided I had gone as far as I dared and gave the pilot a dig in the ribs. He awoke with a start; I advised him that I had done my bit, and it was time for him to complete the trip.

'You have come this far, why not take it on in?' responded the skipper.

'I like living.'[15]

With more regular, predictable flying times, it also became easier to schedule crews and their days off. Rather than the hectic disorganisation of the early days that left pilots exhausted and sleeping under desks or in the cockpits, regular hours were introduced. True, these still required night shifts, but these were now predictable and rewarded regularly with time off. For example, at Flight Refuelling, the routine called for two crews to be assigned to each aircraft. Each crew was expected to fly 50 hours every 8 days. At the end of that time, the aircraft was due for a 100-hour check and the two crews flew their own aircraft back to the UK and received two days' leave while the aircraft was being overhauled. Then they returned with their aircraft for a new cycle.

As an RAF flight engineer put it:

> As time went along things became more organised, crews were allocated numbers, routines more established with an aircraft returning to base for servicing with two or three crew members aboard nearly every day. It worked out that every month we had 5 days home on leave. It became so regular that the barber I went to in Leeds each time thought I was shooting a line when I told him where I was stationed.[16]

Some pilots remember flying for ten days and rotating back to England for four, others recall flying twenty-one days and then going home for a week. As one RAF cynic put it, the system was designed to 'maintain the fiction that the squadron was still based in the UK, thus saving the RAF the expense of providing dependant quarters in Germany'.[17] Regardless of the rationale behind the system, by and large the men flying the Airlift found it a workable and far from onerous rotation system.

Training was another key improvement as the Airlift dragged out far longer than initially anticipated. As Tunner reiterated, a major morale problem for his crews – who could not get home regularly like the British – was the fact that they were on 'indefinite' temporary duty with no idea of when they would see their families again. Only after a system for rotating crews out on a regular basis had been worked out could this problem be solved. Since the USAF had deployed virtually every crew with four-engine experience they had, there was no possibility for rotating crews out until replacement crews had been trained. The USAF recognised the problem early and called up reservists with four-engine experience, but it felt that it would be asking too much of men who had been away from flying for three or more years (and generally had no transport experience) to put them straight on the Airlift.

Instead, on 1 October 1948 a flight school was established at Great Falls, Montana, dedicated exclusively to preparing recalled pilots for Airlift flying conditions. As many as twenty-nine complete crews at a time underwent three weeks of training on a course with navigation beacons set up to replicate the approach from the American Zone into Tempelhof. The course called for 133 hours' flying and included practising flying in blocks, precise timing between beacons, using GCA etc. Plans called for 100 crews to complete training each month, but this proved too ambitious and in fact only fifty crews 'graduated' each month. These were first used to increase the crew-to-aircraft ratio and only later to replace experienced crews. This was in part because the USAF found that despite the three-week course in Montana, the reservists took considerable time adjusting to Airlift conditions – particularly weather – and procedures. Thus chief pilots and check pilots were used by the USAF to ensure that pilots on the Airlift were up to standard – and stayed that way.

With regard to maintenance, once Tunner had control of the facilities at Burtonwood, he instituted what he termed 'production-line maintenance' or PLM. What this entailed was dividing all the tasks required for maintenance into discrete steps and having maintenance crews specialise. In short, the same men performed the same task over and over again on each aircraft while the aircraft moved from station to station – like a product moving down an assembly line. Using this system, Burtonwood operated 24 hours a day, 7 days a week, stopping only if they ran out of aircraft to service because weather had prevented them flying in at the expected rate.

The RAF by contrast not only maintained the principle of a specific crew doing all the maintenance on an aircraft, they rotated the ground crews through various jobs to keep them from getting bored and ensure their ability to perform a variety of tasks. This meant that any of the crew could jump in and perform any routine servicing if a colleague was absent for some reason. Given the high praise earned by RAF ground crews, it is fair to say that what Tunner's system gained in short-term efficiency it lost in terms of well-trained, thinking crews capable of dealing with the unexpected or unusual.

Another RAF innovation was the 'plumber flight'. A little fleet of six Dakotas, including air and ground crews, was dedicated to flying in spare parts and tools for the maintenance of the RAF's Airlift aircraft. The 'plumber flight' ensured that the RAF's mechanics were never reduced to the extremes of Tunner's – buying inadequate tools on the local market. It flew between 400 and 500 tons of parts monthly and it made its vitally important contribution to the Airlift without fanfare.

On the other hand, another of Tunner's innovations was to use the 1,000-hour inspections at Burtonwood to strip unnecessary equipment off the C-54s. Roughly 2,200lb of 'excess' equipment was removed from the Airlift C-54s increasing their payload by a comparable amount. The reduction in equipment had the added benefit of reducing maintenance times since the excess equipment no longer needed to be serviced.

Meanwhile, improvements continued to be made on the airfields as well. The most important of which was the second 6,500ft runway at Tegel. This runway was laid down with an additional 1,500ft base to allow for future expansion. The USAF was already envisaging the day when the C-54s would be replaced by larger transport aircraft requiring longer runways. Also notable was that in the meantime enough heavy construction equipment had been flown in by the method of dissection and reconstruction described above that this second runway could be built by just 400 labourers and supervisory technicians as opposed to the 19,000 Berliners and 165 US Army Corps of Engineers personnel required to build the first runway. At Tempelhof two parallel runways were now also continuously in operation; one for landing and one for take-off.

Improvements in cargo-handling efficiency were fairly steady and incremental as they did not entail massive infrastructure projects. The construction of better roads, more warehousing capacity and better organisation all contributed. Simple things like painting the number of the aircraft in large black letters on the tail fin for easy identification and assigning numbers to the offloading ramps helped both ground crews and pilots get where they belonged rapidly. At all events, by early 1949 the Airlift systems for handling cargo had been continuously improved and refined until they reached a very high standard of efficiency.

At Gatow, cargo-handling now started at the Load Control Centre, a motley collection of Nissen huts a few hundred yards away from the operations building and directly overlooking the airfield. Here all personnel responsible for seeing that cargoes were properly configured and loaded were collected under one roof. There were RAF Engineer Officers, RAF Movement Control (for marshalling aircraft) and Royal Army Service Corps Load Control and Motor Transport Officers. When roughly 20 miles away from Berlin, arriving aircraft radioed in what cargoes they were carrying, particularly if they had awkward cargoes or one requiring special handling. The Load Control Officer estimated offloading time and then assigned a 'load crew' to the aircraft and the RAF Movement Control Officer assigned the hardstanding.

When returning to their home bases, the aircraft again radioed in to report whether they were empty or carrying return cargoes. The RAF Engineer

Officers were then responsible for seeing that refuelling and servicing crews knew where to find the aircraft, while RASC Load Control got the load crew to the same location. As one veteran summed it up: 'We knew exactly how many aircraft were available, how much and what kind [of cargo] had to go into each aircraft and exactly when they had to start-up and take off.'[18]

By the start of 1949, load crews handled 24 per cent more cargo with 24 per cent fewer trucks and 22 per cent less workers. Whereas in the early days of the lift as many as twenty men were in a load crew and worked to the very limits of their physical capabilities, now crews were standardised at twelve men except in special circumstances. There were on average thirty of these crews working each shift at each airfield. The shifts lasted from 7 a.m. to 3 p.m., from 3 p.m. to 11 p.m., and from 11 p.m. to 7 a.m. No one worked overtime as this would have disrupted the shift system. Each load crew usually unloaded between five and six aircraft during a shift or – on record days – ten aircraft. According to one loader, 'the night shift was the least busy, but one used the free time to, for example, bundle the empty cargo sacks and prepare them to send back to West Germany'.[19] Daytimes were generally hectic. Between jobs, the men waited in tents where they could warm up, relax and rest, but when their next assigned aircraft arrived they went to work.

When we rushed out of the tent onto the airport apron to the approaching C-54 another group was just returning for a rest, tired and sweaty from the strenuous exercise. While the propellers of the aircraft were still turning, the wheels slowly grinding to a standstill, an empty truck drew up to the plane, and within seconds a ramp was placed across the plane's cargo door. Then six of our men jumped into the aircraft, the rest distributed themselves on the truck, forming a working cordon to save as much time as possible. The first man picked up a sack of coal, flour or food and threw it to the next man and so on until it was all stacked onto the truck. Within a few minutes the guys from the interior of the plane had moved to the outside with the last sack and all men were back in the truck.[20]

These methods reduced the average time needed to offload a C-54 full of coal from 20–25 minutes down to an average of 7–10 minutes, and then again down to an average of 6 minutes. As the Airlift was winding down after the lifting of the blockade itself, the station commanders of the three airfields in Berlin held a contest for the fastest unloading crew. A reward of $50 and three extra days off work was offered, but most crews were by now motivated by pride. Hans Günther's load crew won with a record time for 180 sacks of coal from a C-54 of 4 minutes and 30 seconds.

Competition was not just between load crews. Tunner consciously and consistently tried to foster competition between the various units under his command and between the different airfields. He set goals for each base and recorded the results daily on huge 'Howgozit' boards where everyone could see – and compare. Tunner claims that:

> The chief topic of conversation on every base was the daily tonnage records. Visitors to the Airlift were amazed by the spirit of competition. . . . The intense rivalry even spread to the loading and unloading groups. . . . We encouraged enthusiasm with prizes – usually cigarettes, worth their weight in gold – for outstanding performances.[21]

And if one was going to keep track of progress and set goals, then obviously one had to go through the motions of celebrating the achievement of goals and the passing of milestones. In fact, these ceremonies became so common that when a York captain found a large reception committee waiting for him on landing he 'thought he must have done something special – the millionth ton or thousand-something sortie. He asked the reception committee, "What's all this about?" To which he received the answer: "Don't you realise you've lost your control tail fin?" It wasn't a reception committee at all but the accident crew come to clean him up off the runway.'[22]

Competition also breeds rivalry which took some odd, unintended forms during the Airlift. It is said that Tudor pilots were so proud of their aircraft that they liked to 'show off' a bit to the C-54s. One Tudor pilot allegedly liked to 'pick on a C-54 about to turn out of the control corridor towards his base, put on all power, dive until he was level with the C-54, then feather both the engines the American could see and roar past with a cheerful smile and insouciant wave'.[23] But the most important competition was that sponsored and carefully managed by the CALTF commander himself.

By April 1949 Tunner had under his command 154 assorted British aircraft and 200 Skymasters in serviceable condition 'hauling cargo'. Selecting a period of predicted good weather – which happened this year to coincide with Easter – he decided to show the world what the Airlift could do, and to fire up his bored ('they can teach monkeys to fly the Lift') crews a little. He stockpiled more coal than usual, and then ensured that in the 24-hour period selected for his demonstration, most of the aircraft would be loaded with this uniform, straightforward cargo. He then very deliberately and not at all subtly incited a spirit of competition between his staff and subordinates and the 'Easter Parade' was on. Tunner describes it:

I shuttled back and forth between Berlin and the bases, applying a needle here, a pat on the back there. At Celle . . . the boys were carrying on their constant feud with Fassberg . . . with a determination greater than usual. The base was running 12 per cent ahead of its quota. It was long after midnight before I reached Fassberg. Things were really humming. Connie Bennett* was down on the flight line with a group of other wives serving coffee and doughnuts. Her husband, Jack Coulter, came up to me with a big grin. He was running 10 per cent ahead of quota, he told me proudly.

'That's fine,' I said, 'but of course it's not up to what they're doing over at Celle. They're really on the ball over there.'

And so on and so forth until:

Dawn was breaking when I reached my office . . . and I went to the cafeteria for breakfast. Then I got the latest word: we had already hit 10,000 tons, with several hours yet to go. Every unit was running well ahead of its special quota, and the weather was improving.

By mid-morning we were no longer able to keep the secret, and I certainly didn't care. General Clay sent his congratulations on whatever it was we were doing, and wanted to know what that was. I sent word back that it was an Easter present for Berlin. Any member of the press corps who hadn't smelled something in the air already got the official word from Clay's headquarters, and the correspondents descended on us in droves. We were nearing the twenty-third and twenty-fourth hour of solid work now, but you'd have never known it; the thrill of accomplishment was more powerful than fatigue. And finally the noon hour drew near, and the Easter Parade would soon be over. Time for only one more plane. Someone toted up the final score and ran out to the plane with a paint brush and a bucket of red paint.

TONS: 12,941
FLIGHTS: 1,398

In the entire daily operation, we had not had one accident, not one injury.[24]

Even more important, the Easter Parade was not a single extravaganza but had a sustained impact on the daily averages. Whereas in the days prior to the Easter Parade daily averages in good weather had been around 6,700 tons, in the post-Easter period the daily averages stood at just under 9,000 tons per day. This was double Clay's initial estimate of Berlin's daily minimum requirement.

April 1949 saw another significant, if more symbolic, milestone. Five aircraft were diverted from the Airlift to fly products from Berlin factories to the

Industrial Fair at Hannover. A total of 120 Berlin companies took part in this, the most important of Germany's industrial fairs. The products were stamped with a Berlin Bear, shown breaking the chain that was wrapped around him, and with the words: Made in Blockaded Berlin. Maybe the products themselves were not the very 'cutting edge' of technology, but they demonstrated Berlin's continued survival, not just as a patient being fed intravenously so-to-speak, but as an entity with the will to support itself again as soon as possible. In short, these products represented Berlin's spirit of defiance and, perhaps more than anything else, helped give Berlin back its pride.

Planning by the Berlin authorities also underwent a fundamental change. Instead of calculating the bare minimum for subsistence, the responsible staffs started to work out schemes to slowly but surely increase the standard of living of the inhabitants. It helped that with the advent of spring, Berlin's many open spaces and balconies could again be turned into kitchen gardens producing fresh vegetables and herbs, but this was not the whole story. The planners were concerned about providing a more varied diet, not just getting the maximum number of calories packed into the lowest volume and weight. They wanted to ensure that hospitals had all the medical supplies required, and they wanted to increase the domestic coal-heating ration. Perhaps an even greater luxury would be delivering electricity throughout the city 6 hours per day. This, in turn, would enable factories to work longer, thereby reducing unemployment. With factories working longer hours, of course, calculations had to be made for the import of more raw materials, spare parts and even replacement machinery. The Airlift could now be expected to meet these needs too – as well as fly out more goods produced in the city. The planners even started to plan longer hours for public transport and to calculate for one-third of the potato ration to be in fresh rather than dried form. To meet all these goals, it was calculated that the daily delivery to Berlin would have to average roughly 11,250 tons per day – or roughly what had been delivered by road and rail before the start of the blockade.

By the time spring came in 1949, virtually no one doubted that this could be done. On the contrary, the morale of the crews and ground personnel on the Airlift was high, not just because the problems with food, housing and rotations had been solved, but because the men involved clearly saw and felt that they were winning. So much so that the Air Forces of Britain and the United States calmly set about working out the details of flying in 12,000 tons a day while assuming that they would be maintaining this huge operation for another two to three years. The question was no longer one of how long the West could maintain the Airlift but rather how long the Russians would insist on their futile blockade.

Chapter 14

'HURRAH! WE'RE STILL ALIVE'

It appears that Stalin came to the conclusion that his Berlin strategy was not paying off at the end of January 1949. January was the critical month in which all had hung in the balance. At the start of the month there was still hope, from Stalin's perspective, that the Airlift would collapse. January started with West Berlin's liquid fuel reserves depleted and coal reserves being drawn down at an alarming rate while even minimum target tonnages were not being met on a regular basis. By the end of the month, however, liquid fuel was being delivered at rates unknown before, coal reserves were not being drawn down and the standard food ration in West Berlin had actually been increased by more than 15 per cent. Under the circumstances, Stalin faced the fact that his last ally, General Winter, had abandoned him. On 30 January he sent an arcane message to the West signalling his willingness to reopen negotiations about the situation in Berlin.

The form used for this message was a press interview with the American International News Service in which – among other things – Stalin listed the conditions for the lifting of the blockade. He cited the need for the West to desist from establishing a West German state and the need for a non-aggression pact with the Soviet Union. What he did *not* mention was a roll-back of the currency reform that had allegedly sparked the blockade in the first place.

Western 'Kremlinologists' – that species of scholar devoted to reading the opaque and obscure signals sent from the Kremlin during the Cold War – interpreted this omission as significant. Via an 'unofficial' channel – namely a chance meeting between the US deputy representative to the UN and the Soviet Ambassador thereto, the US administration enquired if the omission was intentional. Since the Soviet Ambassador did not know the answer, he had to get instructions from Moscow. Eventually, in early March the enigmatic reply came back: no, the omission was not unintentional. Stalin had signalled 'flexibility' on the Berlin issue.

Building on this information and using the same channel, the US groped slowly towards a lifting of the blockade. The negotiations were so secret that not even Gen Clay knew about them. The British and French were not let in on the secret until 21 March. The Foreign Office was miffed, but Bevin ignored the professional pique about the 'amateur' means of the American negotiations and noted in his own hand: 'Watch this. Stalin may now raise the blockade.'[1] Thereafter, both the British and French were involved in the continuing negotiations, but only at the highest levels.

The talks remained highly secret, tentative and – after so much negative experience with Stalin's wily ways – not even those who knew about them really trusted them to produce results. The two Air Forces actually running the Airlift were at all events kept in the dark, and continued to plan on maintaining the Airlift for two, three or even ten more years.

Even more important, the torturous process of drafting a German constitution that would fulfil the criteria of democracy set by the Western Allies also continued. There were many setbacks and unpleasant exchanges; the process was not always conducted in the best spirit of goodwill and trust, but eventually the deal was done. A 'basic law' was hammered out between the leaders of the political parties represented in the Parliamentary Council – which was composed of political representatives from the Western Zones – and the Military Governors approved it. This draft was agreed upon on 25 April 1949 for presentation to a plenary session of the Parliamentary Council on 15 May. The way to the establishment of an independent West German state was now free. This was probably the development that Stalin had been most determined to prevent when he imposed the blockade – and what he was probably still trying to prevent by offering to lift it.

A WAR OF NERVES

Meanwhile, behind closed doors, the Soviets were bickering with the Americans about when the 'traffic restrictions' to Berlin had been imposed – denying any interference with the Allies prior to 30 March. They also insisted on the restoration of Four Power negotiations about 'the fate of Germany as a whole' via a Council of Foreign Ministers. The Allies were negotiating from strength and with time on their side. They could afford to agree to a Council of Foreign Ministers, since they didn't promise to agree to anything proposed or discussed there. They most specifically and tenaciously did *not* agree to stop the process of establishing an independent and sovereign West German state. They set their own (modest) demands concerning the date 'traffic restrictions commenced' (1 March) and the date for the start of the Council of Foreign

Ministers (23 May) and the date the blockade must end: 12 May. The Soviets accepted them all. The results of these bizarre negotiations were made public on 5 May 1949.

They were undoubtedly a press sensation, but they were not greeted with uproarious jubilation in Germany – especially not in Berlin. Neither the Occupation authorities nor the Berliners trusted the Soviets. The Occupation authorities had the added burden of trying to work out all the details not covered in the political agreements worked out in distant Washington and Moscow. Nothing had been agreed about currency, for example, or electricity. Nevertheless, plans went ahead for both road convoys and trainloads of supplies for Berlin to be ready to test the agreement at one minute after midnight on the morning of 12 May. Equally important, the Parliamentary Council approved the 'basic law' ahead of schedule on 9 May 1949.

The Soviets showed their hand the next day. They started imposing arbitrary restrictions on the movement of goods by surface transport even before it had resumed. They insisted that all trains were to be pulled by East German locomotives and manned by East German personnel. Furthermore, there was a maximum limit set on the number of trains per day: sixteen goods trains and six passenger trains. Thus although the lights came on again all over Berlin on the night of 11 May, and barriers on the autobahn came down at one minute after midnight on 12 May, no one really trusted the 'peace'.

What this meant for the Allies was that the Airlift was maintained at full throttle. It did not miss a beat – or take-off and landing, in this case. To be sure, supplies of *additional* goods might now be flowing into Berlin by road, raid and canal, but the Western objective was to build up reserves of all necessities in the city in anticipation of the *next* Soviet blockade. The expectation was that it might come sooner rather than later – if the Council of Foreign Ministers didn't go the way the Soviets wanted. The general consensus was that it was necessary to build up a five- to six-month reserve of supplies and above all to retain the institutions and organisations for running an Airlift intact even after that goal had been attained. Plans called for the resumption of full Airlift operations if and when the Soviets reimposed a blockade.

The Berliners' fear was even greater. They feared that after all they had gone through, and all the determination they had shown in the face of adversity for the sake of political freedom, that the West would still 'sell them down the river' at the Council of Foreign Ministers. Unfortunately for them, there was nothing they could do but watch and wait.

The Council of Foreign Ministers, which convened in Paris on 23 May 1949 turned out to be nothing more than a warmed-over rerun of all previous Councils of Foreign Ministers. The Soviets first condemned the new West German constitution as 'monopolistic capitalism', the Federalist structure was called 'Hitlerite centralism' and majority decision-making was 'non-democratic'. In short, their commentary was pure ideological drivel without content. Rather than sovereignty under such an 'oppressive' constitution, the Soviets suggested that the Germans should be returned to Four Power government – where the Soviet Union had a veto on everything. Dean Acheson allegedly summarised the Soviet position as meaning that 'everything in Berlin would require Kommandatura approval except dying'.[2] The best that can be said for this final meeting of the Council of Foreign Ministers is that it convinced the West they had acted correctly by introducing a sound currency in their Zones and moving forward with an independent West German state – and that they were wise to continue to build up reserves in Berlin. In the second half of July, both the British Cabinet and the American Security Council approved keeping two RAF transport squadrons and two USAF carrier groups respectively stationed indefinitely in Germany.

It was a wise decision. Already the Soviets were showing their muscle on the surface routes. Trains were routinely turned back for 'technical difficulties'; lorries carrying supplies for the civilian population were turned back because the autobahns were suddenly only open for supplies intended for the Allied garrisons; rolling stock was arbitrarily impounded; mail was confiscated wholesale, and it became impractical to send it by surface at all. When the railway workers went on strike demanding payment in West Marks, reinstatement of fired workers and recognition for their independent (not SED-controlled) union, the city of Berlin was again almost totally dependent on the Airlift for another thirty-eight days. Meanwhile, the SED officials insisted both publicly and privately that the lifting of the blockade was just 'temporary'. They claimed it had been undertaken only to clear up some 'bottlenecks' in East German production resulting from the counter-blockade – a backhanded admission of the comparative failure of the Eastern economy. The SED assured its constituents that the blockade *would* be reimposed just as soon as these 'technical' difficulties had been overcome.

What was even more alarming, the Soviets increased fighter activity in the corridors and 'unilaterally' narrowed the corridors from 20 to 9 miles. The Western Allies ignored the latest unilateral 'directive' just as they had ignored earlier ones about filing their flight plans in advance with the Soviet authorities etc. Nevertheless, the signal was ominous.

The Soviets were to make sporadic attempts to put pressure on West Berlin throughout the Cold War. The electricity supplies were disrupted twice in 1950 and stability was only briefly purchased in exchange for selling East Germany electricity from a power plant in Hamburg. In 1952, East Germany abruptly cancelled this agreement and simultaneously announced the end to all electricity deliveries to West Berlin, but they had miscalculated the impact; by then the modern 'Ernst Reuter' power plant, built during the Airlift, was capable of supplying all the electricity that West Berlin needed. The impact of the Soviet move was nil, so the Soviets looked for, and found, a different means of striking out at Berlin: they cut off all telephone connections between West Berlin and the East without warning.

So the war of nerves continued. Khrushchev allegedly bragged that he had the West 'by the balls' in Berlin and needed only to 'squeeze' to make them squeal. He demanded troop withdrawals in 1958. In August 1961, he allowed a massive and militarily defended wall to be built completely around the Western Sectors of the city isolating it physically as well as politically. It was not until 1972, under his successor, that a Four Power agreement finally 'normalised' the situation in and around Berlin, but West Berlin was still enclosed in a wall and governed by Occupation Statutes as modified by agreements between the victorious Powers of the Second World War. Berlin did not become an integral part of Germany until reunification in 1990.

LIFTING THE BLOCKADE

The West kept up the Airlift unabated throughout the summer of 1949. At the end of July it was clear that sufficient stockpiles had been built up to justify a gradual phase out of Airlift operations. Planning was based on the assumption that five months of supplies would give the West time to ramp up a new airlift. Plans called for any such new airlift to be fully operational within ninety days of a new blockade, and the expectation was that it would be able to deploy the larger transport aircraft already in the pipeline. These aircraft would be capable of transporting the same tonnages achieved at the end of the Airlift in far fewer sorties and hence at lower risk and cost.

So the phase out of the Airlift started on 1 August 1949, when the US Navy squadrons and the USAF Group at Celle ended their operations and prepared to return home. The British government started to let contracts with the civilian charter companies expire. On 12 August, the Airlift went on the 'five-day work week' for the first time in its history. On 16 August the last civilian flight on the Airlift was logged. The last Airlift sortie by an RAF

York took place on 26 August and the last Airlift sortie by an RAF Hastings was flown on 6 September. In the meantime, the Combined Airlift Task Force HQ had been closed and command of remaining operations turned over to the Commanding General of the US 1st Airlift Task Force and the AOC of the RAF's No. 46 Group respectively. The RAF closed down its Airlift operations as it had started them: with a Dakota flight. The last Dakota of the Berlin Airlift landed in Berlin from Lübeck on 23 September bearing the message on its nose: Psalm 21, verse 11: *For they intended evil against thee; they imagined a mischievous device, which they were not able to perform.* One week later, on 30 September 1949 the last US aircraft on the Airlift, appropriately a C-54, flew the last Airlift cargo to Berlin. The Airlift officially ended at midnight on that day.

So what had it achieved? First and foremost, of course, a city of over 2 million people had been kept alive for ten-and-a-half months with goods – including not only food but also coal and liquid fuel – by air transport alone. The Berlin Airlift remains to this day the largest and most successful airlift operation in history. In the 77 airlifts which postdate the Berlin Airlift none has come near to the total transportation achievement of the Berlin Airlift; on the contrary, not all of them together carried as much as the Berlin Airlift alone. Sebastian Cox, Head of the Air Historical Branch of the RAF, points out in his article, 'Britain and the Berlin Airlift' that: 'It is to the credit of the United States and Royal Air Forces that they were to prove that their best was better than anyone in Berlin, London, Washington, Paris or, most important of all, Moscow, had a right to expect.'[3]

The ways of measuring that achievement are manifold. There were 277,569 Airlift sorties flown, covering 124 million miles – or the same distance as circumnavigating the globe at the equator 3,960 times. As many as 4,000 take-offs and landings were registered on peak days. In fact, what is now routine at all major airports in the world – parallel runways with take-offs and landings taking place simultaneously, and the system by which an aircraft at the head of the runway is cleared for take-off the minute a landing aircraft turns off onto the taxiway at the other end – was first pioneered during the Berlin Airlift. Gatow was the busiest airport in the entire world at that time, with the number of flights far exceeding New York's La Guardia. There were more GCA approaches made at Tempelhof in the last days of the Airlift than were made at all civilian airports in the United States altogether. In fact the entire air traffic control system introduced on the Airlift, which enabled streams of aircraft of different types to be fed in from different air corridors and be safely directed to different airfields in very limited airspace, was at the time a revolutionary innovation and accomplishment. Veterans of the great bomber offensives of the Second World War and the Airlift attest to the fact that the complexity of air traffic control during the Airlift exceeded the difficulties of assembling the large bomber formations and streams of the Second World War.

The Airlift made lasting contributions to the infrastructure for air transport in Germany. At the start of the lift there were only two major airports in West Berlin, two in the American Zone and one in the British Zone. At the end of the Airlift there were three major airports in West Berlin, and six in the British Zone. Of lasting significance were Tegel Airport, now Berlin's major civil airfield, and Fuhlsbüttel, Hamburg's principle airport. Tegel's runways, built by the most primitive methods and using unorthodox materials to support Skymasters, have proved capable of handling both the Boeing 747 and the McDonnell Douglas DC-10. The Skymaster had a weight of 33 tons fully loaded; a 747 weighs in at 355 tons. Yet perhaps the most astonishing and unique accomplishment was the construction of a modern power plant using materials that had to be transported in pieces on – by today's standards – tiny aircraft. To this day, the power plant built with airlifted components remains the most important source of electricity in West Berlin.

The most common way of measuring the accomplishments of the Airlift is the one Tunner favoured: tonnage. During the first five days of the Airlift, in June 1948, the Allies managed to fly in 1,274 tons in 500 flights – and were proud of it. By the end of the Airlift, they were routinely flying seven times that much each *day*. Or put another way: the daily tonnage improved forty-fold in the course of the Airlift. On the Airlift's best day, Tunner's Easter Parade, the 12,940 tons flown into Berlin corresponded to roughly twenty-two freight trains each composed of fifty cars full of coal, or the complete cargo of a modern bulk carrier of 15,000 dwt. A total of 2,325,510 tons of supplies were flown to Berlin during the Airlift, of which 1,613,119 tons were flown in during the blockade itself, and the remaining 712,391 tons arrived during the summer of 1949 when the Allies were building up the reserves of the city. Of that total tonnage, c. 1,587,000 tons or 68 per cent was coal. Food accounted for roughly 538,000 tons or 23 per cent of the tonnage, and liquid fuel for 92,000 tons or 4 per cent.

But cargo was not all that was being flown to Berlin, and not everything flown on the Airlift was going *into* Berlin. Passengers and mail moved in both directions, and the products of Berlin's industry was flown *out*. Mail service was so good during the Airlift that even the German postal service admitted that mail service was de facto better during the Airlift than when things had moved by rail. After the lifting of the blockade, as mentioned earlier, the Soviets confiscated mail wholesale, so airmail became standard for West Berlin until the Four Power agreements were signed in 1972. Regarding passengers, a total of 227,655 were transported in and/or out of Berlin during the Airlift; over 168,000 passengers were flown out of Berlin, and the remainder were inbound passengers.[4] Last, but not least, 35,843 tons of industrial goods produced in blockaded Berlin were flown out of the city during the Airlift. These products had an estimated value of DM230.5 million – a significant contribution to Berlin's badly damaged economy.[5]

The British contribution in this entire effort was astonishing. Looked at in tonnage terms alone, the British flew 'only' 23.3 per cent of the total inbound cargoes. Since the RAF was by this time roughly just one-fifth the size of the USAF, it was basically carrying its weight. However, the focus on tonnage distorts the picture significantly. Aside from the fact that the early, 4-hour block system, combined with the need to funnel aircraft from six airfields in the British Zone into a single corridor, disadvantaged the RAF's fleet in comparison to the USAF, the British willingness to handle diverse and difficult cargoes made them more valuable to the Airlift while inherently reducing the absolute tonnage carried. The USAF did the workhorse role of flying the bulk (88 per cent) of the coal, but this was also the heaviest of cargoes and the easiest (so fastest) to load and unload. Focusing on tonnage was useful for Tunner in extracting the most out of his crews and keeping them from getting too bored, but it is not the best way for a historian to look at the relative contributions to the Airlift.

In terms of number of flights flown, for example, the British accounted for 31.6 per cent of Airlift sorties. More important, the RAF carried the bulk (c. 80 per cent) of the passengers, all of the return cargoes with industrial products from Berlin's factories, all of the liquid fuels, and all of the salt. The Sunderlands had flown no less than 5,000 tons of the latter into the city along with 1,000 tons of other supplies during their relatively short period of deployment. The USAF had no aircraft that could have done that, just as they had no fuel tankers. In addition, the British carried 45 per cent of the food flown into the city.

The British provided – that is, built or expanded and then maintained – the infrastructure for six out of eight departure airfields and one of the Berlin airfields; or for seven of the eleven Airlift airfields. The Americans were responsible only for four, the two in their own Zone and two in Berlin.

Perhaps most important of all when considering the relative contributions of the British and Americans, are two non-quantifiable contributions which the British lift made to the all-important issue of morale. It was the British who put together an Airlift fleet in a matter of just days and weeks, while the USAF scrambled to pull its resources together from around the world. In the first full month of the Airlift, the RAF accounted for 42 per cent of the cargoes – or more than twice its proportional size. In August, RAF and British civilians together accounted for 38 per cent of the tonnage flown into Berlin. It was not until September that the British portion of the lift fell to roughly its 'natural' proportion of 21 per cent as the C-54s started to replace the USAF Dakotas. By then a crucial psychological battle had been won. In effect, it was the British who showed what could be done and gave Berliners hope in those critical early days.

Nor should the significance of the return cargoes be underestimated. Again, although not quantifiable, the contribution made to West Berlin morale by keeping factories open, keeping people employed and even selling goods abroad was perhaps critical in maintaining Berlin's determination to go on. Certainly it contributed to Berlin's pride, and pride can be decisive in times of adversity.

Likewise, the civilian contribution to the Airlift should not be looked at in terms of tonnage. The tonnage transported in civilian holds was roughly 6 per cent of the total, but only the British civilian charter companies were capable of carrying the liquid fuels. Altogether some 23 companies with 103 aircraft – 31–47 of which were flying the Airlift at any one time – took part in the Airlift. They made 21,980 sorties and carried 146,980 tons of goods into Berlin, of which 92,000 tons was liquid fuels. To put this accomplishment into perspective, this represents 'almost double that of all freight and mail carried by all British civil airlines on scheduled services between 1924 and 1947'.[6]

The contribution of American civilians should not be forgotten either. After all, when Gen Clay ordered the USAF to start supplying the city of Berlin with coal, Gen Le May *said* the USAF could 'carry anything' but *in fact* it was the American Overseas Airline (AOA) that was tasked with that first flight. Altogether the AOA flew 2,366 round trips between Frankfurt and Berlin, carrying 17,242 passengers and 11,356 tons of cargo and mail. It was the AOA which carried the not-just-symbolically important CARE packages to Berlin throughout the blockade. After May 1949, when the blockade itself was lifted, AOA resumed regularly scheduled passenger and freight services to Berlin on a twice-daily basis, using DC-3s (Dakotas) and DC-4s (Skymasters). That first flight, the CARE packages and the re-establishment of regular, scheduled air services – a symbol of 'normality' – were contributions to the Airlift far beyond the nominal payload carried.

The Berlin Airlift had a price too, of course. Various attempts have been made to quantify the monetary costs, but in fact no one kept track and it is almost pointless to try to reconstruct. For a start, it is virtually impossible to come to a consensus on what to include in the costs. Clearly the costs of Airlift aircraft, crew, aviation fuel, spare parts, etc. are part of the costs, but what about the services of the Occupation forces, who were there anyway? Clearly the cost of food, fuel and coal supplied by the Allies are costs of the Airlift – or are they? Food, fuel and coal would have been supplied to Berlin by other means as long as it remained an Occupied territory. As Gen Clay put it, 'there is no place for starvation where the American flag is flying and . . . with the raising of that flag we accepted the responsibility to maintain human values'.[7] And what about the CARE packages which were contributed by Americans as gifts? Or the contributions to Halvorsen's Little Vittles? What about the economic costs of lost jobs and the strain unemployment benefits put on the Berlin treasury? Are those the cost of the Airlift – or the blockade? When the US was pouring millions of dollars into the European Recovery Program (ERP), why should the cost of keeping Berlin free be charged against the Airlift? Surely, the point of the ERP was to keep as much of Europe democratic as possible? The loss of Berlin would have been a disastrous blow to European recovery. Was the deficit in Berlin's budget solely the fault of the Airlift? If Berlin had been taken over by the Soviets, it would certainly have been just as bankrupt by Western standards; the communists never did understand the essentials of accounting any more than they did the basics of finance. The entire communist system survived – and collapsed – on the basis of accounting fictions that bore little resemblance to reality.

All that can be said with certainty is that the USAF calculated the direct costs associated with the Airlift (but not training or the transport of men, machines and materiel across the Atlantic) at $252.5 million. A British historian estimated the British costs at £17 million. German historians have 'guestimated' that the German taxpayer paid altogether DM1.2 billion. Exchange rates for these various figures from their different sources do not exist so a comparison remains illusive. The bottom line is that the decision to supply Berlin by air was a political one, and at no time did the monetary/financial costs of the operation play even a secondary role in Allied or German decision-making.

By contrast, the human cost did play a role. If the Airlift had been costing young men's lives on a regular basis, who is to say that the American public would have remained supportive? If the images coming out of Germany had not been children collecting tiny parachutes with chocolate attached but rather coffins covered with American flags, then the vital will of the West to continue might indeed have broken. In this sense, Tunner's determination to make the Airlift as safe as possible was crucial to its success. Tunner bragged:

> Never, from the very beginning of my command until the end, had I subordinated flying safety to any other phase of operation. Despite our round the clock operation and the miserable weather conditions, our accident rate on the Berlin Airlift was less than the overall average for the United States Air Force. . . . One of the many journalists who visited us, on looking at our accident figures, burst out: 'Why I'm safer on the Berlin Airlift than I am flying between Washington and New York.'[8]

Expressed another way, despite the almost 278,000 sorties and the 124 million miles flown on the Airlift, the USAF recorded only 70 major and 56 minor accidents; or 126 altogether. The RAF reported 46 accidents requiring salvage. The accident figures for the many civil companies have not been tabulated. In all there were 24 accidents ending in fatalities, only one of which was a mid-air collision.

This is not to say that there were not a great many tense and dangerous situations faced by the airmen flying the Airlift. Despite what the airmen claimed about 'teaching monkeys to fly the lift' there were many situations which called for great skill and courage. For example, one veteran of the Airlift remembers:

> A fully laden civilian-operated Avro York suffered engine failure after a night take-off. The captain could not maintain height and could not see anywhere to put the aircraft down in the Stygian blackness. All he could do was prepare for the inevitable crash when suddenly there was a flash of light – the aircraft had struck power cables – and there, just to one side, he saw a clearing in the forest which he managed to pancake into.[9]

In another case:

> An [Navy C-54] loaded with sugar burst a tyre on take-off from Rhein-Main and, although the pilot was able to raise the landing gear and fly to Berlin, the gear would not come down when he got there. Ordered to divert to Erding, the airplane rained 10 tons of sugar across the Soviet Zone as the crew tried to lighten the plane for an emergency landing. It was a success, with no injuries to the crew, although all the propellers on the plane were bent and the flaps were worn off completely.[10]

Another Airlift pilot, Flt Lt Murphy, managed to land on the shorter of Wunstorf's runways with a full cargo but only one wheel.

> He managed to hold the wing, without a wheel, up until the airflow was down to almost a trickle! With the crew doubtless helping by leaning hard to the right!! The port wing slowly dropped, causing a small swerve to the left and minimal damage to the wing-tip and fuselage.[11]

Sqn Ldr Johnstone provides the following account of another 'exciting' Airlift flight. Roughly 50 miles from Berlin the port engine on his Dakota abruptly caught fire. He quickly extinguished the flames and brought the slewing aircraft under control. He was so close to Berlin that he at first thought to continue on. The cargo was needed after all, but he soon realised he was losing altitude and he knew there was no room in Berlin for emergency landings. Reluctantly he dropped out of the stream of traffic and turned back for Lübeck. He was, however, flying without a radio operator on this flight which now created new problems. He could only communicate what was happening by talking via his R/T to the Dakotas ahead and behind him in the chain. They in turn relayed his message to a Skymaster flying higher, whose more powerful R/T transmitted his message on to Lübeck. Lübeck of course wanted to know Johnstone's intentions. By now Johnstone realised he could not maintain sufficient altitude to stay in the corridor, so he had the Skymaster pass on the message that he was dropping out of the corridor and laying a direct course for Lübeck over the Russian Zone. He had to fly maximum power from his remaining engine to be able to keep flying at all. He was now below 3,000ft and still had 90 miles to go. The Dakota was using a great deal of fuel under these conditions, and he was on his last tank of fuel when he and his crew finally reached the zonal border. The Dakota was down to 1,200ft and they still had 20 miles to Lübeck. According to his own account, Johnstone said, 'We'll just about make it', and then things got even more exciting:

> . . . the starboard engine spluttered and stopped. It picked up again, and stopped again. Fuel starvation! Automatically, Johnstone twisted the fuel cock . . . the engine picked up again.
>
> Johnstone hadn't throttled back, and as the engine suddenly roared away again, the Dak skidded and lost another 200ft before he could get it under control. Now he was in touch with Lübeck by R/T. Again, they asked him his intentions. . . .

He told Lübeck control-tower that he was coming in. They stopped everything else and cleared the runway for him, and he turned the Dak back over the Russian Zone again and came in from the east.

Johnstone briefed his navigator.

'I don't want the undercarriage down until we're over the runway. . . . We'll have no flaps either, because I daren't do anything that might cut our speed and make us stall. We've got to keep the speed up. Then so long as we land clear and don't come to a sudden stop, we won't have the newsprint [the cargo] down the backs of our necks. . . .'

. . . right over the runway . . . the navigator slammed the lever down. The undercarriage took a few seconds to descend and lock, the green light came on the same instant the wheels touched the runway. Johnstone let the Dak run on down the runway, then turned into the taxi track at the end of it and immediately switched off. He sat in the cockpit, limp and damp.

Afterwards he watched the ground-crew drain all four of the Dak's tanks. They contained precisely 4 gallons of fuel.[12]

Of course, sometimes mistakes were made too. An American veteran recounts:

> I remember one time, just after a good rain, 444 took off, overloaded of course, when the co-pilot reached for the flap handle and grabbed the emergency brake lever. Naturally that killed the flying speed and the ship ran off the end of the strip, buried itself up to its belly in the mud, and there it sat for a week until the ground dried out so that they could dig it out. Bent up the props some but . . . there was nothing wrong with it.[13]

There was often the risk of fire, particularly for the tankers of the civilian fleet. A fully loaded tanker of the civilian fleet that put a wing-tip in heavy crosswinds exploded right on the runway – miraculously without the loss of life.

Saving lives in such situations took courage and luck. USAF Capt Franklin Crawford saved the life of his co-pilot after their C-54 crashed and burst into flames after the engine failure of three out of four engines on take-off from Celle. The co-pilot was unconscious and Crawford, unable to free him of his harness, managed to wrench the entire seat free and pull it out of the cockpit window with his co-pilot still strapped in.

In another incident, the rescuers were German guards. On one of those dreadful foggy days of November 1948 a USAF Skymaster overshot the runway at Tempelhof, and careened off the tarmac into the Mittenwalder railway that ran perpendicular to the runway at the edge of the field. The aircraft burst into flames. Two of the aircraft's crew managed to get clear of the wreck by their own power, but the captain, Armand Grenadier, got caught in the cockpit door. The incident was remembered by one of the rescuers as follows:

> We could hear the breaks of the landing aircraft screeching unnaturally loud and then we saw in the dusk a heavily laden Skymaster shoot off the end of the runway. It hit the railway tracks, and tore the nose wheel off. After an explosion, the whole front end of the machine went up in flames. When we got closer, we could see what the cargo was. My God, I never would have thought that sugar could burn like that! . . . We saw two men get out of the plane and disappear into the fog, but the third man got caught by his parachute in the door. We couldn't get any closer because of the intense heat, but we kept shouting at him to jump down. Eventually he stumbled and fell – right into a sea of flames. Somehow we inched our way closer, grabbed him and pulled him free, rolling him along the wet ground to extinguish the flames.[14]

This incident came to Gen Clay's attention and he wrote personal letters to all four rescuers. One of which read as follows:

> You and your companions, with utter disregard for your own personal safety, gave invaluable assistance in the rescue of Captain Armand I. Grenadier, who had been stunned and was lying burning on the ground in very close proximity to the burning plane. Two other members of the crew of the plane . . . were having difficulty in attempting to move the victim due to their own injuries and shock, in addition to the intense heat of the burning plane. While your comrades were rendering indispensable aid in removing Captain Grenadier from the vicinity of the burning plane and in extinguishing his burning cloths by rolling him in the mud, you, having returned to get the vehicle, arrived and with the assistance of your comrades, immediately rushed Captain Grenadier and the other members of the crew of the plane to the station dispensary for medical treatment. . . . Although the crash rescue crew arrived at the scene of the crash in approximately 3 minutes, the other members of the plane's crew and you German guards had acted with such efficiency and dispatch that it was not discovered by the crash crews and investigation board until approximately 30 minutes after the crash that the crew had not perished in the burning wreckage.[15]

Unfortunately, not all victims of Airlift crashes were as lucky as the crew of this C-54. Altogether, seventy-eight people lost their lives in the line of duty during the Berlin Airlift, including those killed in accidents on the ground. In addition, seven German civilians lost their lives when the RAF Dakota, on which they were flying out of Berlin, crashed at night inside the Russian Zone. Of the Allied casualties, thirty-nine were British, twenty of whom were Service personnel, and thirty-two were American. Their names, rank, nationality and date of death are found in Appendix C. May the Grace of God be with them all.

Chapter 15

CONCLUSION

The significance of the Berlin Airlift has changed over time as the political situation in Europe, and the priorities and perspectives of those looking back on the Airlift, changed. In the immediate aftermath of the Airlift, as the US and the Soviet Union confronted one another more and more openly around the globe, the Airlift was seen first and foremost as a Western victory in the Cold War. Even though nothing had really been achieved but the *status quo ante*, the Soviet advance had been halted and this seemed like a vitally important victory at the time. The ideological fault line now clearly ran through the heart of Germany, and West Berlin had become an outpost of 'freedom' in a sea of totalitarian oppression. Not only had the Airlift preserved that outpost and beacon, the Berliners' own dramatic and unwavering preference for freedom over communism – even at the price of significant hardship – was raised to the level of legend. RIAS, 'a Free Voice of the Free World', seemed to embody this spirit as did the cabaret 'The Islanders'.

The decade-and-a-half following the end of the Airlift was also a period in which West Germany attained reconciliation with the hereditary enemy France and was integrated into the Western system of alliances, both military and economic. In those early years of the Federal Republic of Germany, Germany was 'rehabilitated' and throughout this period the Airlift was therefore also remembered and valued as the catalyst for the transformation of the former German enemy into an ally.

As a new generation came to maturity in the late 1960s, and the Vietnam War tarnished America's image as the defender of justice and freedom, focus shifted to the negative aspects of the Airlift. It was conceded that the Airlift had saved 2 million civilians from being annexed into the Soviet Zone against their will, but it had also been the beginning and the cause of the, then apparently irrevocable, division of Germany. People noted that not only had enemies been turned into allies, but brothers had been turned into enemies.

The Wall that by then ran through and surrounded Berlin was deadly and cruel. Voices were raised that said: well, yes, the Airlift seemed like a good thing at the time, but are we sure there wasn't another way? Weren't the Western Allies too quick to reject Soviet peace proposals, too quick to go their own way, too bigoted to give joint government a chance? Is it really better to be dead than Red? Indeed, is real existing socialism really all that bad? After all East Germany has day care and equality between the sexes and only the Americans have ever used an atom bomb. . . .

When the Wall came down in 1989 and German reunification followed a peaceful rebellion in East Germany, the Airlift abruptly regained its significance and acquired new appeal. Suddenly the words of Ernst Reuter seemed prophetic – for he had said the job would not be finished until the East Berliners too were free. In 1990 they finally were. The 50th Anniversary of the Airlift was celebrated in the knowledge that the Berlin Airlift had played a critical role in keeping the US engaged in Europe and enabling West Germany to become a powerful and prosperous country. Without both these factors, especially West German economic recovery and the coveted DM, the revolution in East Germany would not have taken place.

Consequently, the Airlift was again perceived as being on the 'right' side of history. Rather than being a contributor to the division of Germany, the Airlift was seen to have contributed to its ultimate reunification. It had ensured that there was a sovereign, independent and democratic Germany capable of playing an active role in international politics rather than an emasculated, satellite state dependent on outside help as in the case of the other colonies of the Soviet Union in Eastern Europe.

Now, sixty years after the start of the Airlift, a generation is reaching maturity who cannot remember the division of Germany and knows of the Soviet Union only from history books. The end of the Cold War has reduced the significance of the Berlin Airlift, and public attention is focused on new enemies and new wars. The Berlin Airlift would not appear to have any particular relevance to the War on Terror or the Clash of Civilizations which now preoccupy us.

But there are 'lessons learned' that should not be overlooked in our haste to turn our attention and resources to new battles. The Berlin Airlift was, as Bob Needham put it, a means of resisting aggression without war. While terrorists would never respect the rules of engagement the way the Soviets did, it is still possible that in the battle for the hearts and minds of the populations which spawn terrorists the example of the Airlift may be useful. Above all, it is important to remember that while the Airlift was peaceful, it was also forceful and entailed most decidedly *not* giving in to pressure. It entailed a determined and dramatic dedication of resources – regardless of the cost – to a cause worth fighting for. The Airlift was, furthermore, a highly successful collaborative effort between Allies, in which each partner brought special skills and made their own unique contribution. All participants report that British and Americans worked well together, respected each other and – if one excludes the food at RAF stations – enjoyed working together.

Yet perhaps the most significant achievement of the Airlift was the inspiring example it set for transforming a spontaneous and improvised stopgap measure into a highly efficient and almost painfully precise operation. From Air Cdre Waite with his rough calculations to Lt Halvorsen with his handkerchief parachutes for chocolate bars, the Airlift owes much of its success to the initiatives of subordinates, acting despite the scepticism of their superiors.

So much of what made the Airlift succeed was experimental – whether it was straight-in approaches and one-way traffic, streams of aircraft flying in blocks, or crushing rubble and re-melting pavement to build runways. Tunner might have been the world's leading expert in aviation transport at the time, but he was always prowling around and asking his subordinates for suggestions on how to make things better.

The Airlift wasn't a General Staff Plan executed perfectly like the German offensive against the West in 1940. It was a spontaneous response to a crisis in which, due to the overall support for the action even at the lowest level, everyone involved was willing to give his or her best. From the Berliners preferring Pom to fresh potatoes in the East, to the cooks keeping the Messes open 24 hours a day, it was very much the ordinary men and women involved in the Berlin Airlift that ensured its success.

Appendix I

Timeline

1939	1 September	Germany invades Poland
	3 September	The British and French declare war on Germany
	17 September	The Soviet Union invades Poland
	30 November	The Soviet Union invades Finland
1940	9 April	Germany invades Denmark and Norway
	10 May	Germany invades Holland, Belgium and Luxemburg
		Sir Winston Churchill becomes prime minister of Great Britain
	13 May	Germany invades France
	15 May	Holland surrenders
	26 May–3 June	The British successfully evacuate over 300,000 troops of the British Expeditionary Force from Dunkirk
	28 May	Belgium surrenders
	22 June	France surrenders
	10 July	Official start of the Battle of Britain
	25 August	First RAF night raid on Berlin
	7 September	Blitz of London begins

	31 October	Official end of the Battle of Britain
	5 November	Franklin D. Roosevelt elected to a second term as president of the United States
1941	11 March	The Lend-Lease Bill is signed into law
	6 April	Germany invades Yugoslavia and Greece
	16 May	Blitz of British cities ends
	22 June	Germany invades the Soviet Union
	12 August	The Atlantic Charter is signed by Prime Minister Churchill of Britain and President Roosevelt of the US stating that their objectives are the restoration of the *status quo ante*, self-determination of peoples, and free trade
	7 December	Japan attacks Pearl Harbor, declares war on the US and the British Commonwealth
	11 December	Germany and Italy declare war on the United States
1942	15 February	British forces surrender at Singapore
	9 April	US forces surrender in the Philippines
	2 November	Allied victory at El Alamein
	11 November	German and Italian forces occupy 'Vichy' France
1943	14–26 January	Roosevelt and Churchill meet in Casablanca: unconditional surrender of Germany is announced as official policy
	30 January	The first Allied daylight raid on Berlin
	2 February	German 6th Army surrenders at Stalingrad

10 July	The Allies invade Sicily
8 September	Italy surrenders
28 November–1 December	Churchill, Roosevelt and Stalin meet in Teheran. Among other points on the agenda, the division of Germany and Berlin into Zones of Occupation is agreed
1944 6 June	American, British and Commonwealth troops land in Normandy to begin the liberation of Europe
20 July	The last in a series of assassination attempts against Hitler fails, dooming the attempted coup d'état
21 August–29 September	Dumbarton Oaks Conference sets the ground work for the establishment of the United Nations and postwar economic order
8–18 October	Churchill and Stalin meet in Moscow, disagreements over postwar aims become increasingly apparent
7 November	Roosevelt is elected to a third term as president
1945 4–11 February	Churchill, Roosevelt and Stalin meet in Yalta. The division of Germany into Zones of Occupation, and Berlin as a separate, jointly occupied area is finalised. The US and Britain agree to reparations from Germany to the Soviet Union without fixing a total sum
12 April	President Roosevelt dies and is succeeded by his vice-president, Harry S. Truman
21 April–2 May	The Soviets capture Berlin

7 May	Germany surrenders unconditionally
17 May	The Soviet Military Administration in Germany (SMAD) appoints the first postwar Berlin government (Magistrat)
5 June	First meeting of the Allied Control Council (ACC) in Berlin
6 June	Re-establishment of the German Communist Party (Kommunistische Partei Deutschlands – KPD)
15 June	Re-establishment of the Social Democractic Party of Germany (Sozialistische Partei Deutschlands – SPD)
26 June	Founding of the Christian Democratic Union (Christlich Demokratische Union – CDU)
1–4 July	US and British troops withdraw behind predefined zonal borders, the Red Army assumes control of the areas thus vacated and British and American forces are at last allowed by the Red Army to take control of their Sectors in Berlin
7 July	Kommandatura for Berlin established
17 July–2 August	Potsdam Conference: Allies agree on 'demilitarisation, denazification, democratisation, and decentralisation' of Germany. Germany is to be treated economically as a single entity
30 July	First sitting of the Allied Control Council in Berlin
6 August	First atomic bomb dropped on Hiroshima
9 August	Second atomic bomb dropped on Nagasaki
12 August	French troops arrive in Berlin and assume control of their Sector, carved out of US and British Sectors
11 September– 2 October	The first meeting of the Council of Foreign Ministers in London

20 November		Nuremburg Trials begin
30 November		The Allies conclude a formal agreement controlling the air corridors from the Western Zones and their Sectors in Berlin
20–21 December		A joint congress of the central committees of the KPD and SPD agree to merge these two parties into one, a Socialist Unity Party
1946	20 January	The first free elections in Germany since 1933 are held in the American Zone
	31 March	West Berlin members of the SPD vote by a margin of 82 per cent against merging with the KPD
	21 April	The Socialist Unity Party (Sozialistische Einheitspartei Deutschlands – SED) is founded irrespective of the vote
	24 April–12 July	The second meeting of the Council of Foreign Ministers in Paris
	9–11 May	The SPD in all three Western Zones elects Kurt Schumacher as Party Chairman
	29 July	American and British governments start developing plans to merge their Zones economically
	13 August	Allied Kommandatura approves a provisional constitution for Berlin
	1 September	The first municipal elections in the Soviet Zone
	15 September	The first municipal elections in the British and French Zones
	10 October	The first free municipal elections in Berlin since 1933: SPD 48.7 per cent, CDU 22.2 per cent, LDPD 9.3 per cent, SED 19.8 per cent

4 November– 31 December	The third meeting of the Council of Foreign Ministers in New York
14 November	Draft constitution for a German Democratic Republic is approved by the SED
5 December	SPD leader, Otto Ostrowski, is elected governing mayor of Berlin
1947 January	Exceptional cold causes fuel shortages, factory closures and extreme hardship, particularly in Berlin
1 January	British and American Zones formally merge together for economic purposes: Bizonia
27 February	The founding of a Parliamentary Council for the drafting of a German constitution under the chairmanship of Konrad Adenauer
3 March–24 April	The fourth meeting of the Council of Foreign Ministers in Moscow. The Soviet Union rejects a federal system of government for Germany and continues to insist on reparations in excess of what the West is willing to accept. The meeting ends without positive results
12 March	Truman Doctrine is announced: the US pledges economic and military aid to Greece and Turkey, both threatened by communist insurgency and/or Soviet expansion
15 March	Gen Clay is promoted from Deputy Military Governor to Military Governor for the US in Germany
17 April	Ostrowski resigns as mayor of Berlin
8 May	Louise Schroeder temporarily replaces Ostrowski as governing mayor of Berlin
20 May	The Economic Council (German advisory board composed of leading political figures) is formed in Bizonia

4 June	The SMAD establishes an Economic Council for the Soviet Zone
5 June	US Secretary of State George Marshall announces the European Recovery Program, better known as the Marshall Plan, for the economic reconstruction of Europe
6–8 June	Meeting of German provincial governors in Munich. Delegation from the Soviet Zone departs before the start of the conference due to differences over the agenda
24 June	Ernst Reuter elected governing mayor of Berlin
25 June	Economic Council reconstituted as Parliament of Bizonia
7 July	Using their right of veto in the Allied Kommandatura, the Soviets prevent Ernst Reuter from assuming his elected position. Louise Schroeder continues to serve as 'acting' mayor
25 November–15 December	The fifth meeting of the Council of Foreign Ministers in London. Meeting adjourned without agreement on policy for future economic and political development of Germany

1948

1 January	The Soviets start to exercise closer control over goods transported through the Soviet Zone to and from Berlin and the Western Zones
14 January	The Soviets unilaterally cancel all licences for travel between the Soviet Zone and Berlin
24 January	The Soviets halt a British military train and remove two cars carrying German passengers
26 January	Renewed harassment of a British military train en route to Berlin
9 February	A High Court is established for Bizonia

23 February	Communist coup in Czechoslovakia
1 March	A prototype Central Bank for the Western Zones is established as 'Bank deutscher Länder'
17 March	The Treaty of Brussels establishes the Western European Military Union, a mutual defence pact for the UK, France and the Benelux countries
20 March	The Soviet Union walks out of the Allied Control Council
25 March	The US commandant in Berlin, Col Howley, orders food reserves for at least one month to be stored
1–4 April	The first blockade of the ground and water transportation routes into the Western Sectors of Berlin
3 April	The Marshall Plan is approved by the US Congress
5 April	A BEA airline is buzzed by a Soviet Yak fighter during its approach to Berlin's Gatow airfield. The planes collide and crash with the loss of all aboard both aircraft: the Soviet pilot, twelve Britons and two Americans
10 April	A Berlin Constitution is approved by the Berlin City Council
16 April	The Organisation for European Economic Cooperation is established
20 April	The Soviets impose restrictions on barge traffic to Berlin
24 April	The Soviets stop civilian passenger traffic between the Western Sectors of Berlin and the Western Zones
25 April	The Soviets introduce new rules for the documentation of all freight travelling to and from Berlin
30 April	A British road convoy is halted and denied transit of the Soviet Zone

20 May	Barge traffic is again disrupted
1 June	Train traffic between the Western Zones and Berlin is suspended
4–6 June	Twenty-six rail wagons full of mail from Berlin destined for the West are seized and confiscated by Soviet officials
7 June	Agreement among Western Foreign Ministers on the administration of the Ruhr and the start of preparations for a German Constitutional Assembly
10 June	Five coal trains destined for West Berlin are stopped by the Soviets for alleged deficiencies in their documentation
12 June	All trains from the West to Berlin are halted in a dispute over 'labelling' of freight
15 June	All trains from the West to West Berlin are stopped and road traffic is halted allegedly because the bridge over the Elbe at Magdeburg is closed 'for repairs'. The only alternative is a ferry operated by hand
16 June	The Soviets walk out of the Allied Kommandatura in Berlin
18 June	The Soviets cancel all internal coach licences and suspend passenger trains and mail service between the West and the Western Sectors of Berlin
20 June	The US and Britain introduce currency reform in their Zones and Sectors
23 June	The Soviets order the Berlin City Council to introduce a Soviet currency exclusively; Western Allies declare the Soviet orders invalid
23–4 June	Establishment of the Warsaw Pact
24 June	The start of the blockade of West Berlin: the Soviets shut down all land and sea routes for passengers and goods from the Western Zones to Berlin. Electricity supplies from all power plants in the East serving West Berlin, and coal deliveries to the power plants in the Western Sectors are also cut off

25 June	The first US aircraft of an improvised and unofficial airlift lands with food supplies for Berlin
26 June	President Truman gives his approval to the Airlift; official start of the American Airlift codenamed Vittles. Foreign Secretary Bevin announces British intention to stay in Berlin to the press, and proposes establishment of a joint US–UK coordinating body for response to the blockade
28 June	President Truman reiterates his determination to remain in Berlin. Marshall agrees to the joint coordinating committee. The British institute their plan for the airlift of supplies to the British garrison in Berlin under the codename Knicker
29 June	The Berlin City Council appeals to the UN
30 June	The Soviets announce the end of Four Power government in Berlin. In parliament, Bevin reiterates British determination to remain in Berlin even at the risk of war and receives ardent support from both sides of the aisle. The British alter the objective of the Airlift to the supply of the civilian population of the Western Sectors as well as the British garrison of Berlin; codename changed to Carter Paterson
1 July	Gen Clay increases the daily ration for Germans in the American Zone and Sector
3 July	Meeting between the Western Military Governors and their Soviet counterpart, Marshal Sokolowski ends without resolution of the crisis. The first York aircraft joins the Airlift
5 July	The first Sunderland flying boats join the Airlift
6 July	The Western Allies send a diplomatic note to the Soviet government demanding the end of the blockade

8 July	Coal shortages force severe cuts in Berlin's public transport network
9 July	The first crash of the Airlift
12 July	Construction of a second runway at Tempelhof commences
14 July	Soviet officials admit that the blockade is not the result of 'technical difficulties' and will only be lifted when the Western Allies agree to resume discussions on the German Question.
16 July	A concrete runway at Gatow is completed
17 July	Rations in Berlin are cut back to pre-1 July levels
20 July	Clay consults with Truman and the National Security Council in Washington
23 July	The US Airlift Task Force is established and USAF Major-General William Tunner is appointed to command
24 July	The Soviets announce that residents in the Western Sectors can register in the East to draw rations
25 July	The second fatal crash of the Airlift when a C-47 crashes into an apartment house on approach to Tempelhof
26 July	The Berlin City Council dismisses the Soviet-appointed police chief; his replacement is in turn not recognised by the SMAD
27 July	The first civilian aircraft, Lancastrian tankers of Flight Refuelling Ltd, join the airlift
29 July	Gen Tunner arrives in Wiesbaden to assume command of US airlift operations
30 July	The Soviets freeze all assets held by Western companies in Berlin
2 August	Ambassadors of the Western Powers meet with Stalin in Moscow to discuss the Blockade of Berlin. The first currency exchange offices open in the British Sector to convert West Marks to East Marks and vice versa

4 August	The official start of the civil airlift
5 August	Construction of a new Berlin airport at Tegel begins
13 August	The Berlin City Council are forced to announce drastic restrictions in electricity. Black Friday: in bad weather three aircraft in close succession crash at Tempelhof and large numbers of aircraft are stacked up with an ever-increasing danger of mid-air collisions; Gen Tunner institutes new rules requiring aircraft that miss their landing to return fully loaded to their base of origin
21 August	Operation Little Vittles is started by Lt Gail Halvorsen
23 August	A second meeting of Western Ambassadors with Stalin about the blockade
26 August	Agitators disrupt the session of the Berlin City Council; Council's request for police protection is refused by the SMAD
30 August	Stalin apparently agrees to the lifting of the blockade in exchange for the withdrawal of the DM (Western currency) from the Western Sectors of Berlin
31 August	The Military Governors of all four powers meet together for the first time since the Soviets walked out of the Control Council the previous March
1 September	The German Parliamentary Council, tasked to draft a new Constitution for Germany, meets for the first time. Five representatives from Berlin participate without voting rights
2 September	The first civilian air traffic controllers drafted by Gen Tunner join the Airlift
6 September	Communist agitators disrupt the sitting of the Berlin City Council. The Council transfers the sitting to the British Sector and the communist delegates refuse to take part in the reconvened session

7 September	The four Military Governors end their negotiations in the face of irreconcilable differences
9 September	Mayor Ernst Reuter speaks before a 300,000-strong rally held in front of the ruins of the Reichstag. He calls for international support for the West Berliners
11 September	Financing from the Marshall Plan is extended to the Western Zones and Sectors of Germany
14 September	Western Allies protest again about the Blockade of Berlin to the Soviet Union
18 September	The Soviets respond that the Western Allies have 'lost' their right to remain in Berlin
19 September	The first fatal RAF crash of the Airlift; an Avro York crashes on take-off at Wunstorf
20 September	The first evacuation of children from Berlin to Bizonia
26 September	The first Commonwealth participants in the Airlift arrive in the form of SAAF aircrew
30 September	The USAF withdraws C-47s from the Airlift; henceforth the C-54s are the backbone of the US airlift
4 October	The Berlin situation is brought before the UN Security Council by the Western Allies
7 October	Gen Clay announces that Berlin will only be charged for the costs of offloading, not the transport to Berlin or the goods supplied
8 October	The Berlin City Council announces new elections for 5 December
14 October	The Combined Airlift Task Force (CALTF) is created to coordinate US and British airlift activities under Gen Tunner's command; RAF Air Cdre John Merer is appointed his deputy
18 October	The US calls up 10,000 aircrew reservists for duty on the Airlift
19 October	The RAF starts carrying return cargoes of freight and passengers

20 October	The street lights are turned off due to electricity shortages
23 October	Construction of a new power plant begins. It is to be made entirely from materials flown in by the Airlift or recovered from the rubble and ruins of West Berlin
26 October	The Soviet Union vetoes a UN resolution calling for the lifting of the Blockade of Berlin. All package post between the Western Sectors of Berlin and the Eastern Sector and Zone is suspended
3 November	Preparations for the municipal elections are forbidden in the Soviet Sector by the Soviet commandant
5 November	The first flight into Tegel Airport by a C-54
8 November	The West Berlin government requests permission to accept refugees from the East into the city despite the blockade; the US Navy sends two squadrons to join the Airlift
9 November	The Soviets increase control of persons crossing the Sector borders to prevent 'smuggling'
11 November	Students and professors protest against the communist ideological straightjacket at the Humboldt University and establish a new university, the Free University, in the American Sector of West Berlin; the RAF employs the first Hastings aircraft on the Airlift
18 November	Tegel Airport officially opens
27 November	The French troops carry out the demolition of a radio tower controlled by the Soviets that is a hazard to air traffic at Tegel
30 November	A new City Council for 'Greater Berlin' is established by 'acclamation' in East Berlin; only 'delegates' hand-picked by the SMAD attend and participate
1 November	Organs of the elected government of Berlin start to move their offices to the Western Sectors

5 December	Municipal elections in Berlin are boycotted by the SED; SPD wins 64.5 per cent, CDU 19.4 per cent, and LPD 16.1 per cent of the votes cast. Construction of a second runway at Tegel commences
7 December	Ernst Reuter is again elected governing mayor of Berlin
11 December	Liberal parties in the Western Zones band together to form the Free Democratic Party (Freie Demokratische Partei – FDP)
12 December	The Allied Kommandatura resumes functions without the presence of a Soviet delegate
15 December	Flying-boat operations are terminated
1949 January	The first Marshall Aid reaches Berlin
18 January	The counter-blockade is tightened
3 February	The Parliamentary Council agrees to accept Berlin as a 12th state in the future Germany
19 March	The German 'People's Council' adopts the Constitution of the Deutsche Demokratische Republik (DDR) in the Soviet Zones
20 March	Western Allies raise the DM to the sole legal tender in the Western Sectors of Berlin
4–8 April	The North Atlantic Treaty Organisation is founded in Washington
16–17 April	A record number of tons are flown into Berlin within 24 hours: nearly 13,000 tons; total tonnage now exceeds 1 million tons
4 May	A new Four Power agreement, calling for a reversal of all hindrances to the free movement of goods and persons introduced in Germany since 1 March 1948, is signed in New York
9 May	The 'basic law' (Constitution) for West Germany is passed by the Parliamentary Council

12 May	The Blockade of Berlin ends by order of the SMAD
14 May	The Allies prevent the participation of Berlin in the new Federal Republic of Germany in order to avoid 'complications' in Berlin
23 May	The Constitution of the Federal Republic of Germany is passed into law
23 May–20 June	The sixth (and last) meeting of the Council of Foreign Ministers is held. The Soviet Union proposes a return to the state of affairs agreed at Potsdam. The Western Allies propose that the Soviet Zone join the Federal Republic of Germany. Neither side agrees to the proposals of the other
1 August	Airlift operations begin to wind down
14 August	The first German parliamentary elections since 1933: SPD 29.2 per cent, CDU 25.2 per cent, coalition of liberal parties 11.9 per cent, CSU Bavarian Christian Party 5.8 per cent, KPD 5.7 per cent, others 22.2 per cent
16 August	The last flight of a British civil aircraft on the Airlift
22 August	The end of night flying on the Airlift
29 August	RAF York squadrons are withdrawn from the Airlift
1 September	The Combined Airlift Task Force is disbanded; Tegel is closed
12 September	Theodor Heuss is elected first President of the Federal Republic of Germany
15 September	Conrad Adenauer is elected first Chancellor of the Federal Republic of Germany
23 September	The last RAF Dakota Airlift flight
30 September	The last USAF C-54 Airlift flight. The Berlin Airlift officially ends

7 October	The last RAF Airlift flight, a Hastings
11 October	Wilhelm Pieck is 'elected' first President of the DDR
12 October	Walther Ulbricht is confirmed as first Prime Minister of the DDR
15 October	The Soviet Union recognises the DDR and ambassadors are exchanged
31 October	The Federal Republic of Germany becomes a member of the OEEC

Appendix II

Contributions to the Berlin Airlift

	Tonnage Short Tons	%	Coal Tons	%	Food Tons	%	Liquid Fuel Tons	%	Outbound Cargoes Tons	%	Total	Passengers Inbound	Outbound	Sorties Number	%
American	1,783,573	76.7	1,421,119	89.6	296,319	55.2	0	0	0			24.000	36.584	189,963	68.4
USAF	1,772,217	76.2										15.379	27.963	185,231	66.7
AOA	11,356	0.5									17.242	8.621	8.621	4.732	1.7
British	541,937	23.3	164,910	10.4	240,386	44.8	92.345	100	35.843	100		35.238	131.843	87.606	31.6
RAF	394,957	17.0												65.685	23.7
Civilians	146,980	6.3					92.345							21.921	7.9
TOTAL	2,325,510		1,586,029		536,705		92.345		35.843		227.665	59.238	168.427	277.569	

Figures are based on the reconciliation of several sources and may be off by marginal amounts in any one category, but not with respect to totals. Where no data is entered, no information was available from the author's sources

APPENDIX III

MONTHLY FLIGHTS AND TONNAGES

	US			British			Total		
	Flights	Tonnage	Tons/day	Flights	Tonnage	Tons/day	Flights	Tonnage	Tons/day
26 June–31 July 1948	8,117	41,188	1,144	5,919	29,053	807	14,036	70,241	1,951
August 1948	9,796	73,632	2,375	8,252	45,002	1,452	18,048	118,634	3,827
September 1948	12,905	101,871	3,396	6,682	36,556	1,219	19,587	138,427	4,615
October 1948	12,139	115,793	3,735	5,943	31,245	1,007	18,082	147,038	4,742
November 1948	9,046	87,963	2,932	4,305	24,626	821	13,351	112,589	3,753
December 1948	11,655	114,572	3,696	4,834	26,884	867	16,489	141,456	4,563
January 1949	14,089	139,223	4,491	5,496	32,739	1,056	19,585	171,962	5,547
February 1949	12,051	120,404	4,300	5,043	31,846	1,137	17,094	152,250	5,437
March 1949	15,530	154,480	4,983	6,627	41,686	1,345	22,157	196,166	6,328
April 1949	19,129	189,972	6,632	6,896	45,405	1,514	26,025	235,377	8,146
May 1949	19,365	192,247	6,202	8,352	58,547	1,889	27,717	250,794	8,091
June 1949	18,451	182,722	6,091	8,049	57,602	1,920	26,500	240,324	8,011

Source: Arthur Pearcy, *Berlin Airlift*, Shrewsbury, Airlife Publishing, 1997. p. 123

Appendix IV

Casualties

AMERICAN

1st Lt Ralph H. Boyd	12 January 1949
Cpl George S. Burns	29 October 1948
AMM3/c Harry R. Crites, Jr	11 December 1948
Capt Joel M. DeVolentine	24 August 1948
Maj Edwin C. Diltz	24 August 1948
1st Lt Eugene Erickson	18 October 1948
Karl V. Hagen	8 July 1948
1st Lt Willis F. Hargis	5 December 1948
Tech Sgt Herbert F. Heinig	12 July 1949
Capt William Howard	24 August 1948
1st Lt Charles H. King	24 July 1948
1st Lt Craig B. Ladd	12 January 1949
2nd Lt Donald J. Leemon	12 July 1949
1st Lt William T. Lucas	24 August 1948
1st Lt Robert C. von Luehrte	12 July 1949
PFC Johnnie T. Orms	2 October 1948
Capt Billy E. Phelps	5 December 1948
Tech Sgt Charles L. Putnam	12 January 1949
Capt William A. Rathgeber	7 January 1949
1st Lt George B. Smith	8 July 1948
1st Lt Royce C. Stephens	4 March 1949
PFC Donald E. Stone	7 January 1949
1st Lt Robert W. Stuber	25 July 1948
Cpl Norbert H. Theis	7 January 1948
Capt James A. Vaughan	18 October 1948
Sgt Bernard J. Watkins	7 January 1949

1st Lt Robert P. Weaver	18 January 1949
Tech Sgt Lloyd C. Wells	5 December 1948
1st Lt Lowell A. Wheaton, Jr	7 January 1949
1st Lt Leland W. Williams	8 July 1948
Sgt Richard Winter	18 October 1948
1st Lt Richard M. Wurgel	7 January 1949

BRITISH

Engineer Officer John Anderson	30 April 1949
Navigation Officer Alan John Burton	22 November 1948
Navigation Officer Edward Ernest Carroll	30 April 1949
Navigation Officer Michael Edwin Casey	22 November 1948
Capt William Cusak	22 November 1948
Flg Off Ian Ronald Donaldson	16 July 1949
Sgt Frank Dowling	17 November 1948
Sig II Alexander Dunsire	16 July 1949
Radio Officer Peter James Edwards	15 March 1949
Capt Robert John Freight	21 March 1949
Engineer II Roy Reginald Gibbs	16 July 1949
Navigator II Lawrence Edward Hope Gilbert	19 September 1948
Capt Cecil Golding	15 March 1949
Ground Engineer Patrick James Griffin	15 January 1949
Sig I John Ernst Grout	24 January 1949
Capt Reginald Merrick Watson Heath, DFC	22 November 1948
Flt Lt Geoffrey Kell	19 September 1948
Capt William Richard Donald Lewis	30 April 1949
Sig III Philip Arthur Louch	17 November 1948
First Officer Henry Thomas Newman	15 March 1949
Ground Engineer Edward O'Neil	15 January 1949
Navigator I William George Page	16 July 1949
Engineer Officer Henry Patterson	21 March 1949
Master Signaller Alan Penny, AFC	22 March 1949
Flt Lt Mel Joseph Quinn, RAAF	22 March 1949
Flg Off Kenneth Arthur Reeves	22 March 1949
Radio Officer Dornford Winstan Robertson	22 November 1948
Flight Engineer Kenneth Arthur Seaborne, DFM	22 November 1948
Navigation Officer James Patrik Lewin Sharp, DFC	21 March 1949
Ground Engineer Theodor Supernatt	15 January 1949
Capt Cyril Taylor, DFC, AFM	22 November 1949

Flt Lt Hugh Wallace Thomson, MC, DFC	19 September 1948
Sgt Joseph Toal	16 July 1948
Sig II Sidney Mark Lewis Towersey	19 September 1948
Pilot I Francis Ivor Trevona	17 November 1948
Capt Clement Wilbur Uttig	8 December 1948
Engineer II Ernest William Watson	19 September 1948
Flt Lt John Graham Wilkins	17 November 1948
Radio Officer Kenneth George Wood	30 April 1949

GERMAN

Will Dühring	unknown
Hans Fiedler	unknown
Richard Neumann	15 January 1949
Kurt Schlinsog	unknown
Herman Schwarz	unknown
Kurt Zühlsdorf	11 March 1949
Unknown driver	April 1949

Notes and Sources

PREFACE

1. Based on a true incident described by Lt Gail Halvorsen in his memoir, *The Berlin Candy Bomber*, pp. 147–8.

CHAPTER 1

* Social Democrats (SPD): 63 seats; Christian Democrats (CDU): 29 seats; Liberal Democrats (LPD): 12, for a total of 104 seats *vs* 26 seats for the Socialist Unity (Communist) Party (SED).

CHAPTER 2

1. Ann and John Tusa, *The Berlin Airlift* (New York, NY: Sarpedon, 1988), p. 2.
2. Tusa, *Berlin Airlift*, p. 25.
3. Lucius D. Clay, *Decision in Germany* (London: William Heinemann Ltd, 1950), p. 32.
4. Michael D. Haydock, *City Under Siege: The Berlin Blockade and Airlift, 1948–1949* (Washington and London: Brassy's Inc., 1999), pp. 47, 68.
5. Clay, *Decision in Germany*, p. 32.
6. Haydock, *City Under Siege*, p. 6.
7. Office of the Military Government, US Sector, Berlin, *Four Year Report*, 1949.
8. Haydock, *City Under Siege*, p. 22.
9. Clay, *Decision in Germany*, pp. 314–15.
10. *Ibid.*, p. 264.
11. Tusa, *Berlin Airlift*, p. 35.

12. Robert Rodrigo, *Berlin Airlift* (London: Cassel & Co.,1960), p. 9.
13. Peter Auer, *Ihr Völker der Welt: Ernst Reuter und die Blockade von Berlin* (Berlin: Jaron Verlag, 1998), p. 82.
14. Clay, *Decision in Germany*, p. 73.
15. Haydock, *City Under Siege*, p. 77.
16. Thomas Parrish, *Berlin in the Balance: The Blockade, The Airlift, The First Major Battle of the Cold War* (Reading, MA: Perseus Books, 1998), pp. 99–100.
17. Richard W. Cutler, *Counter Spy: Memoirs of a Counterintelligence Officer in World War II and the Cold War* (Washington DC: Brassy's Inc., 2004), p. 142.
18. Richard Collier, *Bridge Across the Sky: The Berlin Blockade and Airlift, 1948–1949* (London: MacMillan, 1978), p. 10.
19. Robert Jackson, *The Berlin Airlift* (Wellingborough: Patrick Stephens, 1988), p. 24.
20. Tusa, *Berlin Airlift*, p. 44.
21. Roger G. Miller, *To Save a City: The Berlin Airlift 1948–1949* (Honolulu: University Press of the Pacific, 2002), p. 8.
22. Parrish, *Berlin in the Balance*, p. 120.
23. *Ibid.*, p. 121.
24. Haydock, *City Under Siege*, p. 39.
25. Collier, *Bridge Across the Sky*, p. 30.
26. Haydock, *City Under Siege*, p. 119.
27. Peter Krönig, *Schaut auf diese Stadt! Berlin und die Luftbrücke* (Berlin: be.bra Verlag, 1998), p. 28.
28. Squadron Leader Eric Robinson, letter to the author, September 2005.
29. Gerhard Keiderling, *Rosinenbomber über Berlin: Währungsreform, Blockade, Luftbrücke, Teilung* (Berlin: Dietz Verlag, 1998), p. 46.
30. Haydock, *City Under Siege*, p. 129.
31. Clay, *Decision in Germany*, p. 371.
32. *Ibid.*, p. 354.
33. Haydock, *City Under Siege*, p. 134.
34. Miller, *To Save a City*, p. 13.

CHAPTER 3

1. Haydock, *City Under Siege*, p. 156.
2. *Ibid.*, p. 156.
3. Collier, *Bridge Across the Sky*, p. 73.
4. Clay, *Decision in Germany*, p. 374.

5. Haydock, *City Under Siege*, p. 142.
6. Norman Hurst, letter to the author, 5 January 2006.
7. Clay, *Decision in Germany*, p. 374.
8. Walter Isaacson and Evan Thomas, *The Wise Men: Six Friends and the World they Made* (Simon & Schuster Books, 1986), p. 456.
9. Bob Needham, 'Resisting Agression without War: Berlin 1948–1949', *The Friends Quarterly* (April 2001), p. 276.
10. Collier, *Bridge Across the Sky*, p. 61.
11. Needham, 'Resisting Agression', p. 276.
12. Haydock, *City Under Siege*, p. 146.
13. Erich von Manstein, *Verlorene Siege* (München: Bernard & Graefe Verlag, 9. Auflage, 1981), pp. 346–9.
14. Sir Frank Roberts speaking at the Royal Air Force Historical Society Proceedings on 'The Berlin Airlift, 1948–1949', *RAF Historical Society Journal*, No. 6, September 1989, p. 41.
15. Roberts, 'The Berlin Airlift', p. 41.
16. Tusa, *Berlin Airlift*, p. 144; Haydock, *City Under Siege*, p. 148; Auer, *Ihr Vöelker der Welt*, p. 244. Although the individual numbers for the component factors differ slightly, the sum is always the same: 2,000 short tons.
17. Arthur Pearcy, *Berlin Airlift* (Shrewsbury: Airlife Publishing, 1997), p. 101.
18. Klaus Scherff, *Luftbrücke Berlin: Die Dramatische Geschichte der Versorgung aus der Luft, Juni 1948–Oktober 1949* (Stuttgart: Motorbuch Verlag, 1998), p. 12.
19. Sebastian Cox, 'Britain and the Berlin Airlift', *Royal Air Force Air Power Review*, Spring 2004, p. 28.
20. William H. Tunner, *Over the Hump* (Washington DC: US Government Printing Office, 1964), p. 223.
21. Paul Wood, Royal Air Force Historical Society Proceedings.
22. Parrish, *Berlin in the Balance*, p. 290.
23. Tunner, *Over the Hump*, p. 170.
24. Tunner quoted in Parrish, *Berlin in the Balance*, p. 223.
25. Carter Patterson was the name of a British removals company and Soviet propaganda immediately picked up on this fact and started suggesting that the real purpose of all those flights into Berlin was to 'remove' the British garrison, their family and things in preparation of abandoning the Berliners to their fate.

CHAPTER 4

1. Collier, *Bridge Across the Sky*, p. 66.
2. Parrish, *Berlin in the Balance*, p. 201.

CHAPTER 5

1. 'Friede, Freude, Eierkuche' – a direct translation is Peace, Happiness and Egg-Cake, but the latter does not really translate into English.
2. Gail S. Halvorsen, *The Berlin Candy Bomber* (Bountiful, UT: Horizon Publishers, 1997), p. 54.
3. *Ibid.*
4. *Ibid.*
5. Geoffrey W. Smith, 'The Berlin Airlift 1948/49: Recollections of Berlin and RAF Gatow', essay submitted to the British Berlin Airlift Association, provided to the author by Sqn Ldr Frank Stillwell in his capacity as Secretary of the British Berlin Airlift Association.
6. Axel Freiherr von dem Bussche, in a personal interview with the author.
7. Cutler, *Counter Spy*, p. 69.
8. *Ibid.*, p. 80.
9. Bob Needham, RAF Airlift pilot, in a letter to the author, 28 September 2006.
10. A retired US Army officer and his wife in private conversation with the author, 1983.
11. Capt D.A.R. 'Roy' Day in an email to the author, 10 September 2005.
12. Haydock, *City Under Siege*, p. 105.
13. Erhard Cielewicz in a letter to the author, 18 October 2005.
14. Dr Johannes Semmler speaking at the CSU Party Congress, 4 January 1948.
15. 'Rußland handelt, die Gouverneure kuhhandel. Die Westmächte weichen zurück und verhandeln us', original German quote in Keiderling, *Rosinenbomber über Berlin*, p. 196.
16. Frank Howley, *Berlin Command* (New York: Putnam, 1950), pp. 67–8.
17. Tusa, *Berlin Airlift*, p. 24.
18. *Ibid.*, p. 59.

CHAPTER 6

1. Wartime song: 'Let's fill the air with eagles, let's fill the clouds with men. And we will see a world that's free when we fly home again . . .'

2. Haydock, *City Under Siege*, p. 242.
3. Reg Nash, rigger of No. 77 Squadron, in a letter to Sqn Ldr Stillwell, 10 February 1998.
4. Wg Cdr J.F. Manning AFC, 'The Early Days of the Berlin Airlift', *Through Eyes of Blue: Personal Memories of the RAF from 1918* (Shrewsbury: Airlife, 2002), p. 195.
5. Collier, *Bridge Across the Sky*, p. 79.
6. Rodrigo, *Berlin Airlift*, p. 65.
7. Norman Hurst in a letter to the author, 5 December 2005.
8. *Ibid.*
9. J.O. Bennett, 'Blockade, Reminiscences and Recollections of an Airlift Pilot', in A. Anderhub and J.O. Bennett, *Blockade, Airlift and the Airlift Gratitude Foundation: Concerning the History of the Berlin Crisis, 1948–1949* (Berlin: Press and Information Office of the Land Berlin, 1984), p. 53.
10. Flt Sgt Neville Parker in a letter to the author, January 2006.
11. Tunner, *Over the Hump*, p. 168.
12. Sqn Ldr Eric Robinson OBE in a letter to the author, September 2005.
13. Parker, letter to the author, January 2006.
14. Manning, 'The Early Days', p. 195.
15. *Picture Post*, 18 September 1948, Vol. 40, No. 12.
16. Terence Crowley in a letter to the author, 8 January 2006.
17. Rodrigo, *Berlin Airlift*, p. 47.
18. Flt Lt 'Rusty' Waughman DFC AFC in an email to the author, 21 September 2005.
19. Bennett, 'Blockade, Reminiscences and Recollections of an Airlift Pilot', pp. 63–5.
20. Halvorsen, *The Berlin Candy Bomber*, p. 86.
21. AM Sir John Curtiss KCB KBE, 'The Victory Britain Forgot', provided to the author by Sqn Ldr Frank Stillwell in September 2005.
22. Robinson, letter to the author, September 2005.
23. Victor F. Bingham in a letter to the author, 7 September 2005.
24. Roy Day, email to the author, 13 September 2005.
25. Sqn Ldr Ray Paul quoted from undated material provided to Sqn Ldr Frank Stillwell.
26. Max Chivers DFC quoted in *Saga*, March 1998.
27. Bennett, 'Blockade, Reminiscences and Recollections of an Airlift Pilot', p. 63.
28. Tunner, *Over the Hump*, p. 214.
29. Rodrigo, *Berlin Airlift*, p. 35.

30. Jack Holt, Royal Air Force Historical Society Proceedings.
31. Tunner, *Over the Hump*, pp. 152–4.
32. *Ibid.*, p. 185.
33. Roy Day, letter to the author, 10 September 2005.
34. Arthur Pearcy, *Berlin Airlift*, p. 104.
35. Tusa, *Berlin Airlift*, p. 180.
36. Collier, *Bridge Across the Sky*, p. 127.
37. Reg Denny in a letter to Sqn Ldr Frank Stillwell, 3 June 1998.
38. Collier, *Bridge Across the Sky*, p. 70.
39. Tunner, *Over the Hump*, p. 201.
40. Hans Günther in a letter to the author, 21 December 2005.
41. Crowley, letter to the author, 8 January 2006.
42. *Ibid.*
43. Albert Lowe quoted from the Berlin Airlift Veteran Association (BAVA) website.
44. Peter Day in a letter to the author, January 2006.
45. Lt Donald Measley quoted in Edwin Gere, *The Unheralded: Men and Women of the Berlin Blockade and Airlift* (Victoria: Trafford, 2003), p. 121.
46. Halvorsen, *The Berlin Candy Bomber*, p. 46.
47. Rodrigo, *Berlin Airlift*, p. 125.
48. Flt Lt Dennis Moore in an email to the author, December 2005.
49. Rodrigo, *Berlin Airlift*, p. 156.
50. Hurst, letter to the author, December 2005.
51. Manning, 'The Early Days', p. 196.
52. *Ibid.*

CHAPTER 7

1. Hurst, letter to the author, 5 January 2006.
2. W.L. Ball quoted in Gere, *The Unheralded*, p. 143.
3. Denny, letter to Frank Stillwell, 3 June 1998.
4. Walter Rölz in a letter to the author, 30 September 2005.
5. Collier, *Bridge Across the Sky*, p. 126.
6. *Ibid.*
7. G. Cramp quoted in Gere, *The Unheralded*, p. 155.
8. Jackson, *Berlin Airlift*, p. 81.
9. Lt Col R.J. Royle MA RASC, in an undated essay provided to Sqn Ldr Frank Stillwell.
10. Rodrigo, *Berlin Airlift*, p. 159.

11. Miller, *To Save a City*, p. 65.
12. David Lawrence quoted in Gere, *The Unheralded*, p. 157.
13. Parker, letter to the author, January 2006.
14. Halvorsen, *The Berlin Candy Bomber*, p. 141.
15. Bob George in a letter to the author, 4 January 2006.
16. Halvorsen, *The Berlin Candy Bomber*, p. 66.
17. George, letter to the author, 4 January 2006.
18. *Ibid.*
19. *Ibid.*
20. Rodrigo, *Berlin Airlift*, p. 34.
21. George, letter to the author, 4 January 2006.
22. Miller, *To Save a City*, p. 60.
23. Kenny Swallwill quoted in Tunner, *Over the Hump*, p. 212.
24. Scherff, *Luftbrücke Berlin*, p. 115.
25. Tunner, *Over the Hump*, p. 212.
26. Parrish, *Berlin in the Balance*, p. 273.
27. Cpl George M. Meyer, US Army Engineer, quoted in Gere, *The Unheralded*, p. 107.
28. Jackson, *Berlin Airlift*, p. 75.
29. Tunner, *Over the Hump*, p. 166.
30. Halvorsen, *The Berlin Candy Bomber*, p. 42.
31. *Ibid.*
32. Tech Sgt William Michaels quoted in Gere, *The Unheralded*, p. 111.
33. Joe Trent, BAVA website.
34. Tunner, *Over the Hump*, p. 176.
35. Hurst, letter to the author, 5 December 2005.
36. *Ibid.*
37. John B. Kite quoted in Gere, *The Unheralded*, p. 137.
38. Parker, letter to the author, January 2006.
39. Sgt Robert Van Devort quoted in Gere, *The Unheralded*, p. 96.
40. Collier, *Bridge Across the Sky*, p. 122.
41. Hurst, letter to the author, 5 December 2005.
42. Sgt Thomas Talty quoted in Gere, *The Unheralded*, p. 103.
43. Tunner, *Over the Hump*, p. 171.
44. *Ibid.*
45. Inge Hochgeschwender quoted in a letter to the author from Hans Gunther, January 2006.
46. Rodrigo, *Berlin Airlift*, p. 27.

CHAPTER 8

1. Tusa, *Berlin Airlift*, p. 259.
2. Rodrigo, *Berlin Airlift*, p. 31.
3. Manning, 'The Early Days', p. 195.
4. Cpl Peter Izard quoted in Gere, *The Unheralded*, p. 141.
5. Tunner, *Over the Hump*, p. 204.
6. Rodrigo, *Berlin Airlift*, p. 103.
7. Gere, *The Unheralded*, p. 155.
8. *Ibid.*, p. 120.
9. Günther, letter to the author, 21 December 2005.
10. *Ibid.*
11. Halvorsen, *The Berlin Candy Bomber*, p. 39.
12. Robinson, letter to the author, September 2005.
13. Excerpt from 'Avro on the Airlift', November 1948, further details unknown.
14. Tunner, *Over the Hump*, p. 171.
15. Daniel Bunting quoted from the BAVA website.
16. Klaus Mergner in a letter to the author, January 2006.
17. Rodrigo, *Berlin Airlift*, p. 83.
18. Tusa, *Berlin Airlift*, p. 262.
19. Ulrich Busch in conversation with the author, June 2005.
20. Parker, letter to the author, January 2006.
21. Anita Scholl in a letter to the author, 30 September 2005.
22. Pearcy, *Berlin Airlift*, p. 50.
23. Needham, 'Resisting Agression', p. 277.
24. Pearcy, *Berlin Airlift*, p. 50.

CHAPTER 9

1. Tusa, *Berlin Airlift*, p. 154.
2. *Ibid.*, p. 54.
3. *Ibid.*
4. Collier, *Bridge Across the Sky*, p. 69.
5. Robinson, letter to the author, September 2005.
6. Hurst, letter to the author, January 2006.
7. Royal Air Force Historical Society Proceedings.
8. Pearcy, *Berlin* Airlift, p. 34.
9. Robinson, letter to the author, September 2005.
10. Tunner, *Over the Hump*, p. 41.

11. *Ibid.*, p. 110.
12. Oliver LaFarge, *The Eagle in the Egg* (Boston: Houghton Mifflin Co., 1949), p. 26.
13. Collier, *Bridge Across the Sky*, p. 69.
14. *Ibid.*, p. 71.
15. Tunner, *Over the Hump*, pp. 167, 160.
16. *Ibid.*, p. 171.
17. Miller, *To Save a City*, p. 48.
18. Tunner, *Over the Hump*, p. 176.
19. Halvorsen, *The Berlin Candy Bomber*, pp. 64–5.
20. Tunner, *Over the Hump*, p. 162.
21. *Ibid.*, p. 183.
22. *Ibid.*, p. 187.
* Air Contractors, Airflight, Airwork, Air Services, Air Transport, Aquila Airways, British American Air Services, British European Airways (BEA), British Nederland, British Overseas Air Corporation (BOAC), British South American Airways (BSAA), Bond Air Services, Ciros Aviation, Eagle Aviation, Flight Refuelling, Hornton Airways, Kearsley Airways, Lancashire Aircraft, Scottish Airlines, Silver City Airways, Sivewright Airways, Skyflight, Skyways, Transworld Charter, Trent Valley Aviation, World Air Freight, Westminster Airways.
23. Rodrigo, *Berlin Airlift*, p. 50.
24. Jackson, *Berlin Airlift*, p. 100.
25. Bingham, letter to the author, September 2005.
26. *Idem.*
27. Jackson, *Berlin Airlift*, p. 115.
28. Tusa, *Berlin Airlift*, p. 236.

CHAPTER 10

1. Institute für Zeitgeschichte, München, ED 215. Translation by the author.
2. Ernst Reuter in a speech before the Reichstag, 9 September 1948. Translation by the author.
3. *Neues Deutschland*, 30 November 1948. Translation by the author.
4. Keiderling, *Rosinenbomber über Berlin*, p. 247.
5. Dr Wilhelm Kremer quoted in Rodrigo, *Berlin Airlift*, p. 116.
6. Cpl John Ross quoted in Gere, *The Unheralded*, p. 90.
7. Ruth Andreas Friedrich quoted in Keiderling, *Rosinenbomber über Berlin*, p. 239.

8. Alexander Gunkel quoted in Gere, *The Unheralded*, p. 176.
9. Smith, 'Recollections of Berlin and RAF gatow', p. 3.
10. Daniel Bunting, BAVA website; Bunting was the son of an American officer stationed in Berlin.
11. Alexander Gunkel quoted in Gere, *The Unheralded*, p. 176.
12. Col Frank Howley quoted in Parrish, *Berlin in the Balance*, p. 310.
13. Collier, *Bridge Across the Sky*, p. 84.
14. Doris Bell quoted in Rodrigo, *Berlin Airlift*, pp. 79–80.
15. *Ibid.*
16. Scherff, *Luftbrücke Berlin*, p. 151.
17. 'Der Insulaner' radio show, broadcast 25 December 1948.

CHAPTER 11

1. Cox, 'Britain and the Berlin Airlift', p. 33.
2. Tunner, *Over the Hump*, p. 179.
3. *Ibid.*, pp. 185–6.
4. Tunner, *Over the Hump*, p. 191.
5. *Ibid.*, pp. 191–2.
6. *Newsweek*, 1 November 1948.
7. *Ibid.*
8. Collier, *Bridge Across the Sky*, p. 122.
9. Tunner, *Over the Hump*, p. 193.
10. Parrish, *Berlin in the Balance*, p. 292.
11. Tunner, *Over the Hump*, p. 193.
12. Gere, *The Unheralded*, p. 67.
13. Haydock, *City Under Siege*, p. 244.
14. Collier, *Bridge Across the Sky*, p. 135.
15. Haydock, *City Under Siege*, p. 244.
16. Clay, *Decision in Germany*, p. 383.
17. Collier, *Bridge Across the Sky*, p. 136.
18. *Ibid.*, p. 139.

CHAPTER 12

1. Congressional Record, 27 May 1949.
2. Wg Cdr E.F. Kirby in a letter to the author, 14 December 2005.
3. Derrick Kendrick in an email to the author, 13 December 2005.
4. Haydock, *City Under Siege*, p. 239.
5. Cutler, *Counter Spy*, p. 136.

6. Parrish, *Berlin in the Balance*, p. 9.
7. Tusa, *Berlin Airlift*, pp. 52–3.
8. Royal Air Force Historical Society Proceedings.
9. Bingham, letter to the author, 7 September 2005.
10. Roy Day, letter to the author, 15 September 2005.
11. Hurst, letter to the author, 5 January 2006.
12. Peter Day, letter to the author, January 2006.
13. Halvorsen, *The Berlin Candy Bomber*, p. 54.
14. Clay, *Decision in Germany*, p. 391.
15. Halvorsen, *The Berlin Candy Bomber*, pp. 12–13.
16. Pearcy, *Berlin* Airlift, p. 16.
17. *Picture Post*.
18. Cpl Jack D. Fellman quoted in Gere, *The Unheralded*, p. 88.
19. Sgt John Zazzera quoted in Gere, *The Unheralded*, p. 105.
20. Waughman, email to the author, 21 September 2005.
21. Halvorsen, *The Berlin Candy Bomber*, p. 59.
22. Lt Courtney Latimer, RASC, quoted in Gere, *The Unheralded*, p. 63.
23. Rodrigo, *Berlin Airlift*, p. 81.
24. Tunner, *Over the Hump*, p. 183.
25. D.G. Upward of Flight Refuelling quoted in Rodrigo, *Berlin Airlift*, p. 190.
26. Sgt John Overington quoted in Gere, *The Unheralded*, p. 147.
27. Peter Day, letter to the author, January 2006.
28. Robert A. Hide quoted in Gere, *The Unheralded*, p. 144.
29. Waughman, email to the author, 21 September 2005.
30. Parrish, *Berlin in the Balance*, p. 228.
31. Cielewicz, letter to the author, 28 November 2005.
32. Haydock, *City Under Siege*, p. 223.
33. Tunner, *Over the Hump*, p. 217.
34. Karin Hueckstaedt quoted in Parrish, *Berlin in the Balance*, pp. 224–5.
35. Cielewicz, letter to the author, 28 November 2005.
36. Cliff Wenzel in a telephone call to the author, 22 August 2005.
37. Cielewicz, letter to the author, 28 November 2005.
38. Rölz, letter to the author, 27 September 2005.
39. Hans Günther quoted in *75 Jahre Zentralflughafen, 50 Jahre Luftbrücke*, a pamphlet issued on the 75th anniversary of the Airlift.
40. Ingeborg Lee, BAVA website.
41. John B. Heaton, the author's uncle, in conversation with the author. His brother Kencil Heaton is buried in the British Cemetery in Berlin.
42. Hurst, letter to the author, 5 December 2005.

43. Cliff 'Taffy' Thomas in a letter to the author, 1 November 2005.
44. Halvorsen, *The Berlin Candy Bomber*, pp. 98–105. (Courtesy of Cedar Fort, Inc., Springville, Utah.)
45. *Ibid.*, pp. 117–8.
46. *Ibid.*, p. 131.
47. *Ibid.*, p. 123.
48. *Ibid.*, p. 127.
49. *Ibid.*, p. 137.

CHAPTER 13

1. Tunner, *Over the Hump*, pp. 196–7.
2. BAFO memo cited in Tusa, *Berlin Airlift*, p. 316.
3. Joseph Haluska, published personal account on the BAVA website.
4. Günther, letter to the author, 21 December 2005.
5. Robinson, letter to the author, September 2005.
6. John Dowling, Royal Air Force Historical Society Proceedings.
7. Jackson, *Berlin* Airlift, p. 76.
8. *Ibid.*, p. 79.
9. James Spatafora quoted in Gere, *The Unheralded*, p. 93.
10. Capt Stan Sickelmore in a talk before the Royal Aeronautical Society, 28 May 1999.
11. Jackson, *Berlin* Airlift, p. 127.
12. Peter Day, letter to the author, January 2006.
13. Bennett, 'Blockade, Reminiscences and Recollections of an Airlift Pilot', p. 63.
14. Flt Lt E.F. 'Ted' Edwards quoted in Gere, *The Unheralded*, p. 153.
15. Robert A. Hide quoted in Gere, *The Unheralded*, p. 144.
16. Parker, letter to the author, November 2005.
17. James Peat quoted in Gere, *The Unheralded*, pp. 134–5.
18. 'Avro on the Airlift'.
19. Günther, letter to the author, 21 December 2005.
20. *Idem.*
21. Tunner, *Over the Hump*, pp. 180–1.
22. Talk before the History of Air Navigation Group, Royal Institute of Navigation, 22 September 1999.
23. Tusa, *Berlin* Airlift, p. 250.
 * Film star Constance Bennett and wife of the American Station Commander at Fassberg, Colonel Jack Coutler.
24. Tunner, *Over the Hump*, pp. 221–2.

CHAPTER 14

1. Cited in Tusa, *Berlin* Airlift, p. 334.
2. *Ibid.*, p. 370.
3. Cox, 'Britain and the Berlin Airlift', p. 28.
4. *Ibid.*, p. 37.
5. Keiderling, *Rosinenbomber über Berlin*, p. 138.
6. Haydock, *City Under Siege*, p. 247.
7. Clay, *Decision in Germany*, p. 267.
8. Tunner, *Over the Hump*, p. 218.
9. Roy Day, email to the author, September 2005.
10. Haydock, *City Under Siege*, pp. 260–1.
11. Anonymous first-hand account provided by Frank Stillwell to the author in his capacity as Secretary of the British Berlin Airlift Association.
12. Rodrigo, *Berlin Airlift*, pp. 169–72.
13. William Lance, BAVA website.
14. Account from a Berlin newspaper, provided by Hans Günther. Translation by the author.
15. Gen Clay in a letter to Klaus Mergner, in the possession of Hans Günther.

BIBLIOGRAPHY

PRIMARY SOURCES

Berlin Airlift Veteran Association (BAVA) website, www.konnections.com/ airlift

Bignell, Jim, letter to the author, December 2005

Bingham, Victor F., letters to the author, September 2005

Busch, Ulrich, conversation with the author, June 2005

von dem Bussche, Axel Freiherr, personal interview with the author

Chivers, Max DFC, telephone conversation with the author, September 2005

Cielewicz, Erhard, letters to the author, 18 October and 28 November 2005

Congressional Record, 27 May 1949

Crowley, Terence, letter to the author, 8 January 2006

Curtiss, AM Sir John KCB KBE, 'The Victory Britain Forgot', provided to the author by Sqn Ldr Frank Stillwell in September 2005

Day, Capt D.A.R. 'Roy', letters and emails to the author, September 2005

Day, Peter, letter to the author, January 2006

Denny, Reg, letter to Frank Stillwell, 3 June 1998

'Der Insulaner' radio show, written by Gunther Neuman, broadcast on 25 December 1948

Dieckmann, Anita, Klaus and Hans-Joachim, letter to the author, September 2005

Garretts, Sqn Ldr A. MBE, letters to the author, September 2005

George, Bob, letter to the author, 4 January 2006

Günther, Hans, letters to the author, December 2005 and January 2006

Heaton, John B., conversation with the author

Hurst, Norman, letters to the author, November 2005–January 2006

Institute für Zeitgeschichte, München, ED 215

75 Jahre Zentralflughafen, 50 Jahre Luftbrücke, a pamphlet issued on the 75th anniversary of the Airlift.

Kendrick, Derrick, email to the author, 13 December 2005

Kilburn, J., letter to the author, December 2005

Kirby, Wg Cdr E.F., letter to the author, 14 December 2005

Knowles, Leonard Vincent, tapes of unknown date for Imperial War Museum

Mergner, Klaus, letter to the author, January 2006

Moore, Flt Lt Dennis, email to the author, December 2005

Nash, Reg, letter to Frank Stillwell, 10 February 1998

Needham, Bob, letters to the author, September 2005–January 2007

Neues Deutschland, 30 November 1948. Translation by the author

Newsweek, 1 November 1948

Parker, Flt Sgt Neville, letters to the author, November 2005 and January 2006

Paul, Sqn Ldr Ray, undated material provided to Sqn Ldr Frank Stillwell

Picture Post, 18 September 1948, Vol. 40, No. 12

Reuter, Ernst, speech before the Reichstag, 9 September 1948. Translation by the author

Robinson, Sqn Ldr Eric OBE, letter to the author, September 2005

Rölz, Walter, letters to the author, 27 and 30 September 2005

Scholl, Anita, letter to the author, 30 September 2005

Schulz, Gerhard, letter to the author, December 2005

Semmler, Dr Joannes, speech at the CSU Party Congress, 4 January 1948

Sickelmore, Capt Stan K., talk before the Royal Aeronautical Society, May 1999

Smith, Geoff, talk before the History of Air Navigation Group, Royal Institute of Navigation, 22 September 1999

Smith, Geoffrey W., 'The Berlin Airlift 1948/49: Recollections of Berlin and RAF Gatow', essay submitted to the British Berlin Airlift Association

Stillwell, Sqn Ldr Frank, letter to the author, September 2005, and talk before the History of Air Navigation Group, Royal Institute of Navigation, September 1999

Thomas, Cliff 'Taffy', letter to the author, 1 November 2005

Waughman, Flt Lt 'Rusty' DFC AFC, email to the author, September 2005

Wenzel, Cliff, telephone conversation with the author, 22 August 2005

SECONDARY SOURCES

'A Brief Commentary on The Berlin Airlift 1948/1949', British Berlin Airlift Association, undated

'A Special Study of Operation Vittles', *Aviation Operations*, New York: Conover-Mast Publications, 1949

Auer, Peter, *Ihr Völker der Welt: Ernst Reuter und die Blockade von Berlin*, Berlin: Jaron Verlag, 1998

'Avro on the Airlift', November 1948, further details unknown

Bennett, J.O., 'Blockade, Reminiscences and Recollections of an Airlift Pilot', in A. Anderhub and J.O. Bennett, *Blockade, Airlift and the Airlift Gratitude Foundation: Concerning the History of the Berlin Crisis, 1948–1949*, Berlin: Press and Information Office of the Land Berlin, 1984

'The Berlin Airlift', talk before the History of Air Navigation Group, Royal Institute of Navigation, at Shoreham Airport, 22 September 1999

'The Berlin Air Lift 1948–1949', seminar, Royal Air Force Historical Society Proceedings, No. 6, September 1989, transcript published in *RAF Historical Society Journal*.

Clay, General Lucius D., *Decision in Germany*, London: William Heinemann Ltd, 1950

Collier, Richard, *Bridge Across the Sky: The Berlin Blockade and Airlift, 1948–1949*, London: Macmillan, 1978

Cox, Sebastian, 'Britain and the Berlin Airlift', *Royal Air Force Air Power Review*, Spring 2004

Cutler, Richard W., *Counter Spy: Memoirs of a Counterintelligence Officer in World War II and the Cold War*, Washington DC: Brassy's Inc., 2004

Gere, Edwin, *The Unheralded: Men and Women of the Berlin Blockade and Airlift*, Victoria: Trafford, 2003

Halvorsen, Lt Gail S., *The Berlin Candy Bomber*, Bountiful, UT: Horizon Publishers, 1997

Haydock, Michael D., *City under Siege: The Berlin Blockade and Airlift, 1948–1949*, Washington and London: Brassy's Inc., 1999

Howley, Frank, *Berlin Command*, New York: Putnam, 1950

Isaacson, W. and Thomas, E., *The Wise Men: Six Friends and the World they Made*, Simon & Schuster Books, 1986

Jackson, Robert, *The Berlin Airlift*, Wellingborough: Patrick Stephens, 1988

Keiderling, Gerhard, *Rosinenbomber über Berlin: Währungsreform, Blockade, Luftbrücke, Teilung*, Berlin: Dietz Verlag, 1998

Krönig, Peter, *Schaut auf diese Stadt! Berlin und die Luftbrücke*, Berlin: be.bra Verlag, 1998

LaFarge, Oliver, *The Eagle in the Egg*, Boston: Houghton Mifflin Co., 1949

Manning, Wg Cdr J.F. AFC, 'The Early Days of the Berlin Airlift', *Through Eyes of Blue: Personal Memories of the RAF from 1918*, Shrewsbury: Airlife Publishing, 2002

von Manstein, Erich, *Verlorene Siege*, München: Bernard & Graefe Verlag, 9. Auflage, 1981

Miller, Roger G., *To Save a City: The Berlin Airlift 1948–1949*, Honolulu: University Press of the Pacific, 2002

Needham, Bob, 'Resisting aggression without war: Berlin 1948–1949', *The Friends Quarterly*, April 2001

Parrish, Thomas, *Berlin in the Balance: The Blockade, The Airlift, The First Major Battle of the Cold War*, Reading, MA: Perseus Books, 1998

Pearcy, Arthur, *Berlin Airlift*, Shrewsbury: Airlife Publishing, 1997

Prell, Uwe and Lothar Wilker, *Berlin-Blockade und Luftbrücke 1948/1949: Analyse und Dokumentation*, Berlin: Berlin Verlag, 1987

Rodrigo, Robert, *Berlin Airlift*, London: Cassel & Co., 1960

Scherff, Klaus, *Luftbrücke Berlin: Die Dramatische Geschichte der Versorgung aus der Luft Juni 1948–Oktober 1949*, Stuttgart: Motorbuch Verlag, 1998

Tunner, William H., *Over the Hump*, Washington DC: US Government Printing Office, 1964

Tusa, Ann and John, *The Berlin Airlift*, New York, NY: Sarpedon, 1988

Wetylaugk, Udo, *Die Alliierten in Berlin*, Berlin: Berlin Verlag, 1988

INDEX

149–52, 155, 192, 200, 202,
204, 222–3, 229, 231–2, 249

Halvorsen, Lt Gail 151, 171, 210,
213–8, 246, 255
Hamburg 54, 79, 84–5, 90, 93, 121,
130, 155, 188, 222–3, 241, 243
'hamster' trips 175, 183
Hanau 130
Hannover 53–4, 84–5, 140, 197, 236
Howley, Col Frank 9, 72–3, 167–8,
174
'Hump' – Allied airlift over the
Himalayas in the Second World
War 45, 57, 84, 148, 150

inflation 21, 27
'Islanders', the 180–1, 183, 253

Johnstone, Sqn Ldr 91, 248–9
Jutland peninsula 122

Koenig, General (French Military
Governor) 197
Kommandatura 3, 15, 19, 25, 32,
162, 240
Kotikov, General 174
Kurier 177

Lancashire Aircraft Corporation 81,
109, 112, 223
Leipzig **8**, 118, 195
LeMay, General Curtis 44, 57, 97,
122, 147–8, 152–4, 188
loading 49–50, 52, 54, 57, 78, 86,
120–1, 123, 133–7, 139, 146,
152, 156, 185, 203, 208, 220,
224, 227, 234
Luftwaffe 45, 54–6, 63, 78, 121,
124–5, 196, 204

Mannheim 130
Markgraf, Paul (Soviet Chief of Police)
162–3
Marks (currency)
B-Mark/Berlin Mark 30–1
D-Mark/Deutsche Mark 29–30, 169
East Mark 31, 169, 209
Occupation Mark 27–8, 30–1
Marshall, General George C. (US
Secretary of State) 20, 23–4, 26,
143, 166
Marshall Aid 28, 31–2, 169
Marshall Plan 26, 31, 206
meeting with Stalin 23–4
Merer, Air Cdre J.W.F. 154
military government 166, 168
Military Governors 15, 144–5, 238
morale 97, 100, 102–3, 125–6, 129,
135, 139–40, 159, 186–8, 190,
195, 221–2, 230, 236, 245

NAAFI, Navy Army Air Force
Institute 102, 126, 135, 206
navigational aids 53, 57, 85
Nazi Germany 5, 13, 73
newspapers 15, 47, 62, 162, 176–7
NKVD (Soviet Secret Police) 17–18, 26
Noiret, General (deputy to the French
Military Governor) 197
Nuremburg Trials 67, 201

Oberpfaffenhofen 108, 189
Offenbach 130, 203
offloading 55, 86, 89, 98–9, 126,
129, 131, 135–7, 203, 208,
214, 220, 232
Operations
Little Vittles (*see* also Halvorsen)
217–8, 246
Plainfare 57, 79, 81, 97, 155,